THE BELIEVER BOOK OF WRITERS TALKING TO WRITERS

THE BELIEVER BOOK OF WRITERS TALKING TO WRITERS

Edited by VENDELA VIDA

BELIEVER BOOKS

a tiny division of

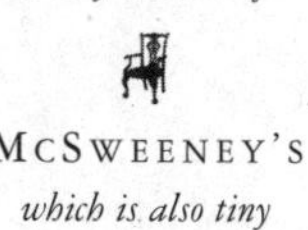

McSWEENEY'S

which is also tiny

BELIEVER BOOKS
a division of
McSWEENEY'S

849 Valencia Street
San Francisco, CA 94110

books.believermag.com

Cover design by Alvaro Villanueva. Illustrations by Charles Burns.

Printed in Canada by Westcan Printing Group.

ISBN: 193-2-416943-97-8

TABLE OF CONTENTS

Notes and Apologies:

- ★ This edition of *The Believer Book of Writers Talking to Writers* contains several interviews that did not appear in the last edition.

- ★ The interviews are arranged alphabetically, by last name of interviewee.

- ★ There are many writers we would have liked to have included in this book. Interviews with these writers may appear in future issues of the *Believer* magazine, or they've already appeared in past issues.

- ★ Whenever possible, the conversations were conducted in person. Many conversations took place in the authors' living rooms, and one took place at a cricket match.

- ★ In all cases, the interviewers proposed the writer they would like to interview. "I'd like to have a conversation with _______," they said.

- ★ Some of the interviews in this book are shorter than others, but all of the interviews are long.

TAYARI JONES

TALKS WITH

CHRIS ABANI

"I AM IN EXILE, BUT NOT ENTIRELY IN EXILE. THE WHOLE THING ABOUT BEING AFRICAN IN THE TWENTY-FIRST CENTURY IS THAT YOUR IDENTITY OCCUPIES A LIMINAL SPACE THAT IS DIFFICULT TO ARTICULATE TO A WESTERN AUDIENCE."

Rites of passage, fictional and real:
Participating in a pro-democracy movement
Writing a third novel
Killing a chicken

In 1985, the Nigerian writer Chris Abani was arrested and imprisoned on suspicion of masterminding a political coup. The evidence: his first novel, a political thriller written two years earlier, when the novelist was just sixteen years old. Since then, Abani has been imprisoned twice more, sentenced to death, and tortured by electric shock; he has also thwarted assassins, published four books of poetry, written eight novels (published three), and won numerous literary awards. His latest novel, GraceLand, *was published by Farrar, Straus & Giroux in February 2004.*

Though Abani's history makes for titillating copy, he should be best known for his detailed, nuanced, and haunting prose. GraceLand *is a sprawling coming-of-age tale that explores the underground world of the slums of Lagos, Nigeria. The author of this beautiful and searing novel, which explores the kidnapping of children for their organs, vigilante justice, civil war, incest, and Elvis impersonation, is not a world-weary and embittered man. Instead, Mr. Abani is thoughtful and soft-spoken—the parlance of California fusing with his British-Nigerian English.*

This interview was conducted by phone from Abani's Los Angeles home. He spoke of hard subjects: colonialism, exile, and war, yet he laughed at the interviewer's jokes and made a couple of his own.

—Tayari Jones (Winter 2003)

I. "ONCE, SOMEONE USING A STONE OR BRICK TRIED TO CRACK MY SKULL BECAUSE HE WANTED TO SEE IF MY BLOOD WOULD BE RED OR WHITE."

TAYARI JONES: I noticed how many of the references in *GraceLand* are American. For example: Hugh Hefner, Elvis. Nigeria being a British colony, I was surprised that the British references were so few. Why does the United States figure so prominently as opposed to Great Britain?

CHRIS ABANI: I think it's a combination of two things. One has to do with the notion of assimilation. There is the old joke we postcolonials have—*Q: What is the difference between the French colonials and the British? A: While the French would see a native African on the street as an animal, or try to civilize you or assimilate you, the British would simply not see you.* British culture is not about assimilation. It is about maintaining the status quo. The whole thing about American culture—because it is driven by capitalism—is this sense of global whiteness through global assimilation. It's sort of a new wave of empire—so I think that was why America had more of an appeal. And also the advent of television and movies. I mean, these were in existence long before I was born. But with my coming into awareness of them, the heroes—even black—were like Shaft.

And Superfly. It was the first time we encountered people of color who had any kind of power. Omar Sharif was a big hit for us. It was easier to sort of find yourself or frame yourself in a global context because of American films.

TJ: I read somewhere that your mother is English and she would call you for tea every day at four p.m. How did your bicultural experience shape your thoughts and ideas about Nigeria and your thoughts about colonialism? How does that figure in to your equation?

CA: Well, that's kind of curious. It might have been a slight exaggeration to say "every day." The thing is, my parents met in the '50s at Oxford. In those days the big thing was for every Nigerian to claim that he was the son of a chief. My father was very clear with my mother that he didn't come from that kind of stuff, that he came from working-class people. In fact, my father was the first graduate from his town and the first one to go abroad. And he knew there would be resistance to his bringing a white wife back, and he prepared her in every possible way for the poverty and the differences. So much so that when my mother went there she was surprised that she could buy everything that she could buy in England. Like her marmalade and her tea.

But certainly the thing is that my father was very insistent that I be raised as a Nigerian. And, more importantly, that we be raised as Igbo men. [The Igbo people are an ethnic group who live mainly in southeast Nigeria. Their traditional language is one of the Benue-Congo subfamily of West African languages.] So I went through every single rite of passage, every initiation, and I speak the language inside and out.

But when you grow up with a mother who is English, you're usually learning to read Western texts and comic books. I grew up on Marvel comics and things like that. It's confusing being biracial in Nigeria. You get treated with a fair degree of specialness and part of it is that you are seen to be weaker and not as strong as everyone else. Once someone using a stone or brick tried to crack my skull because he wanted to see if my blood would be red or white. [*Chuckles*] This was back in 1971.

TJ: Wow.

CA: It was a strange balance. Growing up, I remember listening to all the stories of the Mau Mau uprising [A '50s tribalist guerrilla movement in Kenya]. As a seven-year-old I hated these Mau Mau Kenyans who were killing all these white settlers, because I thought they were going to come and kill my mother. And yet, I did not fully understand the implications of white settlement in East Africa until later.

You have the ability to individuate your mother from the rest of whiteness. And then you are more a product of your environment than race. So I do have the same uneasiness that every other Nigerian would have with colonialism and global whiteness and with racism or white power. It is a very difficult thing to negotiate at home with a mother who has never seen you as "black," but to have to say to her, "Oh, did you realize that what you just said might be construed as racist?" That kind of stuff.

TJ: I feel like you're almost anticipating my questions. You mentioned Kenya and Mau Mau and I was thinking about contemporary African writers and liberation movements. These are two of the themes I noticed in *GraceLand*. And also because I am an African American, I was thinking about liberation struggles here as well. I was wondering if you saw any link between the liberation movements on the African continent and civil rights in the United States. Earlier, you were talking about global whiteness. Do you have any ideas—

CA: About global blackness? I am glad that you picked up on this. All these subtle things that you do as a writer, you think that no one is going to get. Even when Elvis [the protagonist of *GraceLand*] wakes up, the book he is reading is Ellison's *Invisible Man*.

TJ: Yes, it is!

CA: The book falls and cracks apart down the middle. The actual, physical book. That is very interesting. I grew up conflicted about this whole notion. Especially about Pan-Africanism. Especially since Nigeria's independence came quickly and was inspired a lot by Ghana's independence, which was led by [the Pan-Africanist] Kwame Nkrumah. Also in Nigeria was Nnamdi Azikiwe, who was very into Pan-Africanism. But it is interesting that these guys were educated mostly in America. These guys had contact with DuBois and Marcus Garvey long before they came back. You can see this link much more in music. Enslaved Africans brought the roots of the blues with them to the United States and it made its way back to us in Africa. Sailors would come back and teach kids on the docks of Accra and Mali all the American guitar movements, which later produced people like Ali Farka Touré, who plays this hybrid Malian music that sounds so much like the blues. And he influenced people like Fela Kuti. There's that dialogue going on there all the time. And I see a lot of it happening in literature as well. *Invisible Man* becomes such an icon. In the opening of *GraceLand* there's that metaphor of the book falling off Elvis's chest and splitting open. This not only represents the splitting of the diaspora but the ability to enter the text in a way that he wouldn't be able to if he didn't share that fundamental racial heritage.

II. "THERE IS A PARTICULARLY BAD SCENE IN MY FIRST NOVEL WHERE THE GUY GOES TO A RESTAURANT AND SEES A WOMAN HE REALLY LIKES... HE DOES THIS AMAZING SKETCH OF HER AND PASSES IT TO THE WAITER TO GIVE IT TO HER, TO GET HER ATTENTION. I WAS SIXTEEN."

TJ: I spent a year in Nigeria in 1983, the year the civilian government of Shagari was overthrown, and the military regime took over. I was there with my parents—my dad had a Fulbright. But

I was only in ninth grade. Where I was in the north was a quiet town. I was very young. But I remember that people were excited because the coup d'etat gave us three days of uninterrupted NEPA [electricity].

CA: [*Laughs*]

TJ: It was a big thing. And the currency was all changed to a different color. This is what I remember. But what did 1983 mean to you, both in general and with your writing?

CA: Well, I was sixteen at that point. I was just finishing form five, the equivalent of high school. And I had just had my first novel accepted for publication. It won the Delta Fiction Award. My novel actually opens up with a civilian president in power. A mimicry of Shagari. He is overthrown and all this kind of stuff. But how the country was taken over in my novel was not internal, but by neo-Nazis, of all people—don't ask me why; I was sixteen and fascinated by a lot of subjects.

I was born in Nigeria, but left for England halfway through the civil war and returned at the civil war's end. I have memories of the soldiers always being in control of the country. The Igbos were considered the rebels. And there were army cantonments everywhere you went. Roadblocks and such. The Shagari moment (1979–1983) was the first time, for many of us, that we considered the idea that the country had not always been under military control. That the stories our fathers had told us about democracy from 1960 to 1966 actually were true and we had this capacity to return to it. Unfortunately, Shagari's corrupt government led to the sort of disillusionment of that dream, but the subsequent coup sort of marked the beginning of the notion of something we could fight for. I think the seeds for most of the activism were planted then. It's not just myself but a whole generation of people who are now my age who, in one form or another, were involved with anti-government and prodemocracy movements that will never be cataloged, their stories never told. And this is part of the sadness of it all. But that moment, whether we were fully conscious of it or not, marked us. So 1983 was kind of a dark time, and inversely a moment of power.

TJ: What was the title of your first book, the one you wrote at age sixteen?

CA: It was called *Masters of the Board,* because the structural grid of it was a chess game. I sort of had a Nigerian James Bond trying to solve this web of international intrigue.

TJ: Is it available now?

CA: It's out of print. The Library of Congress has a copy, but I'm not very sure how the Library of Congress works.

TJ: Me neither.

CA: The blurb on the back of the book describes me as "Africa's answer to [British political-thriller writer] Frederick Forsyth." [*Laughs*] Crime thrillers were my thing. The novel is very male, very sixteen-year-old. Lots of guns. There is a particularly bad scene in my first novel where the guy goes to a restaurant and sees a woman he really likes and she is across the room. He does this amazing sketch of her and passes it to the waiter to give it to her, to get her attention. [*Laughs*] I was sixteen.

TJ: Not bad for sixteen.

CA: It's still a sophisticated book for that genre, but it's not something I'm really proud of and I hope it never gets reprinted.

TJ: OK, then I won't look for it. You mention your generation quite a bit. I want to know: Who are the writers that you feel are doing important work in your generation? Who are the writers who you think paved the way? Since you do playwriting, I think of Wole Soyinka, the Nobel laureate. And: what do you think is the duty of your generation that is different from those who came before you?

CA: Well, I'll start from the back and work my way to the front. The beautiful thing about being an African writer of my generation is that there is already a rich tradition to mine and build upon. People like Chinua Achebe and Wole Soyinka created a presence for African literature. It's impossible to grow up in that country and not be marked by those books, by those texts. It's sad—I teach here in the United States and I teach young African American men and women who don't realize that they are part of a tradition.

I think for my generation the duty is not just to stand on the shoulders of that tradition but to further it. Like with craft and with language, exploring different forms. For example, a contemporary of mine, Chimamanda Ngozi Adichie, wrote a novel, *Purple Hibiscus,* which is a wonderful book. She does the opposite of what I do. She focuses in on a very detailed portrait of a family, while I try to cover a whole generation of people. There is also Helon Habila, whose narrative structure in *Waiting for an Angel* is highly innovative and original. Someone who I think is very underrated is a writer called Festus Iyayi. I'm not sure if he's my generation or if he bridges my generation and the one that came before. His novel *Violence* inspired what I did with *GraceLand.* He was writing about poor people in a way that is non-voyeuristic. It's just solid and real. His novel *Heroes,* which is about the Nigerian-Biafran civil war, is probably way up there with the Vietnamese book *Novel Without a Name,* written by Duong Thu Huong. It's about character, not about political ideology. Because for a long time what has driven a lot of African literature has been protest against colonialism or internal strife, so the political ideology has sometimes overshadowed the craft and the art.

III. "IN EUROPE YOU ARE GIVEN YOUR FIRST TWO NOVELS TO FAIL AND FIND YOUR VOICE AND BY YOUR THIRD BOOK, YOU ARE READY TO STAND. BUT HERE IN AMERICA IF YOU DON'T COME OUT WITH THIS AMAZING MASTERPIECE AS YOUR FIRST NOVEL, THEN THAT'S IT. YOU'RE DONE."

TJ: As you know, right now in the United States, many creative writers—myself included—come through M.F.A. programs. I want to know about the way that you came to study writing and what you think of this idea of teaching writing in the university.

CA: I am a self-taught writer in many ways. This may have been a good thing. I learned by reading as well as writing. I teach at the M.F.A. program at Antioch University. It seems that people come with the idea that by taking a workshop they are somehow miraculously going to become good writers. And they don't need to read and they don't need to study. They say they don't want to be read because they "don't want to be influenced by it." I want to tell them that they should be so lucky as to have someone read their work and say, "Wow, this is like Toni Morrison," or something. I want to tell them, "You should be so damn fortunate." [*Laughs*]

Personally, I don't think that you can teach people to write. I think you can teach people to read in a more nuanced way. For instance, to look at one of Toni Morrison's books as a writer, say, and not as a cultural critic. To look and see how you can manipulate the body and objects and devices in ways you wouldn't have thought about. My class is bizarre in that I do things like give them a deck of cards and say, "Build me a poem." They look at me like I'm crazy. But I want to teach the idea of convergence and simultaneity. I do that rather than the traditional workshop where people say things like, "I don't like this line," or, "That didn't, like, work for me." Who cares what works for you! [*Laughs*] I don't care what you like. I had one of my students read a book, and she said, "I didn't know what life lesson I was supposed to learn from this book," and I thought, You're here as a writer. This is not a book club! It's not about life lessons. It's about taking this book apart and looking at the characters and seeing how it's built. It's very difficult to get my students to see themselves as craftspeople. The only way I can think of to do it is to trick them.

Because I have been censored in my life and I am very leery of censoring anybody, I am very suspicious of this hierarchical rendering of experience—of whose experience is more fascinating than someone else's. I just think that people are not pushed to go to the places where their stories are, so they just write generic stuff. What professors want, what publishers are looking for, what agents are looking for. But there are plenty of writers in this country who are writing things that will rip your guts out. Percival Everett, for example.

TJ: Yes!

CA: His new book that's coming out, *American Desert,* is about someone who has the DNA of Jesus and is trying to reproduce Jesus and each model fails because when they kill him, he doesn't resurrect. [*Laughs*]

TJ: That's so Percival Everett.

CA: He's incredible. And I must say, having come to the United States, the whole point of my journey here was to meet Percival Everett. Because he turned *GraceLand* from a verbal description into a novel in nine months. He's my most amazing teacher.

TJ: This summer, I met Minnie Marie Hayes, who edits *Story-Quarterly,* one of my favorite journals. She is a great fan of your work. She said that she likes to publish you because you have something to write about. She commented specifically on an excerpt from *GraceLand* when a little boy has to kill a chicken as a rite of passage. She said, "Now *that* is a story."

CA: Minnie Marie often says to me, "I can't stand another cancer story." But I think there may be a cancer story out there that she hasn't seen yet. I don't think that you can overwrite any given topic. Otherwise, we would have all been out of business after the Bible.

But I do think that writers here need to be pushed to find their own raw edges. I think the problem of the M.F.A. is that it smooths things over too much. I think that the pressure on a first novelist in America is too much. In Europe you are given your first two novels to fail and find your voice and by your third book, you are ready to stand. But here in America if you don't come out with this amazing masterpiece as your first novel, then that's it. You're done. It just seems so ridiculous to me. Writing is about growing. In *GraceLand* there are a lot of rough edges.

IV. "I CONSIDER MYSELF TO BE IN EXILE. BUT THAT'S JUST ME. I WENT TO A CONFERENCE ON EXILE AND PEOPLE WERE TALKING ABOUT *BRIDGET JONES'S DIARY* AND BEING EXILED FROM THEIR FEMININITY!"

TJ: Is it right to consider every African writer who is not on the continent to be "in exile"? What does that mean? And I was thinking about Ngugi wa Thiong'o. He writes in Kenya, right? He's home, right?

CA: Actually, he's in Irvine.

TJ: California? Since he writes only in Gikuyu, I just assumed that he must be based in Kenya.

CA: This is part of the dilemma of just being African. He was in exile. He still is in exile. Part of his project has been to recoup an essential African-ness that might have survived colonialism. In Kenya and South Africa it is very different from Nigeria. We were never occupied in West Africa. Our language was never banned as theirs was. And also you have to understand that Ngugi is a Marxist and part of his belief is that your art has no consequence if it can't speak to everybody. Part of his endeavor has been to create his art in his own language so everyone can have access to it. Then it is translated into English as a secondary project. And part of the irony of being African is that he lives in Southern California and does this.

And this brings us to exiles. You have a lot of your intellectuals, writers, doctors, and professionals of all sorts who have had to leave—for economic reasons—to the West, and can't return on a full-time basis to Nigeria because they cannot be sustained creatively, professionally, or economically. And so they have to live in exile in a way. Then you have a second generation born outside of the country whose African-ness, Nigerian-ness, or Igbo-ness is just a received narrative. And who have a sense of exile because they are not accepted by the mainstream community or by the home community. I was a political activist who had to leave Nigeria for my own safety, but there was never a government bulletin saying, "Chris Abani has to go into exile." And even in Soyinka's case—you just leave because you know if you stay any longer, you will die. So in this sense, I am in exile, but not entirely in exile.

The whole thing about being African in the twenty-first century is that your identity occupies a liminal space that is difficult to articulate to a Western audience. If you are in exile, you can apply for a special grant because you are in exile. So you have to navigate through the expectations of these terms. And then there is the resentment at home from people who think that you are benefiting from occupying this liminal space and then you have to make clear in your own head who you are, where you come from. And what your writing will reflect. I consider myself to be in exile. But that's just me. [*Laughs*] I went to a conference on exile and people were talking about *Bridget Jones's Diary* and being exiled from their femininity! [*Laughs*]

TJ: Let's talk about *GraceLand* a little bit more.

CA: You've read it. Tell me. I know you have had some experience of being in Nigeria. But how would you relate to this book, just reading it as an African American?

TJ: So now you're interviewing me?

CA: In a way.

TJ: Actually, it reminded me of *Linden Hills,* a Gloria Naylor novel. The mingling of the recipes with the narrative. I think that part of my culture as an African American is to identify with the struggles of African or dark-skinned people everywhere. Even if I hadn't lived in Nigeria, I would have been able to relate to it. This fear of the police, this is rife in the world that I live in. I've been terrified of police since I was three years old. But on another level, many of the relationships between the characters were just sort of—I hate to use the word "universal," because it usually means something else—but the idea of the son trying to please the father. I read that you consider this book to be a love letter to your father. Could you elaborate on that?

CA: Well, my father died in 2001. I had a very difficult relationship with my father, from when I was, like, six or seven. When I was a kid, Nigeria was still so steeped in tradition and the notion of masculinity as being trained to be a warrior, in many ways. Even though your fight may be a symbolic one in the Ministry of Education. So to have a son who wrote poetry, who was reading Baldwin at nine, and read about homosexuality and tried to defend the idea that love, no matter what kind of love it was, was acceptable—I'm not gay so he couldn't beat me up for that. So my version of masculinity was something he couldn't accept. And he totally hated the idea of my writing. He burnt my first draft of my first book. We had a lot of domestic violence. He really kicked the crap out of us.

In 1991, when I left Nigeria, it was the last time I ever spoke to him. I went from hating him to pitying him to finally being able to understand that in some perverse way, there was actual love between us. I think that occurred when he died. One thing I tried to do in *GraceLand*: Even though it is set in a ghetto and all sorts of terrible things happen, I tried to show a level of love in all of the interactions between the characters. For example, when Redemption [one of Elvis's friends] is showing Elvis how to wrap the cocaine, you get the real sense of tenderness, that Redemption is teaching him something. Terrible thing, but there is not just the homoerotic thing, but a big-brother thing, like the Artful Dodger teaching Oliver Twist.

TJ: That's exactly what I thought when I read it.

CA: Yes, he has a very protective, tender way, but they are preparing drugs. They are going to kill people. And Redemption goes out of his way to protect Elvis from the Colonel, but doesn't tell them that they are moving dead bodies—people killed for their organs and body parts. And yet at every single point in that book, there are moments of frustrated love. Love that can't find any way of expressing itself.

V. THE INVISIBLE WHITE MAN IN THE ROOM

TJ: I remember when I was growing up in Nigeria, there was all this vigilante justice. Someone could point at you and yell, "Thief," and you could be killed by a mob. One of the most devastating scenes in *GraceLand* is when the carpenter is accused of being a thief and the crowd sets him on fire. There are at least five people who get burned alive in this book.

CA: It's not just about the fire and the reality of what the fire does. Apart from that, it has to do with the symbolism of fire. We sort of set ourselves on fire. We sort of self-immolate every time we engage in those kinds of actions.

I grew up in a very violent culture. It's violent because it was colonized violently. Then there was the violence of colonial occupation itself. Intertribal wars and conflagrations. All of this stuff building up to a society that had just come through a civil war.

I went to primary school with people—nine, ten years old—who had been soldiers, who had shot people. People would place bets—"Give me twenty kobo and I will stab myself in the leg." You give them twenty kobo and they would do it.

TJ: Twenty kobo? That's less than a quarter.

CA: You put it in the context of when Nigerian currency had value. It was a little bit of money. Enough for a Coke and a snack. But I grew up watching this. And then there is corporal punishment at school, corporal punishment at home. There's an old Fulani custom: Before you could get married you had to have a hundred slashes with a whip. If you cried, you weren't man enough. The book is soaked through with it. But the real question is how come at least 70 percent of our population seems to be immune to this violence.

TJ: I noticed this with Elvis. He is walking and he hears someone screaming and he doesn't stop walking.

CA: If you live outside of it, you wonder how people carry on. You wonder how people live in Sarajevo, but they do. I wanted to sort of explore that. It is painful for me to write about it. You're torn between representing what you know to be true and worrying how it will be perceived by a Western reader. Will they think that we are all savages?

TJ: Ah, that. What we call the invisible white man in the room. Peeking over your shoulder as you write.

CA: And sometimes it becomes a censor. And that is disingenuous. What I do is similar to what Ngugi is doing, operating under that notion that African art must exist in an appreciative context that is outside of the power of Westernization to reduce or empower. We allow access to the Western reader but also say we don't care about what you think. This is what we are trying to show you. If you get it, fine. If you don't get it, we don't care. ✯

JONATHAN LETHEM

TALKS WITH

PAUL AUSTER

"IT'S CERTAIN THAT THE WORLD'S LARGE ENOUGH AND INTERESTING ENOUGH TO TAKE A DIFFERENT APPROACH EACH TIME YOU SIT DOWN TO WRITE ABOUT IT."

Things novels have swallowed:
Paintings
Songs
Fax machines
Fat women gesturing operatically

P*aul Auster began as a poet, essayist, anthologist, and translator, but since* City of Glass *(1985) he's been recognized above all for being one of our most spare, lucid, and elegant novelists. The protagonists of many of his books, including* The Music of Chance *(1990),* The Book of Illusions *(2002), and* Oracle Night *(2003), are pensive but gentle urban everymen, and some are writers or other artists. They're easy for Auster's many young admirers to identify, rightly or wrongly, as both themselves and the author who put them on the page. In my twenties, when I was becoming a writer, I was certainly one of those young admirers. When I was lucky enough, years later, to have the chance to know Paul, I wasn't disappointed.* —*Jonathan Lethem (Winter 2004)*

I. MUSIC

JONATHAN LETHEM: What were you doing today before I appeared in your house?

PAUL AUSTER: The usual. I got up in the morning. I read the paper. I drank a pot of tea. And then I went over to the little apartment I have in the neighborhood and worked for about six hours. After that, I had to do some business. My mother died two years ago, and there was one last thing to take care of concerning her estate—a kind of insurance bond I had to sign off on. So I went to a notary public to have the papers stamped, then mailed them to the lawyer. I came back home. I read my daughter's final report card. And then I went upstairs and paid a lot of bills. A typical day, I suppose. A mix of working on the book and dealing with a lot of boring, practical stuff.

JL: For me, five or six hours of writing is plenty. That's a lot. So if I get that many hours the other stuff feels satisfying. The other stuff feels like a kind of grace. But if I have to do that stuff when I haven't written—.

PA: Oh, that's terrible.

JL: That's a terrible thing.

PA: I've found that writing novels is an all-absorbing experience—both physical and mental—and I have to do it every day in order to keep the rhythm, to keep myself focused on what I'm doing. Even Sunday, if possible. If there's no family thing happening that day, I'll at least work in the morning. Whenever I travel, I get thrown off completely. If I'm gone for two weeks, it takes me a good week to get back into the rhythm of what I was doing before.

JL: I like the word *physical*. I have the same fetish for continuity. I don't really ask of myself a given word or page count or number of hours. To work every day, that's my only fetish. And there is a physical quality to it when a novel is thriving. It has an athletic component. You're keeping a streak going.

PA: Writing is physical for me. I always have the sense that the words are coming out of my body, not just my mind. I write in longhand, and the pen is scratching the words onto the page. I can even hear the words being written. So much of the effort that goes into writing prose for me is about making sentences that capture the music that I'm hearing in my head. It takes a lot of work, writing, writing, and rewriting to get the music exactly the way you want it to be. That music is a physical force. Not only do you write books physically, but you read books physically as well. There's something about the rhythms of language that correspond to the rhythms of our own bodies. An attentive reader is finding meanings in the book that can't be articulated, finding them in his or her body. I think this is what so many people don't understand about fiction. Poetry is supposed to be musical. But people don't understand prose. They're so used to reading journalism—clunky, functional sentences that convey factual information. Facts... just the surfaces of things.

JL: This relates to the acute discomfort of publicity, so much of which consists of requests to paraphrase the work. Which inevitably results in something unmusical. It's as if you've taken the body away, then drawn its outline and described its contents.

PA: I don't know why the world has changed so much that writers are now expected to appear in public and talk about their work. It's something I find very difficult. And yet one does have some sense of responsibility toward one's publishers, to the people trying to sell the book.

I've tried to pick my spots. I don't do it that often. But every once in a while I'll come out and do it as an act of good faith. Then I hope I'll be left alone again for a while. For example, with the last novel I published, *Oracle Night,* I just simply refused to go on book tours. I just didn't have the stamina for it.

JL: Kazuo Ishiguro has a funny way of talking about it as if it's a giant, consensual mistake all authors made together, by agreeing to this. And then suggesting we need to end it together. It's like a version of the Prisoner's Dilemma. If one of us tours, we all have to tour. If everyone refuses…

PA: He's speaking from deep experience. He did something that no one else I know ever did. He was on book tour for about two years. He went everywhere, to every country in the world where his book was published. In the end, it probably nearly killed him.

JL: Did you read *The Unconsoled*?

PA: I've wanted to.

JL: It's one of my favorite novels by a living writer. An epic, Kafkaesque account of a pianist's arrival in a city to give a recital which never seems to happen. One possible description of it is as the longest and bitterest complaint of a book-touring author ever written.

PA: There's a great entry in Kafka's diaries in which he describes an imaginary writer in the process of giving a public reading. So-and-so is up there onstage, and people are getting restless and bored. "Just one more story," he says, "just one more…" People start getting up and leaving. The doors keep slamming shut, and he goes on begging, "Just one more, one more," until everyone is gone and he's left alone at the podium, reading to an empty room.

II. FILM

JL: It does seem that lately you've managed to reinstate your primary relationship with novel-writing. I mean, judging from the degree of concentration evident in the two recent novels and from your testimony that you're already deep in another one, which is nice news.

PA: Yeah, deep, deep in it.

JL: When you talk about the exclusivity that the novel demands, I'm very much in agreement with you. So I wonder about the years when you were apparently happy in the world of film. Did you feel that you had to retrench?

PA: I stumbled into filmmaking by accident. I've always been passionately in love with movies, to such a degree that even as a young person of about nineteen or twenty I thought maybe I would try to become a film director. The reason I didn't do it was because I felt I didn't have the right personality. At that time in my life, I was mortally shy. I couldn't speak in front of other people, and I thought: If I'm going to be this silent, morose, brooding person, I'm not going to be able to communicate effectively with the actors and the crew and so on. So I gave up that idea. And then ironically enough, it was only after I started publishing novels that I got involved with film—because people started calling me about potential film rights, writing original screenplays, and eventually I got lured into it.

JL: In your recent novels I imagined I'd spotted a subtle turn from film toward fiction—that is to say, the last two books both portray artists. In *The Book of Illusions,* your main character is a filmmaker, and the reader encounters extensive—and beautiful—descriptions of his films. In *Oracle Night* the main character is a novelist, and we read a portion of his novel-in-progress. Does this match a turn in your own attentions?

PA: I want to disentangle this a little bit. During the years I was making films, I never believed I was abandoning the novel. The two films with Wayne Wang took two years of my life. It was a wonderful experience. One of the great pleasures was getting out of my room for a while, working with other people, opening up my mind to new ways of thinking.

Lulu on the Bridge was an accident. I wrote the screenplay for Wim Wenders and then he had a conflict; he wasn't able to direct the film. At his urging, I decided to take on the job myself. And so, boom, there went another two and a half years of my life. But, then again, it was an irreplaceable experience, and I'm glad I did it. Then came the promotional tour, which was far more exhausting than making the film itself. You think books are hard—films are deadly. I can remember doing forty interviews in two days in Japan. Long interviews, one after the other, one after the other. I was so worn out, I got sick and wound up in the hospital. That was when I came to a decision: As much as I enjoyed making films, and as much as I thought I was beginning to get the hang of it, I understood that it's a full-time job. You can't do it as a hobby. In order to go on making films, I would have been forced to give up writing, and that was out of the question. There was no doubt in my mind that what I'm supposed to do is write novels. So, very happily, without any regret at all, I retired. I'm not in the movie business anymore.

But to get back to *The Book of Illusions,* to Hector Mann and his film career: The fact is that Hector was born inside me long before I got involved with the movies myself. He came to me one day in the late '80s or very early '90s, full-blown in his white suit with his black mustache, and I didn't know what to do with him. I thought perhaps I would sit down at some point and write a book of stories that would describe his silent films—each story a different film. I walked around with him for years before the book finally coalesced into the novel it is now. People have said, "Oh, this is a result of Auster's foray into filmmaking," but it really predated all that.

The last thing to say about this little adventure into moviemaking is that it's rare that a person gets a chance at a somewhat advanced age—I'm talking about my mid-forties—to learn something new. To get involved in something you've never tried before. In that way it was good for me. It was good for me not to write a novel for five years. The only piece of prose I wrote during that period was *Hand to Mouth,* my little autobiographical essay about money.

JL: This is something I wrestle with. I am actually in the middle of the longest break from novel-writing of my adult life. I began trying to write novels when I was eighteen.

PA: Me too.

JL: They weren't any good, of course, but I've never been away from the activity since then. But in the past two years I've done a tremendous amount of promotion, and then worked on assembling two collections—a book of stories and a book of essays.

PA: Nothing to be ashamed about.

JL: Thank you. But it means that this body that's been accustomed to this practice for twenty years, as an athlete's body is accustomed to showing up at the clubhouse and putting on the cleats and running, my writer's body is—

PA: Atrophied a little bit.

JL: Yes, atrophied. It's a bit dismaying. I have a friend, a novelist with a delightfully unembarrassed sense of ambition. He's got a bit of that Norman Mailer–getting-into-the-boxing-ring-with-Tolstoy thing. He says a thing that haunts me: "If you look at the record, with very few exceptions novelists are at their best between the ages of thirty-five and fifty. The crossroads of youthful energy and experience." And here I am kissing off a couple of years at the start of my forties.

PA: Just to reassure you, I'm a firm believer that there are no rules in art. Every trajectory is different. My French publisher once told me that a novelist has twenty years, that all his best work will be done in that span of time. I don't necessarily buy that. But the interesting thing is how easy it is not to work. Yes, writing is a necessity and often a pleasure, but at the same time, it can be a great burden and a terrible struggle.

JL: I'm glad to hear you say that.

PA: In my own case, I certainly don't walk into my room and sit down at my desk feeling like a boxer ready to go ten rounds with Joe Louis. I tiptoe in. I procrastinate. I delay. I take care of little business that I don't have to do at that moment. I come in sideways, kind of sliding through the door. I don't burst into the saloon with my six-shooter ready. If I did, I'd probably shoot myself in the foot.

III. PLACE

JL: You've reminded me of another thought I had when you mentioned going to your little apartment. I hope you don't mind me saying you have an extraordinary house. The sort of house which, in my fantasies, I would never leave. There'd be a beautiful office in it and I would write in that office. But in fact, you've actually arranged to slip out of this house. That slippery, crabwise kind of movement is one the writer thrives on. Or, anyway, another thing I identify with.

PA: It's complicated. When we lived in a crowded apartment with children, there was nowhere for me to work, so I found a little studio apartment for myself. I worked there for six or seven years, and then we bought this house. In the beginning, there were tenants downstairs, but eventually they left and I decided to move my operation here. For quite a number of years, I contentedly worked downstairs. But last year we started doing work on the house. We were invaded by contractors, carpenters, plumbers, electricians, painters. There was so much noise. The doorbell was ringing all the time. The phone was ringing all the time. I realized I wasn't able to concentrate. And I thought, Maybe I should go back to the old way. I found a little apartment in the neighborhood about nine months ago and I find it good, very good. This is a magnificent house. It's the product of Siri's [Siri Hustvedt, Auster's wife] tremendous aesthetic sense, her brilliant eye for harmony and order. But I think working in a rougher, meaner environment is good for me. I've always been a kind of Caliban. I feel happier in a bare space.

JL: My equivalent, perhaps, is that I enjoy an indirect relationship to place. People understandably think I moved back to Brooklyn in order to write about it, but the odd truth is that I've written the majority of these Brooklyn books in Toronto or Saratoga Springs or German hotel lobbies. I seem to write most happily about Brooklyn from a little distance, glancing back, yearning for it.

PA: Like Joyce and Dublin. As it happens, I'm writing about Brooklyn now, as well. The last book, *Oracle Night,* was Brooklyn twenty-two years ago. Now I'm writing about the Brooklyn of today. I can tell you the title of the new novel because I'm not going to change it: *The Brooklyn Follies.* It's an attempt to write a kind of comedy. I've never been in this territory before, and I'm having a lot of fun with it, doubting every word I write, and yet finally, I think, producing something that's interesting. I hope so, anyway.

JL: I can't wait.

PA: You try to surprise yourself. You want to go against what you've done before. You want to burn up and destroy all your previous work; you want to reinvent yourself with every project. Once you fall into habits, I think, you're dead as an artist. You have to challenge yourself and never rest on your laurels, never think about what you've done in the past. Just say, that's done, now I'm tackling something else. It's certain that the world's large enough and interesting enough to take a different approach each time you sit down to write about it.

JL: Anyway, your voice is going to be helplessly your own. And so the books will be united despite your attempts to ignore your own earlier work.

PA: Exactly, because all your attempts to flee from yourself are useless. All you discover is yourself and your old obsessions. All the maniacal repetitions of how you think. But you try. And I think there's some dignity in that attempt.

JL: I'm laughing, because now, as I'm about to begin a new novel at last, the only thing I'm certain of are the exclusions, the things I'll refuse to do again. I'm avoiding Brooklyn. I'm going to avoid writing about parents and children. And I've noticed that each previous book, as different as I thought they were, had mortal stakes attached. Someone was capable of pulling a gun on someone else. So I decided to restrict myself to emotional stakes.

PA: Well, that's good. When you become aware of what your limits have been so far, then you're able to expand them. And every artist has limits. No one can do everything. It's impossible. What's beautiful about art is that it circumscribes a space, a physical and mental space. If you try to put the entire world into every page, you turn out chaos. Art is about eliminating almost everything in order to focus on the thing that you need to talk about.

IV. TECHNOLOGIES

JL: Do you find it difficult to include certain technologies, now deeply imbedded, such as email and cell phones, in your fiction? I find that technologies invented beyond a certain date—for me it might be 1978, or 1984—don't seem to belong in the realm of fiction.

PA: That's a very interesting question. In *The Book of Illusions,* which is set in the late '80s, there's a fax machine. Something very important happens through a fax machine. So, I'm not, per se, against talking about technology. In the book I'm working on now, there's a reference to email. Also to cell phones.

I'm one of the few people left without a computer. I don't write on a word processor, and I don't have email and I'm not really tempted to get it. I'm very happy with my pen and my old portable typewriter, but I'm not against talking about anything, actually. I think the glory of the novel is that you're open to everything and anything that exists or has existed in the world. I don't have any proscriptions. I don't say, "This is not allowed because..."

JL: Not an ideological boycott, of course, but more a tendency to flinch from including those things. I email frequently. But if I include it in fiction I begin disbelieving the fiction instantly. It seems to disqualify the reality of the page.

PA: But this leads to a much larger and more interesting question that I've debated with various people over the years. You know, there are the enthusiasts for technology, and they always say—and this has been happening now for probably 150 years—they say that new technology is going to change the way people think and live. It's going to revolutionize our lives. Not just our physical lives, but our inner lives as well. I am not at all a believer in this view for the simple reason that we have bodies. We get sick. We die. We love. We suffer. We grieve. We get angry. These are the constants of human life whether you live in ancient Rome or contemporary America. I really don't think that people have changed because of the telegraph or the radio or the cell phone or the airplane or, now, computer technology.

Seven or eight years ago, I was invited to Israel by the Jerusalem Foundation and stayed at an artists' center called Mishchanot. A wonderful place. I was fifty years old, and I'd never been to Israel, a Jew who had resisted the idea my entire life. I was waiting for the right moment, and when the letter from Teddy Kollek came and he said they wanted to invite me for three or four weeks to stay here and live in this building and write and do whatever I wanted, I thought it was the appropriate moment to go. Siri and Sophie [their daughter] went with me. At one point, we took a tour around the country. We visited the town of Qumran, where the Dead Sea Scrolls were discovered. There's an extraordinary museum there with the scrolls and other artifacts that were found in the cave and around the site. These artifacts are so fascinating because there are plates that look like plates you could buy in a store today, with the same patterns, the same design, or baskets that any French or Italian person would use to take to the market today. And I had a sudden revelation about the extraordinary sameness of human life through the ages. That's why we can read Homer and Sophocles and Shakespeare and feel that we're reading about ourselves.

JL: I spent my early twenties in the Bay Area during the late '80s. I was witness to this extraordinary boom in the ideology of computing, the birth of *Wired* magazine and all that gave it context. There was a tremendous excitement at the idea that human life would never be the same once virtual reality existed. But if you read Dziga Vertov, the great Russian theorist of cinema, a hundred years earlier he was making the same claim for film. And then, if you search just a decade or so earlier, the advent of radio was surrounded by the same rhetoric.

PA: It must have seemed revolutionary then. The world—people from distant places—were suddenly in contact. This isn't to say that there aren't dangers in technology. We're all too aware of teenagers today spending their lives in front of their computer screens, dulling their senses, not living fully anymore. But I think as they grow up and life begins to impinge on them, they're going to join the rest of us.

JL: The sweet irony is that so much of the online world takes a written form. What was meant to be a postliterate or visually literate culture is now obsessed with epistolary exchange. Letters. Or diaries.

PA: Exactly. That gets us back to the question of fiction. Over the generations, countless people have predicted the death of the novel. Yet I believe that written stories will continue to survive because they answer an essential human need. I think movies might disappear before the novel disappears, because the novel is really one of the only places in the world where two strangers can meet on terms of absolute intimacy. The reader and the writer make the book together. You as a reader enter the consciousness of another person, and in doing so, I think you discover something about your own humanity, and it makes you feel more alive.

JL: I like your emphasis on the privacy of the experience. No matter how enormous a novel may become, the physical act of reading determines that there's no way it can become a communal experience. To read is intimate. It's almost masturbatory.

PA: There's only one reader of a novel. That's, I think, the crucial fact about all this. Only one person. Every time, only one person.

V. EKPHRASIS

JL: I'm also fascinated by this notion of the novel's capacity for extensive descriptions of other art forms. It seems to me one of the novel's defining strengths: that it can swallow a song, a poem, or a film—

PA: Or a painting.

JL: Or a painting. It has a scope that other art forms are denied, because a novel can't be recapitulated in some other art form.

PA: I think the word is *ekphrasis,* which is a rhetorical term meaning the description of imaginary works of art. It's so interesting to me that one of the things that novels have tended not to concentrate on over the centuries is the fact that people read books. I show books and the experience of reading as part of the reality of the world. And the same goes for film. Why not describe movies? After I published *The Book of Illusions,* I sent a copy to my friend Hal Hartley, the filmmaker. And he said to me, "You know, I think maybe written films are better than real films. You can see them in your head and yet everything is exactly as you want it to be."

JL: Novelists get to direct the perfect films. We get to cast every part. We dress the set exactly as we wish.

PA: With a book you can read the same paragraph four times. You can go back to page 21 when you're on page 300. You can't do that with film. It just charges ahead. It's often difficult to keep up, especially if you're watching a film you admire very much. Good films demand to be looked at several times in order to be observed completely.

I think one of the mistakes I made with *Lulu on the Bridge* was that I wrote the script too much as if it were a novel. I think the film has to be seen several times before you can really penetrate what's going on. There's a moment early in the film when Harvey Keitel is walking down the street and there's a little graffito on the wall that says BEWARE OF GOD. I had seen this on a T-shirt and liked it very much. It's the dyslexic BEWARE OF DOG. Later on, I very consciously put a barking dog in the distance. That dog, to me, was a deity. And that's when Harvey's character discovers the dead man in the alley. Nobody, nobody could possibly understand what I was trying to do.

JL: A reader, encountering a sentence about a barking dog, would have to dwell on why that choice was made at that moment. Everything in a novel is explicitly chosen, whereas some of what a film captures feels incidental, according to the vagaries of photography and sound recording.

PA: Exactly.

JL: Meanwhile, I just can't help noticing that while you described that, a dog was barking in the distance, here in Brooklyn.

PA: Yes.

JL: So what's your fondest example of ekphrasis—the work of art depicted in another work of art?

PA: There's a great moment in *War and Peace* when Natasha is taken to the opera and Tolstoy deconstructs the whole experience. Rather than write about it from an emotional point of view or an artistic point of view, he depicts it simply from a raw, physical point of view. You know, "Then some fat woman came onstage and started gesturing, and then a gong sounded in the background, and then lightning struck, and then a skinny man sang an aria that no one understood." And I think that's probably the funniest description of a work of art I've ever read. But probably the best and most beautiful, and I'm doing this right off the top of my head—

JL: That's ideal.

PA: I hate to bring this so close to home, but I think it's Siri's last novel, *What I Loved*. The painter's artworks are of a sublime profundity, and the artworks are part of the novel. It was so beautifully articulated. I don't know that I've read another novel in which art has played such an integral role in the story.

JL: I'm remembering the description of a painting in which the artist's presence is shown, just barely, at the edge of the frame.

PA: A little shadow.

JL: Yes.

PA: Over the years, I've been intensely interested in the artificiality of books as well. I mean, who's kidding whom, after all. We know when we open up a book of fiction that we're reading something that is imaginary, and I've always been interested in exploiting that fact, using it, making it part of the work itself. Not in some dry, academic, metafictional way, but simply as an organic part of the written word. When I was a kid, I'd pick up a novel written in the third person, and I'd say to myself, "Who's talking? Who am I listening to here? Who's telling this story?" I can see a name on the cover, it says Ernest Hemingway or Tolstoy, but is it Tolstoy or Hemingway who is actually talking?

I always loved the books in which there was some kind of excuse for the fact that the book existed. For example, *The Scarlet Letter,* where Hawthorne discovers the manuscript in the custom-house and then proceeds to print it in the subsequent pages. It's all a ruse. Art upon art upon art. And yet it was very compelling to me. I think that's why most of my books have been written in the first person rather than the third.

JL: When you first started out, did you think that would be the case? I too gravitate toward the first person, but when I was a young reader, I thought of third person as the more pure. It seemed to me in some way the higher form of fiction.

PA: Perhaps, but I like the low. I'm very interested in the low, the close to the ground, something that's almost indistinguishable from life.

JL: At what point in a project are you certain of which form you'll choose?

PA: I think in every case, I've known from the beginning. The only time I was confused was when I was writing a book of nonfiction, *The Invention of Solitude.* The first part of that book is written in the first person, and then I started the second part in the first person as well. But there was something that I didn't like about it. I couldn't understand why I was dissatisfied. I wrote, I wrote, I wrote, and then I had to stop. I put it away, meditated for several weeks, and understood that the problem was the first person. I had to switch to the third. Because in the first part I was writing about somebody else—my father. I was seeing him from my point of view. But in the second part, I was mostly writing about myself. By using the first person, I couldn't see myself anymore. By shifting to the third person, I managed to get a certain distance from myself, and that made it possible for me to see myself, which in turn made it possible for me to write the book. It was very strange.

JL: You use the word *distance.* And it seems to me one aspect of your work—omnipresent, but very elusive, and difficult to speak of—is a quality of reserve.

PA: This might come as a surprise to you, but I tend to think of myself as a highly emotional writer. It's all coming out of the deepest feelings, out of dreams, out of the unconscious. And yet what I'm constantly striving for in my prose is clarity. So that, ideally, the writing will become so transparent that the reader will forget that the medium of communication is language. So that the reader is simply inside the voice, inside the story, inside what is happening. So, yes, there is a certain—I wouldn't call it reserve, but precision maybe, I don't know. At the same time, I'm trying to explore the deepest emotional questions I know about: love and death. Human suffering. Human joy. All the important things that make life worth living.

JL: Yes, I certainly didn't mean to suggest I experience the books as dispassionate. I found *Oracle Night* a wrenchingly emotional book. I'm not surprised by that. I do think you're right, that what I'm trying to characterize proceeds from the precision of the prose, its exacting quality. The effect is one of timelessness.

PA: I want to write books that can be read a hundred years from now, and readers wouldn't be bogged down by irrelevant details. You see, I'm not a sociologist, and the novel has often concerned itself with sociology. It's one of the generating forces that's made fiction interesting to people. But that's not my concern. I'm interested in psychology. And also certain philosophical questions about the world. By removing the stories from the morass of things that surround us, I'm hoping to achieve some kind of purer approach to emotional life.

JL: What's lovely is that you grant that same imperative to the characters themselves. They are often looking to purify their relationship to their own lives.

PA: I suppose in a way most of my characters are nonconsumers, not terribly interested in all the little baubles and artifacts of contemporary life. Not to say that there aren't many specific things mentioned in my books; it's just that I don't dwell on them excessively.

JL: Yes, even the most contemporary references in your work seem to float off into a timeless place.

PA: I'm very concerned that every word, every sentence in my book is pertinent. I don't want to indulge myself in the luxury of writing beautiful paragraphs just for the sake of making beautiful writing. That doesn't interest me. I want everything to be essential. In a sense, the center is everywhere. Every sentence of the book is the center of the book. ✯

BEN EHRENREICH

TALKS WITH

JOHN BANVILLE

"I AM OLD-FASHIONED ENOUGH TO USE THE WORD *BEAUTY* WITHOUT BLUSHING OR GIGGLING."

Art originates in:
Thought
Feeling
Earthy things like flesh

It is not:
Self-expression

It becomes:
A sudden access of self-awareness

There is a long-dead painter who pops up in more than a few of John Banville's thirteen books, a Nabokovian wink of a character whose name, Jean Vaublin, is roughly anagrammatic with the author's own, and whose work inspires Banville's cast of unfortunates to frequent reverie and occasional murder. "He is the master of darkness, as others are of light," Banville wrote of Vaublin in 1993's Ghosts. *"Even his brightest sunlight seems shadowed, tinged with umber from these thick trees, this ochred ground, these unfathomable spaces leading into night." It's hard not to read this as jokey self-portraiture, so apt a description is it of the gloomful world of Banville's novels, with their less than heroically doomed protagonists wriggling desperately about for a glimpse at something that might resemble rest. They sometimes catch it for a moment or two, but more usually the only light to be found is the stuff gleaming through the wit and polish of Banville's nearly perfect prose. That's plenty light enough.*

In a body of work stretching over thirty years, Banville has taken readers from his early Birchwood *(1973), in which a boy runs off with a tattered circus in famine-plagued Ireland; through a trio of historical novels about Copernicus, Kepler, and (sort of) Newton, in which the famed cosmologists do their best to eke a little harmonic order out of a world where it is far from immediately evident; through another triad of books chronicling the repentant flailings of a maid-murderer named Freddie Montgomery; to 2001's* Eclipse, *about a defeated actor returned to his childhood home in search of self among "the jumble of discarded masks"; and at last to* Shroud *(2003), his most recent, about a vicious drunk of an academic superstar with his share of nasty secrets. Banville's themes are the big ones—the shifting grounds of truth, time, and the ever-shaky self—and he digs at them with doggedness, ambition, and a vocabulary that will bring even the most casual logophiles to their knees in bliss.*

This interview took place over two months and two continents (Banville lives in Dublin), and employed two technologies of communication (email and phone). —*Ben Ehrenreich (Spring/Summer 2003)*

BEN EHRENREICH: Do you find that you're able to like any of your books?

JOHN BANVILLE: No. I hate them all. With a deep, abiding hatred. And embarrassment. I have this fantasy that I'm walking past Brentano's or wherever and I click my fingers and all my books on the shelves go blank. The covers are still there but all the pages are blank. And then I can start again and get it right. I hate them all. They're all so far below what I had hoped they would be. And yet one goes on. Here I am starting a new book. This is the absolute best stage of it, because when you're writing the opening pages of the book, anything is possible, you might actually get it right this time. In my heart, of course, I know that I won't. In a couple of years' time when I finish the book, I'll hate it just as much as the others. I won't deny that every now and then I write a sentence and I can hear a chime, I can hear that ping that you get when you hit your fingernail on the side of a glass, and I think, Yeah, that's right. Why would I sit here day after day doing this stuff? I certainly don't get any money for it.

BE: Your protagonists are generally a pretty wretched lot—broken by time, by the lies they've told themselves, by their weaknesses and fears, but struggling desperately, even when they know better, for some form of redemption. And they do find it, not any lasting sort with harps and hymns, but shards of transcendence, brief salvations. And these transitory redemptions seem to come almost exclusively from art or from sex.

JB: I have an elderly friend who holds that he is like the census form—broken down by age, sex, and religion (he's the same corpulent friend who adapted Connolly's famous dictum to "Outside every thin girl there's a fat man trying to get in"). I suppose one might say the same of my sorry lot of marionettes. They do seek some form of redemption for themselves, although I'm surprised you see so much sex in my work (not half enough, my publishers feel). Art offers them brief moments of transcendence, but they always come crashing back to earth, usually making a messy landing in something soft. I'm acutely aware that *redemption* and *transcendence* are more of those big words that so troubled Stephen Dedalus, and as such one must beware them. Art, in one formulation, is transcendental play—with an equal emphasis on adjective and noun—and play should always involve earthy things, such as clay, flesh, human beings, as well as dice, of course. I like your "not any lasting sort with harps and hymns, but shards of transcendence, brief salvations." Brief salvations is nice, implying as it does that there is more than one way of being saved.

BE: Why "dice, of course"?

JB: Well, play involves chance, of course, hence the dice.

BE: Your characters are very conscious of the role chance plays in their lives, of the degree to which they are marionettes to what Freddie Montgomery (in *The Book of Evidence*) calls "the ceaseless, slow, demented drift of things." They are often quite stubbornly dismissive of any notion of responsibility or volition, of any substantial self capable of making choices. But their narratives are largely confessional—stabs at selfhood, blunderings toward forgiveness for crimes they recognize as theirs. Would you allow that, in this sense, your novels are highly moral creatures?

JB: I don't think—in fact I'm sure, in my case, at least—that artists ever set out to make art with a moral purpose in mind. It simply would not work. One can only make art for its own sake, otherwise there is adulteration. This is what makes Orwell, for instance, such a good political satirist and such a dreadful novelist. However, the artist's intentions are not everything—in fact, they may be negligible, once the work is finished—and it's perfectly possible for a work of art to have a moral force, even a moral direction, of its own devising, as it were, even of its own volition. My characters twist and turn, reel and writhe, not out of moral anguish, but in the awful, salt-on-the-snail's-back agony of trying to be authentic. It is this—vain—quest for authenticity that drives them all, I think.

But this is the artist taking on the role of critic in regard to his own work, which is always dangerous. I look on my books with a mixture of bafflement and shame; half the time I don't know what I'm doing when I'm doing it, and the other half I am in doubt that I should be doing what I'm doing. What is it Kafka says?—I do not speak as I think, I do not think as I should, and so it all goes on in helpless darkness (in German he would not have set two "-ess" endings in sequence).

BE: Yes, I don't mean moralistic or moralizing at all, just that their concerns are moral ones, are the most basic moral ones—the possibility of choice, of becoming, to paraphrase Nietzsche (and I won't dare to speculate on his German), an animal capable of making promises. I suppose I want to push you to unravel for me the notion of "art's own sake," because it seems that you do have your purposes, conscious or not, which are not adulterating but actually fundamental, that you grapple with the same problems in different ways in different books, and do so with such precision and grace that I can't believe it's entirely unconscious.

JB: Well, I read a lot of philosophy, for the beauty of the thought if not for the rigor, and I suppose some philosophical concerns must seep into my literary thinking. I do like fiction to have a "mind," I mean, to have a sense that it originated in thought as well as in feeling. Kundera is disparagingly good on the present-day hegemony of feeling over thought, emotion over reason; he remarks somewhere that far more and far greater crimes have been committed for heartfelt than for rational reasons. Probably it is not possible to be a thinking being without a concern for the moral.

But any question of the moral inevitably raises—for the artist, at least—the question of the beautiful. I am old-fashioned enough to use the word *beauty* without blushing or giggling. Yet one has to be suspicious of what one might term "unattached" beauty. Hermann Broch held that to say "art for art's sake" is not much different from saying "business is business" or "war is war." I'm not sure I agree with him—in fact, I'm not sure I understand him—but the remark has been lodged in my mind for many years. Certainly one has to beware the overly burnished surface.

Recently I came across again a wonderful observation by Proust, I don't know from where, in which he contrasted Flaubert with Balzac. Flaubert's style, he said, replaces the object, the "mere" object, with a highly polished metaphor, so that his work is everywhere uniform, seamless, gleaming; Balzac, on the other hand, leaves all kinds of bits and pieces of things lying around, and consequently his work has the rawness and roughness of real life. I hasten to add that of course I greatly prize Flaubert over Balzac; but one knows what Proust means (indeed, Proust would most likely have detested Scott Moncrieff's daintified translation of *À la recherche*...). As to Nietzsche ("Nietzsche I loved, and after Nietzsche, art..." Sorry), I wonder if you know this wonderful aphorism from *The Gay Science:* "I fear that the animals regard man as a creature of their own kind which has in a highly dangerous fashion lost its healthy animal reason—as the mad animal, as the laughing animal, as the weeping animal, as the unhappy animal."

What were we saying...?

BE: I'm not sure exactly, but Nietzsche and other unhappy animals provide a convenient transition—in *Shroud,* your latest novel, philosophy is more in the forefront than ever. It's set in Turin against the backdrop of Nietzsche's famous breakdown, and its protagonist, Axel Vander, has a little Althusser in him and more than a little Paul de Man. What about those men grabbed your interest, and what brought them together for you?

JB: All my books since *The Book of Evidence* have been more or less concerned with the quest for authenticity. I wrote about a murderer, an actor, a spy. De Man had been in my mind for a long time, ever since I became friendly with the Belgian scholar who unearthed de Man's wartime journalism, Ortwin de Graef. Then I read Althusser's marvelous, frightening memoir, *The Future Lasts Forever* (I recommend it to you, if you don't know it already), which begins with his account of murdering his wife. (Recently I met an old friend of the Althussers', who gave it as his opinion that the only moment of true sanity in Althusser's life was when he killed "that woman.") So I blended de Man/Althusser into a kind of Frankenstein's monster, and came up with Axel Vander, a man who has lived a lie for decades, who has stolen another man's identity, who denies even his Jewishness, for no good reason that he can think of. The quintessential Banville protagonist, no?

In Vander I think I at last expressed all my thinking about the problem of authenticity—now I can move on.

BE: There were a few moments in *Shroud* in which you seemed to be—and this may be a simplistic way of putting it—explaining Vander's theoretical work, which in some ways echoes Paul de Man's, through his life. So of course he felt that "every text conceals a shameful secret," as he put it, because he saw his own shameful secret everywhere he looked. Is it right to read into the book an implicit critique of the sort of literary criticism that de Man engaged in?

JB: No. I mean, it's a travesty of de Man. I'm surprised I haven't had hate letters from de Man scholars. Fiction is absolutely conscienceless and cannibalistic. It gobbles up material wherever it can find it. I suppose I wanted to find an emblematic figure from that period. I have no interest in commenting on the great issues of our time. I just wanted to find a public figure, so I blended these two together, shamelessly, and made a fictional character.

BE: So you weren't interested in engaging with de Man's work?

JB: I find de Man's work very interesting. I think it is very... shrouded. It's written in an extraordinarily guarded, obtuse style. Frequently it is extremely difficult to find out what he's talking about, and I'm not sure whether that's intentional or not. Certainly after Ortwin de Graef discovered these anti-Semitic pieces, people leapt on de Man's work and said, "Oh, the whole thing is an elaborate smoke screen." I find that extremely hard to believe. These were pieces that he wrote at an extraordinary time in twentieth-century history, an extraordinarily dangerous time. Everybody's loyalties and politics were obscure, and I can't imagine that a man of his intellect would lead his life and erect critical systems on a peccadillo from during the war. Certainly one of the pieces he wrote is pretty disgracefully anti-Semitic. He famously said that if the Jewish element were removed from Europe, European culture would lose nothing, which is disgraceful, no doubt about that. But so many people did so many appalling things—look at the early books of Graham Greene, which are dripping with anti-Semitism. And one only has to mention Eliot. Most of the modernists with the great and notable exception of James Joyce were fascistic in tendency and most of them anti-Semitic.

So I don't see that de Man would have felt all that guilty. He did have something to hide, but who hasn't? Certainly if you lived through the period that he lived through in Europe and then went to America, it would be extremely difficult not to have something to hide. And I don't like to think what I would have done if I had been invited to write for a collaborationist newspaper in Belgium in the early '40s, but that doesn't mean that I don't reprehend the stuff that he wrote. Anti-Semitism always seems to me an extraordinarily *stupid* attitude, and extraordinarily dim. I'm always amazed that people with such delicate and finely honed sensitivities, an Eliot or even a Graham Greene, would be anti-Semitic. I just don't know how they could do that. But I didn't live through the period that they lived through. Everybody in the '30s seem to have been casually anti-Semitic.

But this is going wildly off the subject, because I had no intention of writing about these subjects in *Shroud*. From my point of view, a book manifests itself and then the only task I have is to get rid of the damned thing, throw it away. Someone once asked Joyce why did he use Homeric parallels in *Ulysses,* and he looked at him as if he were mad and said, "Well, it was a way of working." In other words, it didn't mean any more than that it was a method of working. I think that's true of practically all art that's real. I don't think art has a conscience of any kind.

BE: Let me ask you a hopelessly nineteenth-century High Romantic question of the sort that you're not supposed to ask (or, God forbid, try to answer) with a straight face these days. What do you believe is the task of literature? The word *task* is perhaps a bit didactic. Maybe *mission* would be better, or *end,* but among the many things that literature does and can do, is there any one thing that you can pinpoint that it must do to be worthy of the name?

JB: As usual, it's easier to say what literature is not than what it is or should be. Certainly it's not self-expression, as so many imagine, including some writers who should know better. I'm rather inclined to agree with Auden that poetry—all art—makes nothing happen. Real art is perfectly useless, if by useful we are thinking of politics, morals, social issues, etc. Cyril Connolly put it well and simply when he declared that the only business of an artist is to make masterpieces. And yet the work of art is always moral, even though the artist harbored no moral intentions in making the work. The moral quality arises from the fact that the work of art represents the absolute best that a particular human being could do—perhaps even a little more than he could do. I realize, of course, that the same can be said of science, which is all right by me—but what about sport? Does the ephemerality of the sporting moment somehow make it less significant than the work of art?

You ask me what a work of literature must do in order to be worthy of the name. I suppose I would say it must have a quality of the transcendent. I do not mean metaphysical transcendence, but a kind of heightening. In the work of art, the world is made for a moment radiant, more than itself while at the same time remaining absolutely, fundamentally, mundanely, utterly itself. So the artistic act is almost like the sexual act: in the glare of its attention, the Other, in a sudden access of self-awareness, takes on a transcendent glow. High talk, I know, but we are, I take it, talking of high art.

BE: You said earlier that several of your novels addressed what you called "the problem of authenticity," which in a way surprised me, because so many of your characters seem to reject the whole notion of authenticity. Freddie Montgomery at one point in *The Book of Evidence* says, "To place all faith in the mask, that seems to me the true shape of refined humanity." Do you agree with him?

JB: I don't know. I don't know that I have any opinion. And I don't know that my opinion counts very much. I don't either agree or disagree with the feelings and the thoughts of the characters that I invent. I don't think fiction works that way. I don't think art works that way. Again I would with Joyce say that that was a way of working. I spent I suppose ten years, damned near twenty years, following that vein of writing. I've now finished it. *Shroud* is the last book I'm going to write like that. (I'm now writing a book about childhood and the seaside!) I felt that in *Shroud* I had gone as far as I could go in that direction. Many people would say I've gone at least one book too far. But I had to try to get it right, and I didn't get it right. I think that the problem of authenticity for characters like Freddie Montgomery and Axel Vander is in a way precisely what you say, that they don't believe in authenticity. And yet, if one doesn't believe in the possibility of authenticity, then how is one to live, literally—how is one to find a solid piece of ground to put one's foot on? This is the question that they all are following, all those characters from Freddie Montgomery right through to Axel Vander. How does one find a solid place to stand?

BE: About the new book, I was about to ask, "What could be more quintessentially un-Banvillean than childhood and the seashore?" but then the protagonist of *Birchwood* was a young boy, wasn't he?

JB: He was, but this is a much simpler book. I've only started it, so God knows what it will become. It may turn into some horrible, dark, monstrous thing, as they usually do. I hope not. Again I suppose I will be writing about an essential inability to absorb reality. I think this is the predicament of all artists, that they stand outside the world looking on in amazement. The only passage in fiction that I've ever written that I thought came close to a direct statement was in *The Book of Evidence* where he says, "I've never felt at home on this earth. I feel that our whole presence here is a sort of cosmic blunder, and the people who were meant for here are out at some other planet on the other side of the universe, and," he says, "they'd be extinct by now in the world that was made to contain us."[1] I suppose if you wanted to extract a testament from the books, that would be it. I'm constantly astonished by the world. I have been since childhood and I've never got used to it.

I'm sitting here looking at clouds going across the sky. Clouds have always fascinated me. They seem the most unreal things. Skies always look to me like things out of a science-fiction movie. And yet I've been looking at skies for the past fifty-seven years. I should've got used to them by now, but I'm not. I look at people in the same way. People do the most extraordinary, outlandish, bizarre things quite ordinarily. I've always felt that if you were a Martian and you came to earth, and you'd coped with everything—half the population scraping its face with a blade every morning and things like that—and thought you had it all down pat, and then somebody sneezes, or somebody yawns and stretches their arms in that sort of silent howl. You'd say, "Oh no, I've got to go back and rethink this whole thing. Obviously these human beings are far stranger than I thought they were." I find the world constantly an astonishing place. Not because of the mysterious things, but because of the quite ordinary things.

BE: I suppose there's a real Martian quality to childhood.

JB: Yes, I think that's why I'm going back now to do this book, which is probably the one I've been practicing to do for the last forty years.

BE: In what sense do you mean that?

JB: I'm pushing sixty now. I find it hard to believe, but I am. One

---

[1] The exact quote is: "I have never really got used to being on this earth. Sometimes I think our presence here is due to a cosmic blunder, that we were meant for another planet altogether, with other arrangements, and other laws, and other, grimmer skies. I try to imagine it, our true place, off on the far side of the galaxy, whirling and whirling. And the ones who were meant for here, are they out there, baffled and homesick, like us? No, they would have become extinct long ago. How could they survive, these gentle earthlings, in a world that was made to contain *us*?"

starts to look backward and try to see clearly one's beginnings, and I feel that I was formed very much by, for instance, those prepubertal loves. To fall in love at the age of eleven is one of the most extraordinary, tender, and anguishing experiences that one can have. One never forgets them. There are girls that I fell in love with seaside summers when I was a child whom I still remember as vividly as people that I was in love with last year, perhaps even more brilliantly. Of course the danger is that our friend Proust has been there already, and it's going to be very hard to do it, not to mention Nabokov in *Lolita,* which has the quintessential seaside adolescent love affair in the opening pages. I don't know if there's much to do after Nabokov and Proust, but one does one's little bit. One scribbles one's little sentences and hopes for the best.

BE: Many of your novels are interconnected. The story of Freddie Montgomery was told in three volumes published over six years, and Cass and Alexander Cleave reappear in *Eclipse* and in *Shroud*. Do you conceive of your novels as complete works in themselves or do you look at the broader picture?

JB: I think in general there is a Book and all of the books that one writes are volumes in it. When I finally drop off the twig, what will be left will be a work. Each one grows out of the previous one. I planned to write a quartet of books when I did *Copernicus* and then *Kepler* and then *The Newton Letter*. I never got around to writing the fourth novel, about a twentieth-century physicist, which is what I wanted to do in the first place.

BE: Who would that have been?

JB: It would have been an amalgam of Heisenberg and Einstein and Niels Bohr and people like that. In the '70s I read a lot of science. I have no training in it whatsoever—I was purely fumbling my way in the dark—but I was fascinated by the ideas that science was throwing up then. I haven't kept up with it. It's practically impossible now; things change so quickly. I still feel a quickening of the pulse when I hear talk of superstrings and things like that.

I planned to write those four "science" books and I set out intentionally to do that, but I didn't intend there to be any more books about Freddie Montgomery than *The Book of Evidence*. The next one, *Ghosts,* started off and suddenly there was Freddie speaking again. I hadn't got his voice out of my head, and I don't think I got the voice out of my head until I had written *Shroud*. It's the same tone throughout. I'm surprised that people hadn't thrown up their hands in despair and said, "Is he ever going to speak in any other kind of voice than this one? We're getting sick of it." And maybe they do. Since I don't read reviews anymore, it may well be that they're all saying that. But I do think that each book grows out of the previous one.

That's one of the reasons that I'm so interested in this little book that I'm starting now, because I can't quite see where it came from. It may be a transition book; it may be a radical shift; I don't know.

BE: It's a very different voice?

JB: It is. It's a much simpler voice. It's a much less malign voice. It's a much more forgiving voice, I think. But let's face it: every writer has only one voice. Even Joyce, somewhere behind all those styles there is a style, there is a voice. Because we can't be more than ourselves. We can't be more than one, no matter how hard we try.

BE: How fully do you plot out a novel when you start?

JB: I used to plan books. *Kepler* is the most extraordinarily planned book. I based the whole thing on Kepler's notion of the five perfect solids in geometry. Each section has the same number of sides as a cube or a dodecahedron or whatever, and I planned it practically to the number of words in each chapter and each section. I knew when I wrote the first line what the last line was going to be and how far away it was going to be. I don't do that anymore. I think *Mefisto* was a transition book for me. It was an extremely difficult book. It took me five years. It almost killed me. My wife insists I had a nervous breakdown when I was doing it. I didn't know where to go with it, I didn't know what to do with it, and I think it was a kind of breakthrough. I don't think that the book was successful in formal terms but I think it has a kind of peculiar coherence that I didn't intend. I wrote about a lot of things and I didn't know why I was doing them. I still don't know why I did them. So now I don't really plan at all.

Eclipse and *Shroud* started as one book. I spent a year or two writing it, and Axel Vander was in that book, in *Eclipse.* I just couldn't get anywhere and it was getting worse and worse and I was thinking of abandoning the whole thing and I suddenly realized there were two books in it and I went ahead and wrote *Eclipse* and then *Shroud.* They were each written quite quickly, in the space of about two years. So there was an instance of something that certainly wasn't planned. It was a bore to be stuck with Cass Cleave in *Shroud* and try to accommodate her fate in that book, but I quite liked writing about poor Cass. It was a relief from writing about these filthy old monstrous woman-killers that I've been writing about since the '80s. So maybe Cass is the one that sent me—this thought has suddenly occurred to me—maybe Cass is the one that sent me back to childhood. That may well be. Maybe this next book is Cass's book.

BE: Are you still editing?

JB: No. I was the literary editor of the *Irish Times* for about ten years but I gave it up about two years ago.

BE: So now you're freelancing?

JB: Yes. I still review for the *Irish Times* and I review for the *New York Review* and the *New York Times* and various places.

BE: It seems like I see your name at least once a week.

JB: [*Laughs*] It's terrible. I remember there was a used-book dealer in

London many years ago. He said he was going to open up a special section of his bookshop devoted to books recommended by Anthony Burgess. When people ask me for blurbs now, prepublication, I say, "My name is such a debased coin, you're better off without it."

But I like the discipline. It's so different from writing fiction. You sit there and you do it, like a piece of Zen archery or something. You do it and if you get it right it can be quite satisfying, and it's not as shaming as fiction.

BE: Shaming?

JB: I can write a review in a day. It would take me a day to write a couple of lines of fiction and even then they wouldn't be right. It's an entirely different discipline. And I suppose I feel that if I have any public duty it's to keep people reading, keep people interested. I had an extraordinary experience a couple years ago when Louis Menand's book *The Metaphysical Club* came out. It had been published for about six months and I read it and I said to the *Irish Times,* "Look, I want to review this." We gave it a full page. The book became a best seller here, just on the strength of that review. I was astonished. I always assume, and I suspect that most reviewers assume, that nobody ever reads reviews.

BE: Or maybe the first and last paragraphs.

JB: Exactly. Before I gave up reading reviews that's what I used to read, the first and the last, because you knew that in the middle it was just the plot summary.

BE: Do you find it difficult to balance writing novels and writing as a critic?

JB: No. In the matter of fiction and criticism I have a split personality, although no doubt each pursuit informs the other, in superficial ways. I was a newspaper copy editor for nearly twenty years; it must have taught me something about precision, clarity, punctuation, etc. Reviewing—and I consider myself a reviewer, not a critic—is a kind of knack that one develops. When one is young one expects to be able to say everything in a review that one feels and thinks about the work under consideration, but rapidly one comes to realize that the demands imposed by word length and deadline and so on mean that one must choose a couple of ideas and reactions and concentrate on them. Fiction—making art—is an altogether more mysterious business, which involves and invokes everything one has to give.

I might put it this way: For me, reviewing is done while I'm awake, and thinking as far as possible in a straight line; art is done while I'm in a form of hypnagogic state that is not quite dreaming and not quite waking. I know all this sounds hopelessly nineteenth-century High Romantic, but there you are.

BE: What is the distinction for you between a reviewer and a critic?

JB: It's quite simple. A book reviewer reviews new books that the public has not seen yet. My job is to introduce people to the book and say, "Look, this is worth your attention." I'm in the happy position now that I can choose what I want to review, so I don't review books that I don't like. My wife always says to me, "You're giving an entirely false image of yourself, because you seem like the nicest person in the world. You like everything you read. It's only because you only review books that you like." She says, "You should take a book now and then that you don't like and take a flying kick at it." I say, "What's the point of that?" There are enough critics around, enough book reviewers around, who are tearing the guts out of books. What I try to do is get people enthusiastic about books.. ✯

DAVE EGGERS

TALKS WITH

JOAN DIDION

"I'M INVISIBLE SCARLET O'NEIL IN WASHINGTON. I MEAN, IT DOESN'T HAVE ANY CURRENCY. BEING JOAN DIDION MEANS NOTHING."

Unfortunate decisions California citizens have made:
Electing two movie-star governors
Building prisons to create jobs
Neglecting the public school system in favor of short-term gains
Committing a lot of sane people to mental institutions

This interview took place in San Francisco, in the fall of 2003, as part of a series of onstage interviews presented by City Arts & Lectures. The venue was the Herbst Theatre, which seats about nine hundred. Didion had done interviews at the Herbst before, and while watching her previous event, I'd learned that she seemed to prefer to chat than to be asked to expound. Ponderous, open-ended questions—"Why do you write, Ms. Didion?"—were not going to work. So on this night I tried to keep the mood buoyant and conversational, especially given that the subject matter of her then-latest book, Where I Was From, *was not sunny.*

That book, by the way, is no less brilliant than The White Album *and* Slouching Towards Bethlehem, *the collections of her pieces—part journalism, part cultural critique, part memoir—that established her as a writer of uncommon acuity and a voice that spoke to and about a certain generation at a critical point. Like those early books,* Where I Was From *showcases her perfectly calibrated style, and like all of her recent work, including* Political Fictions, *it has lost nothing on her reputation-making books of the late '60s and '70s. As always, her prose is both precise and fluid, cruelly accurate while often revealing the vulnerabilites of its author.*

Didion has, of course, written great novels too, and has said that each time she starts writing a novel, she re-reads Joseph Conrad's Victory. *Though the style of that book is a bit more rococo than Didion's minimalist prose, it's evident why it would seem to inspire books like* The Last Thing He Wanted *and* A Book of Common Prayer. Victory *concerns intrigue among travelers in the islands of the Far East, a cast of misfits of whom most are wanderers, abandoners. They leave husbands, children, their countries, and they get involved in very tricky business. These are the characters that populate Didion's fiction, and her heroines are among the most complex, even opaque, in contemporary fiction.*

Because Didion's prose is so extraordinarily sharp, some expect that in person Didion would be a kind of ranconteur, a spewer of devastating bons mots. But she's far more personable than that. She is a person, actually, very much a person, even though her name now has about it the sound of legend. The Legend of Joan Didion—*that could be a western, or a book by James Fenimore Cooper. "The Ballad of Joan Didion"—maybe a song by Bob Dylan? It means so much, that name, Joan Didion, even if she denies it.*

—Dave Eggers (Fall 2003)

DAVE EGGERS: So we're going to just get started. I have the questions printed on blue cards.

JOAN DIDION: It's beautiful type, too. [*Laughs*]

DE: That means they're going to be good. [*Laughter*] So we met about six or seven years ago when I interviewed you for *Salon*.

JD: Yes. And I didn't even—I wasn't on the net at the time. And I did not know what *Salon* was. As a matter of a fact, I wanted to cancel the interview because I had so many things to do and I thought, What is this? Why am I doing this? [*Laughs*]

DE: Yeah, and there were many years after that when people were still wondering. [*Laughter*]

JD: That was 1996. It was only seven years ago.

DE: At the time, one of my favorite answers that you gave was when I asked what you missed most about California. Do you remember what you said?

JD: No.

DE: Driving. You talked about how you missed that uninterrupted line of thought that you had when you drove. And you've written about it, about L.A.

JD: My husband and I moved to New York in 1988, and to negotiate going to the grocery store meant you had to go out on the street and deal with a lot of *people,* you know? You had to maybe run into a neighbor—certainly run into somebody in the elevator, run into a doorman. It took you out of your whole train of thought. Whereas if you walked out of your driveway and got in your car and went to the store, not a soul was going to enter your mindstream. You could just continue kind of focusing on what you were doing.

DE: You still have a California driver's license.

JD: I do.

DE: With a New York address on it.

JD: Yes, it does. Mm-hm. [*Laughter*] You know how I got it?

DE: No. How would that work?

JD: Well, my mother was living in Monterey and I was visiting her.

I had to renew my license, so I went up to—I think it was Oceanside. And I said, "Uh, you know I'm not *actually* living in California right now; I'm living in New York. Can I put that address on?" She said, "Put wherever you want us to send it." [*Laughter*]

DE: And another thing, when we talked then, we talked about a book called *Holy Land,* written by D. J. Waldie, about Lakewood, California. And then shortly around that time you wrote about Lakewood yourself, and that would become the first piece—

JD: Part of *Where I Was From.* And in fact, when I wrote about Lakewood, it was 1993. It was a piece for the *New Yorker*—Tina Brown was then the editor and she was interested in this. When I said I wanted to do Lakewood, she was crazy for me to do Lakewood because there was this group of high-school boys called the Spur Posse who were all over shows like *Montel* at the time. They did this totally predictable and not very unusual thing for high-school boys: They kept a point system on girls they had slept with, right? And for this, this somehow gained them all this notoriety. But anyway, what interested me about Lakewood was that it was a defense-industry town, and the boys gave me a reason to go into a town where there was a Douglas plant that was clearly the only employer in town. And it was during the middle of the defense cutbacks, and so I thought that would be an interesting thing to do. And I met D. J. Waldie then, and he was doing this series of pieces—not *pieces,* they were pieces of a *novel,* it turned out—which he was publishing in little literary magazines. And he gave them to me and I was just *stunned*—I mean, they were so good.

DE: *Holy Land* is an incredible book. And the Lakewood section is one of the primary elements in *Where I Was From.*

JD: Well, what happened is, I finished that piece, and I realized that, even though it was eighteen thousand words long or whatever—I mean, it didn't run that long in the *New Yorker,* but that's how long I'd written it—that I hadn't *answered* the questions I had.

That it'd raised more questions about California than I'd answered. I hadn't even thought of it as about California when I started it; I thought of it as about the defense industry, right? The kind of withering of the defense industry in Southern California. But then it turned out to raise some kind of deeper questions about what California was about. So then I started doing some more reading and started playing around with the idea of doing—of trying to answer those other questions about what California was about. And finally—I didn't realize—it was only quite late, when I was writing this book, that I realized that was what Lakewood was about. The person who would explain what Lakewood was, was Henry George, who had written this before the Southern Pacific, when everybody in California was excited about the glories the railroad would bring. He wrote this piece—it was the first piece he ever wrote—for the *Overland Monthly* called "What the Railroad Will Bring Us." And Lakewood was really an answer to what the railroad had brought us. I mean, it was the answer to what the ideal… It's too complicated. [*Laughter*]

DE: Lakewood was like a Levittown. And it was supposed to be bigger than that, and it went up overnight and all the houses were identical.

JD: They all went on sale the same day. It was bigger than the original Levittown, actually. And it was designed around a regional shopping center. If you look at the *Thomas Guide* book—this is what got me excited about it—to this day, you see the shopping center in the middle of town. You see a public golf course, nine holes, over on the corner of the town. And then down below, you see the Douglas plant. This is a kind of really simple town. And the houses were all identical. I mean, I think there were something like eight basic models, but they were all pretty much alike. They came in various colors and you couldn't have two of the same color next door to each other.

DE: They had a choice of colors and models—

JD: Yeah, but you had to rotate them on a block. And they were really quite small. They were two- and three-bedrooms, but they were nine hundred and fifty to eleven hundred square feet, which is—I mean, I've lived in apartments which were eight hundred and fifty square feet, and it's not a lot of, you know, space. For a three-bedroom house.

DE: But the piece about Lakewood crystallized a lot of the issues that you've been writing about.

JD: *Opened* a lot of the issues. Yeah. I mean, really, it raised all these questions. That's why I started writing this.

DE: So in this book—you've been writing about California for so long, but never with such, I think, *finality.* You know, you really come to conclusions here. Basically, you mentioned the Southern Pacific Railroad and how California has this history of selling itself out for the short gain—you know, short-sightedly—selling its land to the Southern Pacific Railroad, for example. And in some ways, your book is fatalistic, because California hasn't changed that much in its shortsightedness. Can you talk about that, about the process of realizing that the state has always sort of been this way?

JD: Well, all these things kept happening. I kept thinking that this was evidence of how California had changed. I mean, one of the things that really deeply shocked me was when I realized that California no longer had a really functioning public school system. That its scores were now on a par with *Mississippi's*. And that the University of California system was no longer *valued* as it had been. And that the investment at the state level was not being made there. And yet we were building all these new prisons. I thought this was evidence of how California had changed, but it wasn't. I mean, I finally realized it was the same deal. It was selling the future, selling the state, in return for someone's agreement—short-term agreement—to enrich us. People want prisons in their town because they think it'll bring jobs, right? Well, it doesn't even bring jobs, and what does it bring for the future?

DE: But now everything's changed. We had a recall, and we have a new governor, he was an action star—I think we've been really far-sighted about that, at least. [*Laughter*] So you must be thinking optimistically, now. Finally there's a break, and we're thinking of the future—looking ahead. [*Laughter*] But you commented on Arnold's election somewhere, I think. I didn't see it firsthand, but didn't you say, "Nothing good can come of this."? [*Laughter*]

JD: I probably did. [*Laughter*] I was so sort of thrilled over the weekend: I saw in the *Los Angeles Times* that part of the way the budget had been balanced by Gray Davis included getting rid of a huge number of state jobs. But as things progressed, he didn't—Gray Davis didn't—have a chance to get rid of those people. I mean, he could do it now, but he's not going to. And so it will fall to Arnold Schwarzenegger, who will have to make a decision: either to follow through on the job cuts or to find that money someplace else. Where will that money come from? And he keeps talking about bringing *new business* in. Where is this new business coming from?

DE: Well, it was interesting: you talk about how California has this history of individualism and self-reliance, but from the beginning the state has depended pretty heavily on federal money.

JD: Yeah.

DE: And here, Bush came to the state, and Arnold was crowing about how George will come back and give us some money and he'll bail us out. He called himself the Collectinator.

JD: And he himself was deeply into that individual effort, yes. He's almost an exemplar of the kind of error that we've seen over the years in California. [*Laughs*]

DE: Well, the whole map is right here in your book, the blueprint for how this state is run. It's amazing that—well, I don't know. If everybody had read this, I think we might have had a different result with the whole recall effort. It's all there.

Let's back up a little bit and talk about the writing of your book. California has always been a very personal subject for you, and you've woven together the state itself and your upbringing here. And at the same time, this book is sort of about the loss of a certain California that you knew.

JD: Yeah, well, I don't think I could have written it before my parents died. I don't mean that we would have had a fight about it—we wouldn't have had a fight about it at all. But I just couldn't have done it, because it was not their idea. That's one thing. The other thing is that the death of my parents started me thinking more about what my own relationship to California was. Because it kind of threw it up for grabs. You know, when your parents die, you're not exactly *from* the place you were from. I don't know, it's just an odd—it's an odd thing.

DE: Early in the book you trace the paths of many of your ancestors in coming to California. And it connects a lot with the heroines in many of your novels. I think you find sort of the DNA for them in this passage that describes many of your—[*DE gives JD the passage in question*]

JD: Everybody in my family moved on the frontier. I mean, they moved on the frontier, through several centuries. Wherever the frontier was, that's where they were. [*Reading*]

> These women in my family would seem to have been pragmatic and in their deepest instincts clinically radical, given to breaking clean with everyone and everything they knew. They could shoot and they could handle stock and when their children outgrew their shoes they could learn from the Indians how to make moccasins. "An old lady in our wagon train taught my sister to make blood pudding," Narcissa Cornwall recalled. "After killing a deer or steer

you cut its throat and catch the blood. You add suet to this and a little salt, and meal or flour if you have it, and bake it. If you haven't anything else to eat, it's pretty good." They tended to accommodate any means in pursuit of an uncertain end. They tended to avoid dwelling on just what that end might imply. When they could not think what else to do they moved another thousand miles, set out another garden: beans and squash and sweet peas from seeds carried from the last place. The past could be jettisoned, children buried and parents left behind, but seeds got carried.

DE: And when we spoke many years ago we talked about connections between the heroines in *A Book of Common Prayer* and *Run River,* and that passage connected a lot of them together, these women that were—

JD: Even the woman in the last novel—Elena McMahon, in *The Last Thing He Wanted*—she was similar in some ways.

DE: Right. When you were writing *Where I Was From,* did you realize the connections between all those characters in your novels, that their DNA was that of the frontier women in your family's history?

JD: No. No. No, I didn't.

DE: So we just, right now, we just did it. We just figured it out. [*Laughter*] Wow, that was good. That was easy. [*Laughter*] But so there's this idea of "I'm debunking the myth of California" that runs throughout the book, and in many different ways. But you've also said that you see this book as sort of a love letter to California. Can you explain that?

JD: Well, you don't bother getting mad at people you don't love, right? I mean, you just, you don't. I mean, why would I spend all that time trying to figure it out if I didn't have a feeling for it?

DE: There's a passage near the end, when you're driving from Monterey to Berkeley and your mother's asking, "Are we on the right road? This doesn't look familiar, are we on the right road?" And you keep reassuring her that you're on 101 North, that this is the correct road. And then she finally says, "Then where did it all go?"

JD: Mm-hm.

DE: And there's also a passage, way back, from *Slouching Towards Bethlehem* that went, "All that is constant about the California of my childhood is the rate at which it disappears."

JD: Yeah. Well, at the time I wrote that line, very little of it had disappeared compared with the amount that has disappeared now. I think I was thinking specifically about the *one subdivision* that had been built that was visible from the road between Sacramento and Berkeley. Well, now it's a little bit more built up than that. [*Laughs*] What Mother was talking about when we were driving up from Monterey, that had happened just in a few years. I mean, suddenly, suddenly, suddenly everything had disappeared—suddenly all the open space on 101 south of San Jose was gone. I mean, it had been gone north of San Jose for some time. First Morgan Hill went. Then Gilroy went. Salinas may be next. We were just north of Salinas when Mother was so troubled.

DE: There's a man that you cite in one of the pieces, Lincoln Steffens, who talks about deep ecology, the belief that humans are inevitably going to destroy themselves, and so we shouldn't worry so much about things like recycling. Are you fatalistic about the future of California?

JD: Well, you know, if you extrapolated from the history, you would not be optimistic. But I keep thinking that we're all capable of learning, you know? That somehow we will, we will see—we'll realize the value of what we have and actually make a commitment to invest in the university, keep some open land, you know, just some basic things.

DE: Switching back: Tonight Michael Moore is speaking at San

Francisco State, and you and I talked a little bit before about the political climate right now. You've always been—to I'm sure everyone here—an exemplar of someone who can find nuance and who doesn't necessarily look for the black and the white and the easy answers in your political writing. But right now we're at a point where there is a shrillness to the debate. You turn on the TV and find MSNBC and Chris Matthews and everything else, all so loud and abusive. What's your political diet? What do you watch? What do you read?

JD: Oh, I read a lot. You know, I get five newspapers. But in order to follow what's going on, you actually have to look at television at certain points, because otherwise you don't realize how *toxic* it's become. You get no sense of the confrontational level of everything. I don't know what it is. The obvious answer is it's 24/7 television, it's cable. But how cable took the form of people shouting at each other, I don't know.

DE: In a way, it's a positive thing that Michael Moore is being read so widely, and that Al Franken has a number one book. But then these books keep reacting to each other. I don't know when it's going to end. And I don't know who's *buying all of the books*—

JD: But somebody is. There's a secret there. Ann Coulter's book, for example—is she the *Treason* or the *Liar* one? I can't—

DE: There's a *lie* somewhere in there.

JD: Yeah.

DE: And her face on the cover, which is nice.

JD: It has a little—there's a little code icon next to it on the best-seller list in the *New York Times*, which indicates that a lot of its sales have been in bulk. [*Laughter*]

DE: Oh, that's true.

JD: And so that's where some of it's coming from. But who the bulk is, I don't—[*Laughter*]

DE: No, that's how it works. But now, *Fixed Ideas,* which is your short book that New York Review Books put out, begins on the stage we're sitting on, when you were here in 2001, in September.

JD: Yeah, it was just after. It was like a week after the event.

DE: Right, and it talks about you touring in the weeks after 9/11 and fearing the quality of discourse. And the people that you met along the road were all afraid of the inability to speak out after that and—

JD: I don't know if they were afraid. They were speaking out, they were absolutely speaking out. I mean, I was amazed. I had sort of arrived from New York like a zombie to do this book tour, which seemed like the least relevant thing anybody could possibly be doing, and to my amazement, every place I went people were making connections between our political life—which is what the book was—I was promoting *Political Fictions.* There are many connections between our political life and what happened on September 11. Connections I hadn't even thought to make. I was still so numb. And so then I got back to New York after two weeks, and I discovered that everybody had stopped talking in New York. I mean it was—everybody had flags out instead. And the *New York Times* was running "Portraits of Grief," which were these little sentimental stories about—little vignettes about the dead. I mean it was kind of—it was a scary, scary thing.

DE: In *Fixed Ideas,* you wrote that the people you spoke to recognized that "even then, with flames still visible in lower Manhattan… the words 'bipartisanship' and 'national unity' had come to mean acquiescence to the administration's pre-existing agenda—for example, the imperative for further tax cuts, the necessity for Arctic drilling, the systematic elimination of regulatory and union protections, even the funding for the missile shield." Do you feel that the quality of debate has gotten better since then?

JD: No. I mean, the president is still using—is now using September 11 when he's asked about *campaign funding*. [*Laughter*] No, it's true. He was asked why it was necessary for him to raise *x* million dollars, or whatever it was, for his primary campaign when he was unopposed, and he said that he remembered the way this country was, that he'll never forget September 11. [*Laughter*] And that it was important for him to remain in office, too. [*Laughter*]

DE: Do you have plans to cover the next campaign?

JD: I don't have any plans to cover it. No, I just don't have the heart to cover it. I mean, I might read about it and then write about it, but I'm not going to get on those planes now. [*Laughs*]

DE: No?

JD: No.

DE: Was there a point in your career when being Joan Didion got in the way of your being a reporter? When you couldn't hide anymore, you couldn't just observe?

JD: I think I can usually hide. Especially around politics. I'm Invisible Scarlet O'Neil in Washington. I mean, it doesn't have any currency. Being Joan Didion means nothing. [*Laughs*]

DE: There's a great passage in *The White Album,* in a piece you were doing about Nancy Reagan. And who was that for? And why?

JD: I had a column every other week for the *Saturday Evening Post,* a magazine that no longer exists. So I decided to go to Sacramento, to interview Nancy Reagan, who had become the governor's wife.

DE: And there was a camera crew there, and you were there, and there was a lot of discussion of how to make her seem like she was having a normal day.

JD: Yeah, the camera crew was there to see what she was doing on an ordinary Tuesday morning in Sacramento. This was, like, her first year in Sacramento. And I was there to see what she was doing on an ordinary Tuesday morning in Sacramento. [*Laughs*] So we were all kind of watching each other. And then she said, "I might be picking… I might be picking…" and the cameraman asked her if she might be picking roses. And she said, "I might be *picking* them, but I won't be *using* them!" [*Laughter*]

DE: I never got that part. Did you get it? I never understood what that meant.

JD: It was just—she wasn't having a dinner party. She didn't have dinner parties in Sacramento. She only had them in the *Pacific Palisades,* so she wouldn't be *using* the flowers. I think that's what *she* meant, but what I heard was, it was, you know, sort of a bad actress's line. [*Laughter*] More animation than was required.

DE: You wrote about a trip with Bush Sr., when he was vice president, going to Israel and Jordan. They would always have to have the right backdrop. In Jordan, Bush's people made sure that there was an American flag in every frame, and a *camel.*

JD: A camel. [*Laughter*] I guess that was to clarify the setting, you know?

DE: And at one point they said they wanted Bush to be looking through binoculars at enemy territory. Who knows why. So they give him a pair of binoculars, and then they realized the direction he was looking was Israel. [*Laughter*] When you were following Dukakis, and when they had him playing ball, you wrote that it was "insider baseball." That was also a title of one of the pieces.

JD: "Insider baseball," yeah. It was astonishing.

DE: Yeah. Because they wanted to make them seem real, so everywhere they would go, Dukakis and one of his guys would play baseball—play catch outside the airplane.

JD: On the tarmac, yeah.

DE: And then you would be invited to watch—

JD: Right, and then if anybody missed it—I don't mean if *I* missed it, I could have missed it and they wouldn't have even noticed, but if one of the *networks* missed it, they wanted everybody to film it, right—if anybody missed it, they would do it again. [*Laughter*]

DE: And why does everybody—you're astonished by it when you're covering these campaigns, but everybody goes along with the same sort of events. "OK, now we're going to go out, and the candidate is going to eat broccoli, and that's going to lead the next day's news." But everybody goes along with it. They're trading access; they want the access and then in exchange, the campaign gives them this moment.

JD: Yes. You don't want to get thrown off the campaign. That's the key thing about covering a campaign, for people who cover them, is you can't—

DE: You don't want to get thrown off the plane.

JD: Right. You want to be there. So it's a trade for access. In case something happens, right? But nothing is going to happen—

DE: Well, somebody's going to fall off a platform one of these days, right?

JD: Somebody did, remember?

DE: That was Dole.

JD: Yeah, in Chico.

DE: OK. Now we're going to do a quick speed round. With these questions, you're allowed to answer only *yes* or *no*. [*Laughter*] OK, here we go. Will there be another recall, this one of Arnold?

JD: No.

DE: Should there be one?

JD: No, I don't believe in recalls.

DE: Just yes or no, please. [*Laughter*] Will you ever move back to California?

JD: I can't answer that *yes* or *no.* [*Laughter*]

DE: Can you believe how well this interview is going? [*Laughter*]

JD: Yes.

DE: Have you written a screenplay where you were happy with the final product?

JD: Yes.

DE: What was that? You're allowed to answer.

JD: *True Confessions.*

DE: Is that the one with—

JD: De Niro and Duvall.

DE: Oh, right. And—

JD: And it was directed by… I know him as well as I know my own name: Ulu Grosbard. We had a good time on it, and I was happy with it. In fact, I see it on television and it still makes me cry.

DE: So it was written by just you and your husband?

JD: Yeah. In fact, we did all the changes during shooting; we did them on the weekend. Ulu would come over—we were shooting in Los Angeles and he would come over and we would make the changes while he sat there on Sunday afternoon. It was really easy.

DE: So you were on set the whole time?

JD: No, we weren't on set. We were at a house in Brentwood. [*Laughs*] But Sundays they had off, so he would come over on Sunday and we would do it.

DE: OK, a few more in the speed round. Can Wes Clark beat

George Bush?

JD: If he were nominated, yeah.

DE: Can Howard Dean beat George Bush?

JD: I doubt it.

DE: And finally: really, though, can you believe how well this is going? [*Laughter*]

JD: Yes.

DE: There's a line in the new book where you say, "Not much about California, on its own preferred terms, has encouraged its children to see themselves as connected to one another." Can you explain that?

JD: People in Northern California grew up with the whole founding myth of California, the whole crossing story, et cetera. Southern California was founded on a different story. The only time when I felt, really, a big connection between Northern and Southern California—and I've lived in both—was when PSA was flying. [*Laughter*] No, I mean, literally, PSA connected the state where you could fly—

DE: Explain what PSA is.

JD: Pacific Southwest Airways. You weren't here then, probably. They had these planes with these big smiles painted on them. And you could fly from Sacramento to Los Angeles for I think sixteen dollars, and you could fly from Los Angeles to San Francisco for twelve. And there was what they called a Midnight Flyer, so you could fly up for dinner, in San Francisco, and then fly home, to Los Angeles, or vice versa. I mean, it gave a great sense of mobility around the state, which has been—which we never had before, and I haven't felt it since. I mean, going from Los Angeles to San Francisco on a plane now is so unpleasant that my brother always drives—you know, he does this all the time.

DE: So you're talking mostly regionally there, between coastal, inland, north, south.

JD: There were a lot of things I was thinking about there, I suppose. I was also thinking, the idea, the ethic that everybody kind of believed represented California, was one of extreme individualism, and we did not feel very responsible for others in the community. Community wasn't a big idea.

DE: And that's something you feel is prevalent throughout this state? Is that something grounded in the myth of California?

JD: In the way it was settled, yeah. I mean the kinds of people who settled it. The idea was, basically, California was settled by people who wanted to strike it rich, in a way, at the simplest level. And *as* individuals. This ethic kind of took hold; it became a big point of pride even though everyone in the state was heavily dependent on federal government. We didn't feel very responsible for those around us. One of the things that really knocked me out when I was writing this book was the thing about the committal to mental hospitals in the early days of the state. And right into the early twentieth century, people were committed at a higher rate than almost anywhere else in the country. And it was explained that they were kind of unhinged by the ups and downs of life on the frontier, in the gold camps... This wasn't it, I don't think. It was just an extreme disregard for, and a refusal to tolerate, the people around them. I mean, people were being committed in San Francisco for—one older woman was committed by her sister. This was a study done by somebody who had gotten hold of all these records. One woman was committed by her sister because she had lost all interest in crocheting. [*Laughter*]

DE: And the national committal rate was, what, 3,900 people committed one year. And 2,600 of them were from California, or something like that.

JD: Yeah, I mean huge, huge numbers. And they were committed basically for life. I mean, it wasn't one of those forty-eight-hour deals.

DE: We talked about a passage that I was going to ask you to read, and you asked me to read it, that I think sums up a lot of what is central—both your love of the state and then ambivalence, and also the sense of loss. After your mother died, you flew back to California, and this occurs late in the book. Do you want to read it, or should I?

JD: You read it.

DE: "Flying to Monterey I had a sharp apprehension of the many times before when I had, like Lincoln Steffens, 'come back,' flown west, followed the sun, each time experiencing a lightening of spirit as the land below opened up, the checkerboards of the Midwestern plains giving way to the vast empty reach between the Rockies and the Sierra Nevada; then *home, there, where I was from, me,* California. It would be a while before I realized that 'me' is what we think when our parents die, even at my age, *who will look out for me now, who will remember me as I was, who will know what happens to me now, where will I be from.*" ✯

VENDELA VIDA

TALKS WITH

JENNIFER EGAN

"MY BIG DECISIONS IN FICTION HAPPEN INSTINCTIVELY. I SEEM TO NEED THAT GUT FEELING OF EXCITEMENT. AND ODDLY ENOUGH, IT ALSO TURNS OUT TO BE MY BEST GUIDE TOWARD WHAT'S GOING TO REALLY INTEREST ME ON THOSE BRAINIER LEVELS."

Strange things that fascinate Jennifer Egan:
Twins
Medieval architecture
Online dating
Vampire soap operas

There's no such thing as a typical Jennifer Egan novel. Her first, The Invisible Circus, *is set in the '70s and follows a young woman's quest to piece together her older sister's travels across Europe and make sense of her untimely death. Her second novel,* Look at Me, *takes place in New York and Illinois around the year 2000, and addresses issues of terrorism before 9/11. It was a finalist for the 2001 National Book Award.*

Egan's new book, The Keep, *is being published this month. A contemporary Gothic novel, it alternates between a castle setting in Eastern Europe and a U.S. prison. It's unclear how the various stories are going to connect until they do. Maybe that's one thing Egan's novels—and her short stories—have in common: They're all thrillers in their own way. The plots take you in a direction you didn't foresee and you find yourself racing to the surprising conclusion.*

This interview took place in May in Fort Greene, Brooklyn, where Egan lives with her husband and sons. —*Vendela Vida (Spring 2006)*

I. "SHE USED TO COMPLAIN I REEKED OF GARLIC, WHICH SHE THOUGHT WAS VERY LOW-CLASS."

VENDELA VIDA: You're not a twin, are you? Your books all have twins in them, or people whose lives are mirrored by other characters, or other selves. In *The Keep,* two of the central characters, Danny and his cousin Howard, are almost like twins—they're bound together by a childhood trauma. And when we get to the primary setting of the novel, an ancient castle in Eastern Europe that Danny is helping Howard convert into a hotel, we learn that a pair of twins once drowned in the castle pool.

JENNIFER EGAN: Isn't that funny? I don't have a twin. I don't even have a full sibling or a half sibling close to my age. But twins do come up again and again. In *The Keep,* I felt like I'd finally arrived at the perfect place to exploit my twin fixation, because twins are very Gothic. Intellectually, my interest in twins comes from a deeper interest in identity and doubling and doppelgängers, but I think there's more to it than that.

VV: In *Look at Me,* you talk about people's shadow selves. The main character, Charlotte, is convinced everyone has a shadow self, which is the self you see when someone's not looking, when they're not trying to present themselves a certain way. A shadow self is the true self, according to Charlotte.

JE: Exactly. In *Look at Me,* I was exploring twinning or doubling in the context of image culture, asking how reflections of us affect our inner visions of ourselves. But I think on a fundamental level, I'm just fascinated by this idea of a double person. In *The Invisible Circus,* the two sisters, Phoebe and Faith, are essentially twins. The older sister is dead, and people who see the younger one are confused, because she looks so much the same.

As a kid, when I would go to Chicago to visit my father in the summer, I volunteered at a day camp where there was a set of identical redheaded twin girls. I feel like those girls are always cropping up in my work. They're obviously adults by now. I would love to know who they are and what they're doing. I don't know why they're of such interest to me. I was asked to write a story about "vanishing twin syndrome," which is the phenomenon of pregnancies that begin with two fetal sacs and then one is flushed away in the first trimester. There are people out there who feel that having had a "vanished" twin with them in the womb explains a lot of things about their personalities—they've been longing for their lost twin. My article never ended up getting printed, but it was fascinating research. Personally, I don't think you can remember that, as a five-week-old fetus, you lost your twin in utero. But I do think it addresses that feeling of longing that so many people have for some other self—some version of us that can offer a kind of total sympathy and comprehension. That's the longing for the dopplegänger, the other you, which is *so* gothic.

When I was a kid, I would come home from school and watch *Dark Shadows*—which my mother abhorred. I mean it was a soap opera! Who wants a kid coming home and watching a soap opera? But I was electrified by it. One scene I remember vividly: There were twin sisters and one was evil and she was dead and buried in a coffin and there was this hokey scene where she comes out of her coffin and confronts her live twin—of course it's the same actress playing both—and she says, in this whispery voice, something like "One of us is going to die. But it won't be me.... it will be *you*!" It's totally corny, but I've remembered it all these years. Another corny Gothic classic is Daphne du Maurier's *Rebecca,* which is all about twinning: the two Mrs. De Winters. I wouldn't even want to try and re-read that now, it's probably badly written. But when I was eleven, reading *Rebecca*—I couldn't even think about or discuss anything else. Other cheesy Gothic novels... John Fowles's *The Magus* features identical women playing with the mind of the protagonist. I wonder if my twin preoccupation will continue after this. I have a sense that *The Keep* might have exhausted it.

VV: Most of the characters in *The Keep* are male. Was this something you set out to do—write a book with very few females after writing a number of stories and two novels with female protagonists?

JE: It felt like something I'd been moving toward for a while. I've always been interested in writing about men. And not only do I not *like* to write about my own life, but I'm terrible at it—my biggest problem is trying to use material that actually has some root in reality. What better solution than to simply exit from my gender altogether! It felt very natural in that way. I was a little concerned and surprised by how few women there were in the book. It wasn't a plan, although I wanted it to be a streamlined story without a lot of peripheral characters. The crux of the story is a relationship between two men. But I was relieved as I moved through the book to find that a woman is finally the bearer of the story, if not exactly the writer. She's there as a gaze more than a speaker. Also, I really feel like the novel is a love story between Ray and Holly [two characters that start out as minor figures]—she is very present in that way as sort of a destination for him. And then later he becomes the same thing for her.

VV: Where did the idea of the baroness come from? In the book, she's this old woman who's been at the castle for a long time—she's the tie to the castle's past. It's unclear whether she's real or a figment of Danny's imagination. It's also unclear how old she is—from a distance, Danny thinks she's young and alluring, and as he gets closer to her he sees that she's closer to a hundred years old—though this doesn't stop him from having sex with her.

JE: That actually does have a basis in reality. When I first came to New York, I worked as a temp and a word processor at a law firm. It was a nightmare—I had so much trouble making enough money to support myself and still having time to write. And I had no credentials whatsoever. So I got this strange job. I became a private secretary for a woman named the Countess of Romanones—and *she* was actually a writer. She had been a spy during World War II for the OSS [Office of Strategic Services]. She was American-born and very beautiful, had been a model for Hattie Carnegie. How much spying she actually did is a matter of some debate, but she did some work for the OSS and then married a Spanish count and lived in Madrid in great finery and grandeur and had three sons and then after her husband died—by then she was in her sixties—she wrote a book about her experiences called *The Spy Wore Red*. It was a surprise best seller. And after that she suddenly had a career and a complicated publishing life, so she needed a secretary.

And I, meanwhile, was tired of working every holiday and a lot of nights at this word processing pool, feeling like I just *had* to find some other way, so we wended our way together. I worked for her from one to six p.m. for two years and she was a maniac. God love her, she was a genuine character. She was a difficult person to work with—to work for. She used to complain I reeked of garlic, for example, which she thought was very low-class. If I'd had garlic three days earlier, she would complain that it was coming out of my skin. She could *smell* it. So I stopped eating garlic—it wasn't worth it. She was a really complicated and really difficult person. Ever since, I've been wondering, How am I going to use the Countess? and this ended up being the way. I thought, Come on, if I've got a castle....

I originally imagined a doddering old count, but then I thought, This book is full of men—why am I putting in another man? and as soon as I realized that the ancient aristocrat was female, I thought, Wait, I know who it should be! That was really fun because it gave me a chance to dream up an extreme version of her, which I have to say is *less* fictionalized than you would probably think.

II. "I'VE GONE TO EUROPEAN CASTLES BEFORE, BUT FOR SOME REASON, THIS VISIT WAS ENTIRELY DIFFERENT FOR ME. I WALKED IN AND THOUGHT, I HAVE TO DO SOMETHING WITH THIS."

VV: You often write for the *New York Times Magazine.* Do you ever find that your journalism assignments influence your fiction writing?

JE: There's a strange symbiosis between the two. I only pick assignments that really interest me, and often at the time I don't *feel* any connection between those topics and the fiction I'm working on. I used to actually do both at once, but now that I have kids, that doesn't happen as much. I don't work anything like the hours I used to work. But often the same interests that make me take on an assignment are also fueling my fiction, so they do end up intersecting in funny ways. Years ago I did a story for the *New York Times Magazine* about self-injury. I had known someone in college who had that problem, and I'd written a short story touching on it, "Sacred Heart," which is in my collection. So I was interested in the fundamentals of that disorder, and it was great to then learn about the science of it in all this detail, writing for the *Times.* A few of my assignments over the last few years worked their way into *The Keep,* most of them having to do with online culture.

VV: In *The Keep,* one of the main characters, Danny, is addicted to the internet, to being connected. I don't think I've ever seen a compulsion to email, to text message, so well described. And it's so funny. How did the decision to detail this kind of obsession come about?

JE: That started with a piece for the *Times Magazine* about the secret online lives of closeted gay teens. I was almost done with *Look at Me*—I had sold it and everything—and I was just starting to think about what would come next. The editors and I had no idea how to approach this online story. We thought I was somehow going to hang around with these closeted gay teens and *watch* them living their secret out lives online [*laughter*], which was really just a case of old thinking trying to address a new phenomenon. Of course I got nowhere with that strategy. I couldn't even find a way to *suggest* meeting one of these kids, they were so anxious and freaked out. And then I realized that this was what the story was about: *online relationships.* It was not going to be a story about following people physically—forget physicality. And I think having to forget about physicality and conducting journalism in this new way was important for me in terms of my thinking about the internet and its impact.

Oddly, a number of my pieces after that involved the same discovery. I did a cover story about online dating where I never even spoke on the phone with my two main subjects. Early on in that story I tried meeting up with one person I'd been interviewing by email, but it felt weird—I knew all about his sex life and suddenly we were sitting together in a bar. It had the feeling of a date. I was like, "Ahh! Get me out of here! Let's get back online!" Again, I had this dutiful journalistic sense that I should meet my subject, but it wasn't appropriate to the situation, it wasn't helpful. So I think some of those discoveries found their way into *The Keep.* I knew I wanted to write a Gothic novel, and I was very interested in injecting modern communications technology into a Gothic world, which is usually atechnological. It's all about being cut off. If you think about classics like *The Turn of the Screw,* there's always a kind of immersion in which the protagonist, who is usually female, goes into a world and can't get out of it, or at least can't communicate beyond it. So I loved the idea of those remote conditions colliding with modern-day telecommunication.

VV: So how did you know you wanted to write a Gothic novel?

JE: It came about very specifically. After my first son, Emmanuel, was born—this would have been two or three months after the article about the online lives of closeted gay teens was published—we went to France. My husband [David Herskovits] had a directing job in Charleville, so we scooped up our eight-week-old and headed over there. David was really busy, but we had one day of leisure and we drove to Belgium to a castle in Bouillon where, it turns out, the First Crusade began, led by Godfrey de Bouillon. We went to see Godfrey's castle, which was in ruins. I've gone to European castles before, but for some reason, this visit was entirely different for me. I walked in and thought, I have to do something with this. It was this really strong fictional impulse, and I had no idea where it would lead. I thought, Do I want to write a novel set in medieval times? But the logistics of that were mind-boggling; I had a newborn baby, and even just trying to fathom the research was overwhelming. And then I realized that what I really liked was the nostalgic feeling of this decayed medieval past, which is a very gothic sensibility. And so it came to me that really I just wanted to be in that state and write in that state. I'd read Gothic novels over the years, but I wasn't extremely well versed in them, so I began to do a lot of reading.

VV: Where did Howard's vision to transform the castle into a hotel originate? Sometimes it strikes me that writers put business or money-generating plans into their fiction in lieu of pursuing them in real life. Is the idea of a castle-cum-hotel a business-plan idea that you might have pursued if you weren't a writer?

JE: No, no. Actually, I struggled with the question of what kind of enterprise would bring these characters together. I knew there was some sort of building, some old moldering structure, as there so often is in Gothic fiction. A castle, an old house, there's almost always a structure at the heart of it. Gothic literary theory talks about what these structures represent: Is it the body? The past? It seems overtly symbolic in an almost goofy way, which is another thing I love about the Gothic: it's sort of inherently goofy. But trying to figure out what *occasion* would bring a bunch of people to an old castle today was a challenge. I knew that my protagonist was male—I loved that idea because it reverses the classic Gothic setup, which is basically: helpless female, trapped, strange circumstances… is she imagining it or is it real? So I loved the idea of it being a guy—

VV: A goth guy.

JE: [*Laughs*] Exactly. But then the question was: who is he visiting and why? And somehow the idea of the hotel renovation just came to me. It seemed like a good meeting point of past and present. Because I really wanted to make a contemporary novel, I didn't want to set it in the past. And in fact Europe is full of these old castles that have been renovated into hotels. Although the one we were visiting, in Bouillon, had not. It was still a ruin.

VV: I love the title. How did you come up with the idea of the castle in your book having a keep?

JE: The idea of castle architecture preoccupied me for a while. I read books about it. I thought that I might draw—or have someone draw for me, because I draw really badly—an exact floor plan of the castle I was inventing. Later, I gave that up because I felt like what I wanted was for the castle to be unfathomable in some way, so nailing down every room and hallway seemed like a poor idea. Anyway, most castles have a keep of some kind, meaning a tower, although that term *keep* seems to have fallen out of use in recent discussions of castle architecture. But as soon as I read those words—*the keep*—I felt this great excitement. I loved the name and I loved the fact that people don't use the term anymore and I loved the purpose of the keep, which was to serve as a last stronghold inside the castle, a core place where the owner's family could hide if the walls were breached. When I first read the term I felt a sort of shiver that seemed to be, you know, a sign that I was going to use it.

VV: Because of the shiver? [*Laughter*]

JE: It's not an especially cerebral or analytical approach, although I do get very cerebral and analytical later on in the writing process. But my big decisions in fiction happen instinctively. I seem to need that gut feeling of excitement. And oddly enough, it also turns out to be my best guide toward what's going to really interest me on those brainier levels.

III. "IN A WAY, ADDICTION IS THE INVERSION OF THE TWIN FANTASY: IT'S TWO DIFFERENT PEOPLE INSIDE ONE PERSON."

VV: There are a lot of accidents in your work. Have you ever been in a car crash like Charlotte in *Look at Me* or a bad accident like Danny in *The Keep*?

JE: Well, I was in a bad car accident. I was eighteen or nineteen. It happened in San Francisco, driving with my mother down Pine Street, coming back from downtown. Someone ran a red light coming down a hill and just smashed into us. We basically did a 360 and then flipped onto our side. It was bad. I was driving, and my mother ended up hanging in the air from her seat belt. I didn't even have a seat belt on, but my side was on the ground. We were intact, we were completely fine, but the car was totaled and we never drove it again. The gas tank burst, but it didn't catch on fire. I remember we walked out the back window, and that smell of gasoline, it was almost nauseating. My mother had dry cleaning in the back and all these clothes were scattered around the street and it really looked like a wreck where people had died, yet we just walked out. I wouldn't call it a traumatic event, but it certainly was an event that I remember—especially the feeling of the car spinning around, completely out of my control.

One question *I* have is why people are always falling from heights in my books. There's a suicidal dive in *The Invisible Circus,* a comically failed suicide jump in *Look at Me,* and then in *The Keep* there's an absurd fall out a window. I have no idea why that keeps happening. I'm not aware of having any sort of preoccupation with falling in real life.

VV: There's also a lot of addiction described in your work. As I mentioned, in *The Keep,* there's Danny's addiction to being connected. Charlotte in *Look at Me* has a drinking problem that you use to comic effect. But in the same novel, Detective Halliday loses his wife and kids (redheaded twin girls, if I'm not mistaken) as a result of his drinking.

JE: I've certainly known people who were addicted to things. My father was an alcoholic. But none of that quite explains the reaction I had when Christopher on *The Sopranos* shot up again last Sunday. It made me incredibly uncomfortable. And maybe that was because of my father, who finally did get sober and whose life was really much better after that, although he died in an accident not too many years later, and I wish his life could have been better for longer. So seeing an alcoholic fall off the wagon has some personal resonance for me. But when I saw Christopher shooting up I felt extremely distressed. I found myself thinking, I'm not going to watch this show anymore. I can't take it. Never mind the people getting bumped off left and right—it was the heroin abuse that got to me.

I think what's interesting to me about addiction is the way it opens the door for this *other* presence to enter into someone's life and personality. Suddenly a whole different set of priorities and needs that are in direct opposition to all the things you know are good for you blows in and just dismantles your life. Even when I was a kid, I was fascinated by drugs—just theoretically. I'd had no exposure to them. I would read books about junkies. I remember being, like, ten years old and going to the library looking for books about barbiturates, and the librarian saying, "Uh, why?" I still don't know, but I think it's something about the way drugs can obscure a personality and replace it with something else. I find that so wrenching and tragic. I seem to come back to it again and again, but—thank God—I don't seem to have the addict gene.

VV: I was looking at it more in terms of a cautionary tale or a dreaded alternative. Fiction writers can explore what would happen if, say, we took a left at the fork in the road instead of a right. So in a way, the addiction path is not so different from the twin obsession.

JE: In a way, addiction is the inversion of the twin fantasy: it's two different people inside one person. That's deeply uncomfortable to me. It's grotesque, and I think I'm sort of mesmerized by the grotesqueness. And it's also an embodiment of the way in which all of us are different people fighting it out inside one person. And I'm interested in the ways people lose control, and how the threat that they *might* lose control can affect a fictional environment. Like with the character of Anthony Halliday in *Look at Me,* the question is always on the table: will he relapse? It keeps the stakes around him very high. And when Charlotte tries to make him relapse by spitting booze into his mouth when she kisses him, it's such a horrible abuse of intimacy. So in fiction, an addict is a little like the gun in the living room. The question is always there: if and when and how it will finally go off.

VV: Addiction definitely raises the stakes for a character. Something I think about a lot is how hard it is to raise the stakes when writing a contemporary novel. In nineteenth-century novels, adultery and falling in love with someone outside of one's social class were huge obstacles. I'm thinking of *Anna Karenina* and *Jude the Obscure.* But put these same challenges in a contemporary novel and, well, leaving a spouse for another person can be the stuff of chick lit.

JE: I've been thinking a lot about the question of what's at stake in contemporary fiction. I've been re-reading Jane Austen, and I find myself marveling at the fact that she could wrest so much drama and tension from the very short period in a girl's life between the point when she came out into society and her marriage. Everything comes into play in that space of time: power, money, social class, the status of women—it's all there. Can you imagine trying to bring that kind of gravitas to a novel about a girl looking for a husband today? There's just nothing there. [*Laughter*]

But in Austen's time, the stakes couldn't have been higher. It was literally almost of life or death: here's your chance, and either you make this work and find a tolerable husband to support you, or you'll spend the rest of your life in a marginal existence, with no prospect for change. Outside the realm of poverty, there's very little in modern American life that can create those high stakes.

VV: *The Keep* is incredibly different from *Look at Me,* and *Look at Me* was fundamentally different from *The Invisible Circus.* I'm talking about plot, point of view, setting—everything. I'm wondering how you break away from the blueprint. I think once a writer has found a structure that works for them, they have to make a very conscious decision not to abide by that structure. It's hard because the blueprint is almost embedded in your subconscious.

JE: My books are all pretty different from each other—to the point where I'm sometimes told that people are surprised that one person wrote them. One reason is that each book has taken a long time to write, so they've happened pretty far apart from each other in my life. Also, because I don't like to write about myself or even about *lives* like mine, there isn't a through line of my own biography or experience holding them together. I don't really know the story when I begin. And frankly, what gives me the impetus to go forward is partly a sense that I'm discovering something unknown to me, exploring a new set of ideas. And what makes that discovery possible is almost consciously throwing away the books I've already written before I begin.

For me, so long as the *world* of the books feels really different in terms of voice, point of view, time, and place, I'm intrigued enough to go on. *Look at Me* doesn't have a Gothic feeling at all. It wasn't even remotely in my mind until I went to that castle after it was finished. The revelation was: This is something new to me, something different. I just want to be here for a while, I want this feeling. And for me, that sense of time and place—of atmosphere—predates a character, a story, everything else except a few abstract notions that I want to explore. And those conditions have been so different for each of my three novels that I guess it was inevitable that the stories would unfold in different ways. There are definitely similarities, and I start to see them as soon as the books are finished. But I need to *feel* as I work that there are no overlaps, or I'm just not interested in going forward.

IV. "I ACTUALLY STILL HAVE A BUSINESS CARD THAT SAYS 'JENNIFER EGAN, PRIVATE INVESTIGATOR.'"

VV: Where is your next novel set? Can you say?

JE: It's going to be set in New York right after World War II. I'm really interested in the women who worked at the Brooklyn Navy Yard during the war. They did all these amazing things. They would build and repair ships—all the jobs that men had done. Then they were fired the minute the war ended. Not a lot was written about these navy yard women. I've actually partnered with the corporation that runs the Brooklyn Navy Yard now, and we're going to do an oral-history project and try to find some of the remaining women who worked at the yard during the war, who of course are very old now. I'll interview whomever is willing, which I want to do for my own research, but which I also think will be a useful record to have in the world before these people die.

So... very little overlap with *The Keep,* atmospherically. There's no Gothic feeling in this new one. It doesn't feel campy at all, it feels more genuinely romantic. I'm really interested in that immediately postwar period in New York—I'm not even quite sure why. I want to know how it *felt* to be here then. So I've put my stake down there, in that time and place, and they'll definitely require an entirely different voice, story, and everything else than what I've written before. What I have right now is very little: an aesthetic and some ideas. That ain't much, but, you know, I'm trusting that the rest will evolve for me because it always has in the past. And I think that the research is going to be what renders up a lot in my specific plans. It's going to make my mind start working.

VV: Did you ever work in a prison, teaching writing like Holly in *The Keep*?

JE: I thought about teaching writing in a prison, but I decided to wing it instead. I almost didn't want to have *too* much personal experience with it. I felt like that could possibly complicate the situation. I interviewed several people who had taught in prisons. I read pretty much everything I could get my hands on about prison life in the past twenty-five years. I also spent a day at a high-security prison in Ohio with a female corrections officer who's pretty high up in the hierarchy, whom I'd found through one of the teachers I interviewed. She was generous enough to spend one of her vacation days taking me around her workplace. I saw everything, and I talked to lots of prisoners. Basically, I used that prison in *The Keep* in terms of the architecture and atmosphere and all the rules and regulations. And also various other things I touch on, like the reptile program.

VV: You mentioned that you worked as a private detective at one point.

JE: That was for *Look at Me.* At one point, I thought that the private detective component in that novel would be bigger, and

I worked for a brilliant, crazy detective for a few months. What I was mostly doing was transcribing—trying to transcribe—tapes made by hidden recorders placed inside cars of people who were suspected to be mobsters. It was incredibly hard to be accurate. There was car noise, honking, tunnels—you couldn't understand most of what they were saying. Then it would get fantastically quiet just in time for them to have a long discussion of what they should order for lunch. I had zero qualifications for that job, but I loved it.

My father's side of the family has generally gravitated toward law enforcement. My grandfather was a commander in the Chicago police force and my sister is a U.S. attorney right now, doing a lot of work on gangs, and my uncle was a criminal-defense lawyer, and my father was a lawyer too.... I've always been fascinated by cops and all that stuff. So the job satisfied that yen in me. I actually still have a business card that says, "Jennifer Egan, Private Investigator." [*Laughs*]

VV: When was this?

JE: That was about ten years ago. There was a second detective I interviewed a few times, and he was nothing like the one I worked for, but they were both real mavericks: The whole stereotype of this iconoclastic, lonely, slightly outsiderish detective seems to be completely right in my observation. And they were both working on detective novels. I'm not kidding. There seemed to be an assumption that if you were making your living this way you should obviously be working on a novel. Just like now: if you're a mobster, there's probably an assumption that you should also be an actor. So it was research and also something else—I mean, I got paid to do it. It was a paying job.

VV: What books did you read when you were researching *The Keep*?

JE: Well, prison books, as I mentioned. My two favorites were Ted Conover's *Newjack* and *You Got Nothing Coming,* by Jimmy Lerner.

That one is a little controversial, because after it was published it emerged that Lerner had bent the facts surrounding the murder he committed, trying to make himself sound like the victim. But the book is incredibly lively and colorful in terms of prison life. As far as Gothic fiction goes, I read the usual suspects: Poe, James, Hawthorne, Joyce Carol Oates, Stephen King. But I especially loved the crazy old Gothic novels people don't read much anymore: Ann Radcliffe's *The Mysteries of Udolpho,* Horace Walpole's *The Castle of Otranto*, *The Monk,* by Matthew Lewis—these are all eighteenth-century novels. My two favorites, other than *The Turn of the Screw,* are from the nineteenth century: *Melmoth the Wanderer,* which is an absolutely wacky book inside a book inside a book, and Wilkie Collins's *The Woman in White,* which is one of the best thrillers I've ever read.

I've sort of moved away from all that now, but I had a great time with it—I was happy just to live in that world for a while. And the genre is going strong—you know, the Gothic is alive and well and it's happening now. ✯

VENDELA VIDA

TALKS WITH

SHIRLEY HAZZARD

"I AM FULL OF LINES OF POETRY, IMPRESSIONS, EXPERIENCES, WORDS."

Things that seem implausible, either in books or in life:

Two people reading the same book at the same time
Undesired flinging-together
Distant rocks visible only in July

S*hirley Hazzard was born in Sydney in 1931 and left Australia in 1947. She has since lived in Hong Kong, New Zealand, Britain, and France. Now an American citizen, she divides her time between Italy and New York. Between the years 1952 and 1962, Hazzard worked in the United Nations as a clerical employee, an experience which led her to write not only* People in Glass Houses *(1967), a satirical collection of character sketches, but also* Defeat of an Ideal *(1973), a nonfiction book that detailed the weakness of the U.N., and* Countenance of Truth *(1990), about the United Nations and the Kurt Waldheim case. She is also the author of the nonfiction books* Coming of Age in Australia

(1985) and Greene on Capri *(2001).*

It's fiction for which Hazzard is best known. She is the author of the short-story collection Cliffs of Fall *(1963), and the novels* The Evening of the Holiday *(1966),* The Bay of Noon *(1970),* The Transit of Venus *(1980), and* The Great Fire *(2003). She was awarded the National Book Critics Circle Award for Fiction in 1980 for* The Transit of Venus; *in 2003, more than twenty years after her last novel was published,* The Great Fire *was shortlisted for the PEN/Faulkner Award, and went on to earn her the National Book Award.*

Many have compared Hazzard to Henry James, perhaps because like James, Hazzard peppers her novels with clues for the astute reader. In The Transit of Venus, *it's left to the reader to piece together the circumstances of Ted Tice's suicide. Throughout* The Great Fire, *repeated references are made to a thick book Aldred Leith is reading, but Hazzard never blatantly states that it's* War and Peace. *Indeed, Hazzard herself—in her treatment of love and war and the burden of history—is perhaps the closest thing we have to Tolstoy.*

This interview took place shortly after Hazzard won the National Book Award. We met on a snowy afternoon in the Manhattan apartment she shared for many years with her late husband, the translator and biographer Francis Steegmuller. *—Vendela Vida (Winter 2003)*

I. "THE ONLY CARD I HAD TO PLAY WAS LITERATURE."

VENDELA VIDA: In *Greene on Capri,* you recount how you started a friendship with Graham Greene essentially through poetry. He and a friend were sitting at a table next to yours at a café in Capri. Greene was reciting a Robert Browning poem, "The Lost Mistress," but he couldn't recall the last line. As you left the café, you recited the elusive line of the poem to him. In *The Great Fire,* the protagonist, Leith, is reading a book on a train, and when he arrives at his destination he's greeted by a soldier who is reading the same book. In fact, in a lot of your books it's poetry or literature that brings people together.

SHIRLEY HAZZARD: Yes, it's quite intentional. You see, books were a theme of life, a lifetime, for whole populations who grew up before the 1950s, when television broke on the world. In one of his novels, *Travels with My Aunt,* Graham's protagonist remarks that one's life is more formed by books than people. "It is out of books," he says, that "one learns about love and pain at second hand." He once said to me that we—those of my generation and of his—had known a world where poetry cut across the classes and the generations. It was true. People spontaneously invoked lines of poetry without self-consciousness, and weren't considered to be showing off or eccentric. A single allusion, to a familiar book or poem, could create affinity.

My novel *The Great Fire* is set in the late 1940s, before television came on the scene. I've noticed that some reviewers question whether the young people in my story could be so well read. This reflects a generational gap. Critics don't realize that books were central to millions of lives, and were a predominant pleasure and a chief form of education.

Years ago, John Bayley, the British literary critic, wrote of "the solace that great language brings." In my childhood and early youth, men and women who read were all beneficiaries of the comfort derived from a great range of human expression. Through authentic expression, we recognized ourselves and one another, and were no longer isolated. This is a sense of sharing that we can enjoy through all the arts.

Through reading, I grew up. I am still hoping to grow up through reading, through music, through experience. When I was sixteen, living in Hong Kong, I went to work in an office of British Intelligence. The young English officers there knew Asian languages, had fought in the war, were clever and amusing. The only card I had to play was literature. They were all full of poetry, and so was I. We were walking anthologies. That was a great happiness and, in those times, not unusual.

VV: As readers, we find our expectations challenged so frequently when reading your work. One of the things we're continually surprised by is how funny so much of it is. One of my favorite scenes in *The Transit of Venus* is when you write: "The country bus lurched over an unsprung road. The girl thought that in novels one would read that he and she were flung against each other; and how that was impossible. We can only be flung against each other if we want to be."

And then a page later you write: "The bus plunged and bucked, determined to unseat them. We are flung against each other." I thought that was such a beautiful synthesis between life and art, and how what may seem far-fetched or unlikely in novels can actually be true.

SH: In that same book, I say a similar thing: that one wouldn't dare put into a novel the amount of coincidence that occurs in life itself.

VV: Yes, one of the characters says: "I've thought there may be more collisions of the kind in life than in books." Maybe the element of coincidence is played down in literature because it seems like cheating or can't be made believable. Whereas life itself doesn't have to be fair or convincing.

SH: Life doesn't have to prove itself. Life happens; we have to accept it. Reading fiction, the disbelieving, skeptical critic likes to feel in control. Yet his own existence, all existence, is subject to the accidental element, to the inexplicable or magical, or dreadful intervention that cannot be justified by logic. A friend of mine who knew the Shetland Islands told me that in the long light of the northern summer there comes a moment, in July, when a rock becomes visible that lies between the Shetlands and Norway. If the weather is favorable, a watch is kept from a certain promontory, and the rock can be seen. This phenomenon was denounced by scientists as wishful thinking, and quite impossible, but the rock has continued to manifest itself irrefutably: the thing is standing there, indifferent, or perhaps laughing to itself, unaccountable.

VV: That reminds me of the scene in *The Great Fire* that I mentioned before, when Leith gets off the train—I just love that scene. He gets off the train and the soldier who meets him has a book. And as a reader you're thinking, It's not going to be the same book, and at the same time you're kind of hopeful that it is. You think, It's a novel, she can't do that, and then you do it. It's wonderfully surprising, and surprisingly rewarding.

SH: That was important to me. Leith is on the train. He has his father's book. Arriving, he apologizes for the long wait the driver has had. And the young driver says, "It's all right. I had a book." Nowadays the young driver might of course have his cell phone, or an audio tape, or a Walkman. In those days you read a book—which in this case turns out coincidentally to be the book by Leith's father. All that would have been completely natural.

II. "I FEEL THE SURF OF THE CITY BEATING ON MY WINDOWS."

VV: I thought it was interesting that in *Greene on Capri* you put the explanation of why you wrote the book at the end, instead of at the beginning, as a foreword or preface.

SH: It just seemed to fit better.

VV: Did you experiment with it?

SH: No. You shouldn't start a book by telling the reader, "Here is how I feel, and therefore how you ought to feel." Let readers form their own conclusions. At the end, you can say, "Here is how it came about." In some measure, my memoir of Graham Greene was an opportunity for me to write about the life I shared there with my husband. In that sense, it is really a memoir of our own lives. Of course, Graham rampages about the book, just as he did throughout those years when he was a strong element of our Italian times, when we saw him frequently in spring and autumn on Capri, although our own temperaments and days were distinct from his.

VV: As you describe it, your marriage with Francis Steegmuller was an extremely literary marriage.

SH: Yes, that was an indivisible part of the whole.

VV: Was there a great deal of exchanging of work at the end of the day, or what was your typical work pattern?

SH: People often expect—I don't know why—that two writers living together must generate some hostility or friction. With us, it was the contrary; each understood what the other was up against: the need for seclusion, silence, and a need also for stimulus, sociability, sharing. Even the need for interruption, but only if one could dictate the interruption on one's own capricious terms. I had the study there [*she points*], and Francis had the study near the door. In a New York apartment, no room is really distant from another, so that tact and a sense of privacy are involved. Each of us understood that behind the closed door, on some particular day, the other might be going mad over a recalcitrant paragraph. And then, it always does fall to the woman to come and make the dinner. However, I should add that—and in this, as in much else, I was very spoiled—Francis did nearly all of what I call the administration of our lives: documents, taxes, leases, all those things that now fall heavily to me.

As we were fond of each other, we wanted to be reasonable. We didn't have to make an issue of every small thing that came up. That sort of running resentment can become, I think, an outlet for other forms of discontent between couples. We didn't feel like that, didn't hew to that line.

Looking back, I realize what a great change came over our world. When we were first married, over forty years ago, New York was certainly not a quiet place, but there was space for leisure. In the mild evenings, when there was long light, we might walk out after dinner, walk over to Madison Avenue and look into the windows of antique-furniture shops, of which there were many more in those days, or peer into the displays of the art dealers, and stroll home by some roundabout route. Now, one never has any such time. I feel the surf of the city beating on my windows. Whatever I'm doing, I feel I should be doing something else; should be catching up on some insurmountable backlog.

VV: You address the issue of memory, and the dangers of note-taking, in *Greene on Capri*. You write: "Over our years of Capri meetings, I seldom made 'notes' after our conversations with Graham and Yvonne. An underlying intention to record changes the nature of things, blighting spontaneity and receptivity: an imposition, like a snapping of photographs."

I love that description of how our need to record a conversation (surely these present words included) alters the conversation. I felt, when reading this book, that if someone had just given me a transcript of your conversations with Greene, it would have somehow rung less true.

SH: Of course. I didn't keep what would be called a record. And then, I have a good memory for what interests me. Not so good, I admit, for what is useful. We kept, I still do, a little appointment book for each day. I might write "Dinner, Gemma, with Graham and Yvonne," perhaps adding four or five words to recall some matter touched upon: a word or two that evoked the whole evening. Yet sometimes I might clearly recall whole exchanges of conversation long after.

VV: A lot of your novels are rich with detail and place. Do you ever take notes or do you work purely from memory?

SH: Memory. I think I have a fairly remarkable memory. I've always reserved what gave me pleasure, what interested me. Also, what has been poignant: the nature of sadness, the private anguish of tragedy, regret. I am full of lines of poetry, impressions, experiences, words. If remembrance were all pleasure, that would be too easy. I keep hold of matters that can't be resolved—why something went wrong, who was at fault, or how the difficulty was shared. These remain with me—no doubt as they do with many people. I see, too, looking back from that early youth I kept a reserve of what was beautiful, pleasurable, even sad, as a capital to draw on, and perhaps as evidence of a better self that I could consistently summon before the world.

III. "I'M ONE PERSON, NOW, IN THREE PLACES IN THE WORLD."

VV: I was reading an interview you did with Michiko Kakutani after the publication of *The Transit of Venus,* in which you said, "I think there is a tendency to write jottings about one's own psyche, and call it a novel. My book, though, is really a story. And that might have contributed to its success."

All of your books are stories. They often commence with a big event, or in the wake of one—whether it's in *The Transit of Venus,* which starts with the capsizing of a boat in which the girls lose their parents; or in *The Great Fire,* which begins in the aftermath of a war and the bombing of Hiroshima; or the first sentence of *The Bay of Noon,* when a military plane crashes on Mount Vesuvius. Is there something in those tragedies that embodies the seeds of a story? Or in your mind, does the story begin with a tragedy?

SH: I think my books often start out with the arrival of a loner. Ted Tice is "arriving" at the beginning of *The Transit of Venus;* Leith is arriving at the start of *The Great Fire.* The circumstances are obviously quite different, but the loner is appearing on the scene. In *The Bay of Noon,* the lonely girl is arriving at Naples. So there has been a break with previous experience; something new is beginning. The protagonist is in each case relatively young. So the future is before them.

VV: Both *The Bay of Noon* and *The Evening of the Holiday* take place in Italy, where you still spend some part of the year. Where do you go in Italy?

SH: In the south of Italy. On Capri and at Naples. In my early twenties, I spent a year in Naples, and have loved the city ever since. It is a complicated place—but all great cities are difficult now. Its street dangers are intimidating to outsiders. The dangers are far less than those of New York City, but they are of unfamiliar kind. Naples retains its strange, singular, ancient ways.

VV: I think it's the only place I've been in Italy where I felt a little wary.

SH: It requires time. For the last twenty years I've had the use of a pied-à-terre on the property of friends in Naples, right on the sea, very near where I lived in my first Neapolitan incarnation in the late 1950s. In *The Bay of Noon* my heroine lives in the district of Posillipo in Naples. And that is where I now stay when at Naples. However, there is also Capri. For many years we rented a dear shabby old place in an old building of Capri. It was never for sale, and, after my husband's death in 1994, the owners wanted it for their daughter. So I sold a painting that we had here in New York and bought a tiny old habitation on a Capri hilltop, and fixed it up. It has a huge view of the sea and sky, and of the green central mountain of the island.

Thus, New York is my headquarters, and I have the two outlying nests in the Bay of Naples. I'm one person, now, in three places in the world, only one of which I own. Perhaps absurd—financially and otherwise. But continuity—habit, and the memories of habit—are precious to me.

VV: Can you tell me a little about where you lived when you were growing up? Your books are set in so many places, and you, as the writer, seem so knowledgeable about and equally familiar with these various settings.

SH: When I was twenty-five, I looked around and realized that I'd lived in six completely different parts of the world for substantial periods: Australia, the Far East, and New Zealand; in Britain, with repeated returnings; New York; and Italy. In the 1960s and early 1970s, we lived half the year in Paris. Wonderful. My husband was writing on Jean Cocteau.

VV: Which won him the National Book Award.

SH: Yes. He had it twice—the second time for translating. [*The Letters of Gustave Flaubert,* 1981]

VV: It must have been fun, for lack of a better word, when you won the National Book Award, too.

SH: Of course. I thought the other evening [at the National Book Awards ceremony] how we would have shared the pleasure—the fun, as you say. I thought, when I was required to say a few words, that I would talk about him, but then—

VV: At the dinner?

SH: Yes. Well, everyone had been talking about their spouse—how helpful, how devoted. So I said to Francis, on the quiet, "Forgive me, but I won't join the crowd. I'll make it up to you in some other way."

VV: [*Laughs*]

SH: He was lovely.

IV. "YOU DON'T KNOW WHAT YOU WILL DO THAT MAY PLEASE YOU MORE, LATER ON."

VV: This might be a hard question, but which book are you most proud of?

SH: I don't think I can separate them just like that. Perhaps I can touch on it by invoking William Maxwell, who, as the chief fiction editor of the *New Yorker,* took my first work out of a slush pile and published it. Divine intervention. He was a marvelous man, who became, with his wife, Emily, a great friend to me.

I wrote a number of short stories rather quickly at the time. And then suddenly I was writing a novel. I said to Maxwell, "It's markedly different from my previous work. Perhaps I've grown up as a writer, or the material's different, but I begin to wonder whether some of my first stories will eventually seem quite juvenile to me."

Maxwell said, "I wouldn't count on that. Rather, you'll look back on them as things absolutely fresh and spontaneous, with a kind of innocence that you will only rarely recapture in later work. Your later work may be more mature, riper, more imaginative, more inventive perhaps. But there will always be the freshness about the first work."

I'm aware of the truth in this. A very early story—the second story, really, that I ever wrote, called "The Worst Moment of the Day"—continues to please me, just for a mood or a feeling, or a sentence or two that stand on their own. You don't know what you will do that may please you more, later on. Of course an entire novel exists differently: to bring it all together, you feel, yes, that you've achieved something. But what is that something?—it's hard to know. On occasion, the authentic moment can be conveyed in just a sentence.

All the same, I like my novels. If I re-read one of them, with a lapse of years, I don't wish it away. The later books—*The Transit of Venus* and *The Great Fire*—are closer to the way I feel now. But I have an attachment to *The Bay of Noon;* and to some particular stories in *People in Glass Houses*—satirical stories that are on the side of truth. People in power, even if it's only petty bureaucratic power, are rarely good news. They become unreachable, unless by satire. Alexander Pope sees them as "Safe from the Bar, the Pulpit, and the Throne, / Yet touch'd and sham'd by Ridicule alone. / O sacred weapon! left for Truth's defence, / Sole Dread of Folly, Vice, and Insolence!"

VV: I've read that you're an avid reader of Elizabeth Bowen. Who else do you think has been an influence? Do you read D. H. Lawrence?

SH: Elizabeth was a great friend of ours, an incomparable person. The best of her writing is singular, inimitable. As an influence—I really don't know. So many poems and novels have influenced me, have developed my ear. Too varied to discuss here. Browning was the first perhaps, when I was nine or so. The great poems of Hardy, first read at sixteen when I was in Hong Kong; and, later, his excruciating novels. Conrad, whom I first read at school in his stories, remains a companion. His novel *Victory* travels with me.

And one of the greatest of all short stories, "The Secret Sharer," told on so many levels that the reader has to wonder—are there two men here, or is there only one? Consummate. Graham Greene said that the spell of Conrad over him in youth was so powerful that he sometimes avoided re-reading him. Greene himself broke on me early, in adolescence: *The Heart of the Matter* was the first for me, perhaps the best. D. H. Lawrence?—I haven't read him in years. I appreciate him, but I don't turn to him eagerly. There have been particular books—Nigel Balchin's *The Small Back Room,* Jean Rhys's *Wide Sargasso Sea,* Nabokov's *The Defense,* Muriel Spark's *The Girl of Slender Means*—many others—that eccentrically touch the imagination.

Whether any of this amounts to "influence," I can't really say. It's just that certain books moved you, and you never forget them. They become intimate, indelible. I'm often linked to the influence of Henry James, yet I had written for years before I settled in to read James, as in youth I'd never really liked him. He has some greatness, but there are even now reservations in my feelings about Henry James. Similarly I'm told that Patrick White has influenced me. He hasn't; but I consider his *Voss* one of the greatest novels of the twentieth century. God help us, the other day someone wrote that I was influenced by Somerset Maugham. Maugham was a splendid writer; he told a fine story. It's true that some sympathy is lacking in his work, but he is a master of narrative language and its deployment. I see nothing in my work that reflects Maugham. But once someone says it, it will go on being said.

VV: Right. [*Laughs*]

SH: In the same vein, people will tell you that you clearly had this or that happen to you at an early age, and you consequently respond in such and such a way. But they don't know what else may have happened, since what is most important for you, you keep to yourself. The greatest literary influence lies in arousing us to words, to expressive speech. That comes through reading, through the pleasure and excitement of reading that creates receptivity. These are wide impressions, not narrow, particular ones. Such matters can scarcely be critically addressed. As I consider our modern lives, I feel that, due to the growing uncertainty of the world, people anxiously want to believe themselves on top of things, in control. Especially in the United States just now, at the height of world power, there is the impulse to settle on what is attestable, to pronounce and explain; to exclude mystery, imagination, the intuitive powers of individual existence. What about the *inattestable,* that informs all that most matters to us? What about the accidental nature of our life? The salient events of private life are always tinged with the accidental. If I hadn't gone to a party that Muriel Spark gave down the road here in the Beaux Arts Hotel, I would never have met Francis Steegmuller.

VV: Which brings us back to the coincidences and collisions in your work.

SH: From the psychiatrists and sociologists, we never hear a word about the accidental, the inattestable. Max Beerbohm said, of this era of explanation, "They explain because they can't understand." Which is perhaps why, with so much elucidation, we're still in the dark. ✯

SARAH MANGUSO

TALKS WITH

AMY HEMPEL

"ANY TIME YOU HEAR SOMEONE SAY '*THAT'S* NOT A STORY,' I THINK YOU SHOULD QUESTION THE PERSON, NOT THE STORY."

On Amy Hempel's desk:
The first sentences of stories
Forensic pathology textbooks
Reams of paper
Manuscripts
The last sentences of stories

The miracle of Amy Hempel's stories is their extreme compassion despite their extreme brevity. Dense and undecorated, they exemplify short literary form, but they also awaken a deep empathy that seems more appropriate to long company with characters through hundreds of pages. This mysterious and elusive effect has earned Hempel recognition as a master of short fiction.

Hempel was born in Chicago in 1951, went to high school in Denver, spent some dozen formative years in San Francisco, then moved to New York. She studied at Columbia with the renowned writers' mentor Gordon Lish, who was a champion of her work and who edited her first two collections, and whose name appears in print often preceded by the word legendary. *Hempel's books include* Reasons to Live *(1985),* At the Gates of the Animal Kingdom *(1990),* Tumble Home *(1997), and* The Dog of the Marriage *(2005). With Jim Shepard she edited* Unleashed: Poems by Writers' Dogs *(1995). Her* Collected Stories *appeared in 2006 and was released in paperback in 2007. She has won a Guggenheim Fellowship, taught at a number of colleges and universities across the country, worked as a veterinary surgical assistant, and provided foster care to seeing-eye dogs in training. She's currently a faculty member in the graduate writing programs at Bennington and Sarah Lawrence.*

This interview began in a diner on Manhattan's Upper East Side, continued during a dog walk with Wanita, Hempel's yellow Lab, and finished via email. —*Sarah Manguso (Spring 2007)*

SARAH MANGUSO: Your stories are recognizable as yours—whatever it is, wherever the story came from, it passed through Amy Hempel. What I'm wondering is this: Does writing feel to you like progress toward Hempelianness, or progress away from it? In other words, do you ever feel as if the goal is to sound like—or unlike—Amy Hempel?

AMY HEMPEL: The goal is always to sound unlike myself. In life I am filled with doubt, I am not tough—or I wasn't when I started writing—and I often use more words than I need, doubling back to make sure I got a point across when it's not necessary. So what shows up on the page is an idealized version of what I think I sound like, having had time to axe anything hesitant or redundant. And with luck there will be a hint of the sounds of the voices I hear every day, the people I'm in touch with daily, such as Julia Slavin's incomparable humor, or the poets I read and re-read daily.

SM: I know you re-read books and that you claim to have an untidy apartment that was recently put in order during an "apartment intervention." Everyone's untidiness is particular, but many writers admit to owning too many books, especially in New York, where the apartments are all so small. Do you own mountains of books? And, secondary to that, do you use libraries? I have a neighbor who goes to the library every week and takes out books and reads them and returns them on time. It seems a remnant from an earlier age, before the advent of online used booksellers. I have a New York Public Library card but I haven't used it in years.

AH: Yes, there *is* something quaint about library cards. I have one for the New York Public Library, and if I ever used it, it was many years ago. I don't remember ever checking out a book. I haven't used a library in as long as I can remember, not here in New York. Maybe it's because I'm a writer, but it always seems like the decent thing is to *buy* a book, you know? But I'm happy to give them away, too. It's key to find a couple of good charities that welcome books—then you don't end up bruising yourself when you turn a corner in your apartment and a tower of books brains you.

SM: Is that a kind of compensatory behavior, having an untidy apartment? To offset your stories, which are absolutely empty of clutter?

AH: I don't know, but the apartment intervention was the kindest thing anyone's ever done for me. I used to have this straw basket, while I was writing my first book, and I got rid of the basket eventually, but I used it to keep slips of paper that I'd write the first sentences of stories on.

SM: I've read that you first write the first and last sentences of a story, and then somehow see the shape of the rest of it that needs to be filled in.

AH: Yes… and for a while the slips of paper with the opening lines on them were just around the apartment, like everything, and the other day I opened a Lucite box, and it was filled with the sentences! A box full of sentences! I keep finding things in my apartment. Surprises.

SM: You've said you experience the world not as a coherent narrative, but as a series of variously disconnected moments, which seems a reasonable evaluation of how being alive feels. On the other hand, forensics (which I've read is one of your interests) is a field of inquiry that seems based on tracing cause to effect to effect to effect, in a concatenation that seems altogether different from a series of nonintegrated moments. Could you talk about that?

AH: You've landed on one of the big draws of forensic psychology for me—that it relies on logic of a kind that is foreign to me, so it's like learning another language. More than that, it's learning to think in a different way. It forces me to make connections it would not otherwise occur to me to make; it's a challenge, and the stakes are very high in this realm. I like considering experience in both ways—in the associative way I always have, and in this new way that's exciting and endlessly surprising.

Chris Kennedy, a poet at Syracuse, sent me his new manuscript. I left it sealed in its envelope, so it wouldn't just get lost in all the paper. So it lay on my desk unopened for about a month.

SM: That's the opposite of what I would do. I fetishistically enjoy throwing things away. I'd recycle the envelope right away.

AH: Then I was walking the dogs one day and found part of a block taped off in yellow. It was right near Petco, where the girls like to drag me. Later I found out someone had jumped from the sixteenth or seventeenth floor and been impaled on a NO PARKING sign. I got home feeling shaken. To distract myself I opened the envelope. The title of the manuscript was *Encouragement for a Man Falling to His Death*.

SM: Knowing the first line and the last line seems an efficient way of working, but it seems to contradict the old saw that many fiction writers repeat, that they never know quite where a story is going to go until it goes there by itself—I recall reading about Flannery O'Connor not knowing that the "Good Country People" girl's artificial leg would be stolen until a sentence or two beforehand. Do you feel any contradiction between your knowing the last line of a story and your not knowing quite where it's going?

AH: I don't have a problem with knowing the last line of a story getting in the way of discovery on my way *to* that last line, because I don't know how I'll get there. It's not as though I've figured it all out before I start, that I just color it in and stay inside the lines. It has to do with knowing that a certain last line made me teary when I thought of it, for example, and so I hope/expect it will do the same to a reader. That's worth working toward, I think. There's still plenty of room for the story to go wherever it ends up going en route to the closest I have to a sure thing, my last line.

SM: Your stories exhibit what Rick Moody called in the introduction to your *Collected Stories* a "nearly Japanese compaction." Do you ever think about the ideal length and form of a story? Would the perfect story be one sentence long, or one word long, or maybe no words at all? Do your shortest stories seem more successful because of their brevity?

AH: Some of my shortest stories seem successful because they approach a kind of poem. I don't think there is an ideal length, though I like the idea of a story in one sentence, and plan to try more of these.

SM: I know you read a lot of poetry as well as a lot of fiction. But how do you distinguish between poetry and fiction? Is it even important to do that? And what about prose poetry? I teach a whole class on it every semester and still don't know what it is.

AH: The best definition I know is that if I write one it's a short-short, and if you write one it's a prose poem. I think there is a lot of leeway. I like the idea of the prose poem being image-driven, but that describes a lot of short-short stories too. I don't really worry about it.

SM: Your stories are small machines, but they aren't simple. There's been plenty of discourse about *difficulty* in texts, which I think is supposed to mean a sort of earned incomprehensibility. How can a reader tell the difference between a text that's necessarily difficult and a text that's just an encrypted banality? And how can a writer tell the difference?

AH: I think what some people would call *difficult* isn't really difficult. And I think what some people would call difficult I'd just call *boring.*

SM: So it's an instinctual way of knowing. If you're bored, then the so-called difficulty is unnecessary.

AH: Yes. But it doesn't really matter what you call it, difficult or whatever else. It's either good or not.

SM: That seems reasonable: either good or not good. Like the equally beside-the-point debate about the difference between poetry and fiction, which reminds me: I read that you designate your new work as prose poetry rather than fiction.

AH: Well, it seems more lyrical, more—what do people say about poetry—image-driven. But there are image-driven stories. And non-image-driven poems.

SM: So how are these pieces different from your previous stories?

AH: That piece that ran in *O* magazine [a short-short/prose poem titled "Sing to It" that appeared in the magazine's recent Reading Issue]—it uses repetition in a way I've never used it before.

SM: They have lyric refrains.

AH: Yes, but more than that, they feel different to me as I write them. They move differently. Something that happens to me very infrequently is this: I dream of the rhythm of a sentence, not the words of it, but just the rhythm of it, and wake up with the beat of it in my head: da-DA-da-DA-da-da-da-DA. And that's happened much more lately, with these pieces, and so I'm calling them poems.

SM: So the name itself isn't what's important—what's important is that the name designates a different category of work from what you've done before.

AH: The stories all came out in a book together, and then I thought, Well, why not? Why not just do this completely new thing?

SM: I understand and share your deep respect for the sentence as a rich, malleable unit of expression. Yet you read a lot of poetry, at least some of which I assume is in verse. Do you experience versed lines differently from the way you experience sentences?

AH: Yes—lines are different from sentences, and I often don't know why a line breaks in a poem, why the poet made that decision. I don't have a feel for lines the way I do for a sentence. I know when I've made a good sentence, and I know how to edit sentences for my students sometimes. I don't have the same experience with the line. It's frustrating, and I wish I did! I thought I could bring it on by reading a great deal of poetry, but I can't seem to make it happen.

SM: In "Jesus Is Waiting" (from *The Dog of the Marriage*) a character says, "Maybe people should be trained like dogs. But people aren't dogs. And a dog won't speak to you either." And at the end of "The Uninvited," a dog's owner is asked by a vet's assistant to wave a chain above a dog's hips to determine whether the dog's pregnant, but the dog owner misunderstands: "I gave her back the chain. I got down on all fours." You mentioned that during a visual-association exercise, when someone said *face,* you pictured a dog's face. What do you think are the real differences between humans and dogs?

AH: Dogs are like our best selves. The difference? Dogs don't live long enough.

SM: Do your dogs leave you alone while you write, or are being with dogs and writing interpermeable experiences—or the same experience?

AH: James Dickey wrote a poem called "A Dog Sleeping on My Feet" that begins: "Being his resting place, I do not even tense / The muscles of a leg / Or I would seem to be changing...." I love it when this happens, but the moment there's any motion—the tensing of a muscle—then I'm fair game, and my dogs figure I'm there to entertain them. I have to wear them out before I can work with them in the apartment. But the trade-off is that in the miles a day of "walkies," I can sound out sentences, and sometimes a problem gets solved *because* I'm not sitting at my desk.

SM: You entertain the dogs and work in the apartment—do you ever entertain yourself? When in New York, what do you do most: go to readings, look at art, go to concerts, or watch films? I should probably include sports events and lectures and things, too.

AH: I've been spending a lot of time outside the city the last few years, though I live here at least half the time. The number one activity is walking the dogs, so the number one activity includes being in the park, and trying to pull my dogs' heads out of the barrels of cookies at Petco, as you have seen. After that: movies. I'm easily overwhelmed by how much of everything there is here, but it is usually possible for me to walk into a theater and find an aisle seat. My friend Kathy Rich and I see every Korean horror film that opens here—that's a subset of what I'll see. I'm happy to watch almost anything.

SM: Do you regularly read any journalism?

AH: I rely largely on my friends who do to tell me what I should know about. Mainly I read forensic psychology and forensic science textbooks, which, added to the teaching, doesn't leave a lot of time for regular reading of much else.

SM: After working as a journalist but not having attempted fiction, you arrived at Gordon Lish's class more or less a fully formed fiction writer—your almost unbelievably good story "In the Cemetery Where Al Jolson Is Buried" (from *Reasons to Live*), according to legend, was your first attempt at writing fiction. But was there a point of transformation between your being a journalist and your writing that story, a point that marked your becoming a fiction writer?

AH: I did *not* arrive a "fully formed fiction writer" when I took Gordon's class! I didn't know anything about writing fiction, hadn't done it before. That story was a direct result of what went on in those sessions at Columbia—my material, his issued challenge to dismantle our sense of ourselves. The "transformation" from beginning journalist to fiction writer—there was not a defining moment, but more of an accumulation of evidence. Each new story helping to make the case for it. A writer writes—I started to have proof.

SM: Do you ever feel the impulse to write what could be called *memoir*?

AH: I have written maybe three or four personal essays that included things that really happened to me, and I found them very difficult to do. Sticking to the facts—I refer to a reporter in an early story as being officious, "really into accuracy," and that enters in. I love to read memoirs—I'll read a less-than-perfect memoir where I won't read less-than-wonderful fiction. But in terms of trying to do it, I'm more interested in what happens when I *think* I'm going to write about something that really happened, and see where I start to veer away, and why, and where I end up.

SM: Do your students ever slip into mimicry? Padgett Powell answered this question by asking: *What is one doing in a classroom finally but peddling his biases?*

AH: I like Padgett's question. And sure, you see influences, if not outright mimicry. For example, George Saunders has an enormous influence on students I've worked with recently. I can see it, so I say it—"You've been reading George Saunders," and I've always been right, and it's a compliment, the students love his writing,

I love his writing—and then the job is to find the ways in which the new writer can hold on to the inspiration and look at ways in which s/he can be different from George Saunders. He is a writer who has amplified what a story can do and be, and that's thrilling.

SM: Lazy critics declare some of your stories not to be stories because they don't resemble the stories they've seen in some magazine or other. But I wonder whether you have a positive definition of a story. How do you know a story's a story?

AH: I have an increasingly open sense of what a story is. Why not make room for more instead of being restrictive? There are so many kinds of stories! Any time you hear someone say, "*That's* not a story," I think you should question the person, not the story.

SM: You've said that the first sentence of "Tumble Home" indicated to you that it would have to be a novella, but can you explain how you knew? Was it something about the sound of the words?

AH: The first sentence of "Tumble Home" that I wrote was this: *The trees are all on crutches, on sawed-off braces of deadwood notched into Y-shaped crooks for support.* See what I mean? I saw that, and as I've said before, my heart went through the floor—*Oh no, this will be long.* There is an exchange in Mary Robison's novel *Why Did I Ever* where a guy asks his paramour about something she just said, he says, "What's that mean?" And she says, "Same as the words mean." I love that, and somehow I think that was the exchange here, for me. What the words mean, what they meant to me, was that here was a landscape both physical and emotional that I'd be spending some real time in.

SM: This thing you understood continues to obsess me. I want to find something literally different in that sentence from the rest of your opening sentences. Like the word *Y-shaped,* which doesn't appear in any of your other opening sentences. That must be it. I realize the misguidedness of this pursuit, but I can't help it.

AH: I can't say—it was just a certainty and I didn't question it.

SM: "Offertory," the last story in *The Dog of the Marriage,* is hailed as the first appearance of explicit sex in a Hempel story. But most of the sex isn't really sex! It's one character describing (via dialogue) a prior sexual arrangement to another character. And then at the end of the story, as in your famously unreliably narrated story "The Harvest" [from *At the Gates of the Animal Kingdom*], this character (via first-person narration) reveals that the story she's told might be inaccurate. This narrator's description of a Polish porn film is more explicit than her dialogue about the sex she may or may not have had in the past, which is in turn more explicit than the "real" sex she has within the action of the story. Was this a conscious attempt to distract the reader (or… the writer) from the story's "real" sex?

AH: I love this question! All I had when I started (besides the first and last lines, of course) was that I wanted to show the moment when power shifts between two people. And the way I wanted it to shift would involve manipulation of several kinds, all of them delivered in the form of stories, withholding and then bestowing truths. I had been told that the only sex scenes that worked were those that were about something else. I think I would have felt awkward writing some of the things I wrote here if that had not been the case. And I had a good time writing moments of misalignment—as when the man urges the woman to tell him a salacious story again, and she says, *Oh, don't you have something like that on video?* But you asked about distracting a reader from the "real" sex in the story—I tried to look as closely as I could at these acts of love and sex; I was trying not to be distracted, so I don't think I tried to distract a potential reader, no.

SM: Speaking of readers, real ones, does recognition for stories ever change your opinion of them? Does the recognition of "In the Cemetery Where Al Jolson Is Buried" make you like the story more or less than you did before it was widely anthologized, or more or less than your other stories? Do you have steady favorites from among your work?

AH: There are stories I can rely on when I will be giving a reading, stories that tend to work read aloud. Was it Picasso who answered that his favorite painting was his next one? I'm probably most pleased with the last story I've written, so that means it's the *O* magazine piece. Most of what I want to do next is there. ★

ZZ PACKER

TALKS WITH

EDWARD P. JONES

"ALL THE WRITERS THAT WENT UP TO THE 'HOUSE OF SLAVERY' WENT IN THE FRONT DOOR, WHICH IS BLACK-AND-WHITE WITH NO SHADES OF GRAY IN SIGHT; AND I JUST DECIDED TO GO AT IT FROM THE SIDE, AND OPEN A DOOR THAT HADN'T REALLY BEEN OPENED VERY OFTEN, AND THAT WAS THE DOOR INVOLVING BLACK SLAVEHOLDERS."

The ultimate novel-writing mix tape:
Judy Collins, "That's No Way to Say Good-bye" [six times in a row]
Opening-credits theme, The Life and Times of Judge Roy Bean
[Get up and walk around while tape is rewinding; play again]

Edward P. Jones has earned renown as a writer of consummate understatement, control, and unflinching honesty, even as his range extends from the intense ode-like short stories in his collection Lost in the City *(1992) to the Miltonic scope of his novel* The Known World *(2003). His prose style is often so clean as to appear initially neutral, and yet the cumulative effect is that of an interrogation; Jones tests our moral hesitancies until we are surprised to find ourselves in an epistemological corral of our own reckoning.*

Set in Washington, D.C., Lost in the City *forsakes the corridors of power to funnel the reader through a peripatetic tour of D.C.'s most in-*

digent neighborhoods, its denizens trapped black Washingtonians who cling to their humanity while sometimes questioning the dubious gift of it. In The Known World, *Jones's canvas is grander and his sense of irony keener. The novel begins with the death of Henry Townsend, a black slaveholder in pre–Civil War Virginia whose life and death become a manifest for slavery's more absurdist particularities. Through the novel's scores of characters, Jones artfully widens the focus from race onto all of mankind, suggesting that the question of slavery is the ultimate litmus test of any civilization.*

Jones was born and raised in Washington, D.C., received his B.A. from the College of the Holy Cross in Worcester, Massachusetts, and his M.F.A. from the University of Virginia, Charlottesville. Jones was shortlisted for the 1992 National Book Award for Lost in the City, *which went on to win the PEN/Hemingway Award for that year. In 2003, Jones was again shortlisted for the National Book Award, this time for* The Known World, *which went on to win the National Book Critics Circle Award and the Pulitzer Prize. He is a recent recipient of the MacArthur Foundation "genius grant."*

This interview took place over the course of two long phone conversations.

—ZZ Packer (Spring 2005)

I. "MAYBE I'LL WRITE A STORY WHERE A MOTHER JUST ABANDONS HER CHILDREN, BUT I'D HAVE TO DIG DEEP TO CREATE HER. IT'D BE LIKE WRITING A STORY WHERE A HUMAN BEING DECIDES TO EAT ANOTHER HUMAN BEING."

ZZ PACKER: I remember a certain writer came to Iowa to read, and he was praising your collection *Lost in the City,* but he also said, "It's remarkable, he got through a collection of stories and there wasn't one white person in it."

EDWARD P. JONES: How many black people are in Hemingway's stories? How many black people are in Chekhov stories? If there are no Martians in the world you live in, why should you be condemned for writing stories with no Martians?

ZZP: A kind of unconscious racism.

EPJ: One reviewer condemned me for not having many men in *Lost in the City.* People get up in the morning and the world is horrible for them, so they have to find a way to take it out on somebody else. It's as if, if you're an atheist, you have to find your religion by beating up on other people's religion.

ZZP: Family, as a structure, dominates both *Lost in the City* and *The Known World,* particularly the devastating effects of its absence. In what way did your portrayal of families in *The Known World* and *Lost in the City* come from your sense of family and how you grew up?

EPJ: I try to make everything up, but I was quite aware growing up that my father wasn't around. I remember one night when I was in high school; we used to take the trash can and put it up on a table because the mice would get into the trash can at night and cause a ruckus... so we set it up there [on the table], but in the middle of the night one night, the trash can fell and we thought someone had broken in to the place. I got up and got this little vase to go out there, and my sister was behind me and my mother was behind her, and I remember thinking, This is what a father is supposed to be doing—protecting his family. That was the best example of that, but there are probably many others that I've since forgotten.

ZZP: There are quite a few dead mothers in your stories. I'm thinking of "The Girl Who Raised Pigeons," "Young Lions," "A Rich Man"—

EPJ: My mother died when I was twenty-four. After that I thought, God, I don't know what would have happened to me and my sister if she had died when we were kids. Maybe we would have gone to live with an aunt in Brooklyn. There were times when I was a child and she was very ill, and it was a scary thing—there was no one else in Washington that would have taken us in. And probably, though it's not on any conscious level, that's in the back of my mind, and I'm sure it comes up in the work.

But sometimes the mother has to be out of the equation. In order to get where you're going people have to be sacrificed... Being the kind of person I am, the way I lean is toward the great tragedy of life being the loss of a mother.

My own mother died January 1, 1975. Then my father died that March. I was in Philadelphia and didn't learn about it [my father's death] until a couple of months later. Not until my sister and her new baby came down in May and went to where my father had lived; the woman my father lived with said he'd died.

I was glad I hadn't been close to him. I don't think I could have taken two losses in such a short time.

ZZP: How often did you end up seeing him?

EPJ: Over the years, he and I had twenty visits. In sixty-five, we went to visit my aunt in Brooklyn. We came back and my mother had moved. But none of us had telephones and my mother couldn't read or write. Luckily we'd found out she'd moved in to this place around the corner; they had condemned the place we'd lived in, so she had to move. We lived in one room and there was a hole in it—you could literally see up to the second floor. We could see the light, we could see the *ceiling* of the second floor. So my mother had moved around the corner to a tiny room. The locks were flimsy and people were always stealing stuff from her. God knows how we all slept those nights in that tiny room. My aunt took it upon herself to find us a new place and went out and saw this place on N Street, and it looked fine, so she said we should live there. Well, it was diagonally across from where my father was living. And mother didn't want to do it, but we were in dire straits and so we moved there. So for several years we lived across the street from him.

ZZP: Did you talk to him? Did it feel odd, after not having had regular contact with him for so long?

EPJ: I went over a few times and talked to him. I was in high school, so in a certain sense he was just a person across the street. Before then, we'd spoken maybe ten times.

He knew absolutely nothing about my life. I didn't go and share anything about my life with him—it would have been like sharing my life with a stranger. If my mother had been the kind of person like my father, who just up and left, I don't know what would have happened to us. So I guess I was writing "The Girl Who Raised Pigeons" with that in mind. The father is alone on the street, and his baby girl can't talk, so the father could have up and left.

Maybe I'll write a story where a mother just abandons her children, but I'd have to dig deep to create her. It'd be like writing a story where a human being decides to eat another human being.

ZZP: In "The First Day," a young girl discovers that her mother is illiterate. You said your own mother couldn't read or write.

EPJ: I saw how hard she was struggling, so I always endeavored to be a good kid, a good student. One of the things I was doing early on was reading comic books; then I graduated on to books. A lot of it came from this understanding that we had that she wanted me to get the most education that I possibly could. [*Starts laughing*] I remember once she came home with this paperback some customer of hers had left at the restaurant. On the cover there was the back of a woman, naked, down about to her waist, and there was a man embracing her.

She didn't know what it was about. She just knew it had words and she wanted me to be involved with words. And she knew I read a lot, and here was another book she could help me have. It wasn't a memorable book, and it didn't have much sex in it, either.

ZZP: When did you discover that your mother couldn't read? Did you ever find yourself in a role of translating for her?

EPJ: Well, I remember when I was very young; my brother was retarded and he lived with us until I was about four—he was a year younger than me. A letter came from the court system, but she couldn't read, so she had to find somebody there to tell her what it was about. The letter said they were taking my brother and putting him in an institution.

ZZP: How often did you see him?

EPJ: We would go out to this place in Laurel, Maryland, at least once a month, sometimes every third week.

ZZP: You were homeless once. Can you talk about what that was like?

EPJ: It wasn't for very long: it was in seventy-six. After my mother died I went to Philadelphia, then I came back [to D.C]. I stayed in this mission downtown. You could get a room free for the night if you listened to this religious stuff. A lot of singing and all that. When you're faced with being out on the street versus a cot in a room with about fifty other men, you sort of choose the latter.

ZZP: What got you out of that?

EPJ: I'd written to my sister and asked her to send me fifteen bucks for the Trailways bus up to Brooklyn. I was going to stay with her. I thought maybe my chances would be better up there. .

So my sister sent the money, but that week I got the job at *Science* magazine, and the people in Philadelphia finally forwarded one piece of mail that *Essence* magazine had sent—

ZZP: And that was the first piece that you'd ever published, right? In *Essence*?

EPJ: Yeah. All that happened in one week.

ZZP: What was the story called?

EPJ: "Harvest." My sister for a long time had been getting *Essence* and I would read the stories every month. And I thought, God, these stories are horrible! So when I was in Philadelphia, I wrote that story and sent it off. And a year later they were going to publish it.

ZZP: Was that the first time you considered yourself a writer?

EPJ: No. After it came out, I still had the job at *Science* magazine, and George Washington University had this thing where writers can teach a course to people with regular day jobs. So I went to a writer's house—Susan Shreve's—and did the writing thing.

ZZP: I wonder if there was pressure to be something other than a writer. Weren't you a tax analyst for quite some time after *Lost in the City*?

EPJ: I got a job after graduate school, and my heart was never really in it, but I had to have a place to live and something to eat. It was a nonprofit organization called Tax Analysts, and they were publishing this esoteric magazine for tax accountants and lawyers. I would summarize two or three pages out of 120 pages of really dense stuff—court opinions, tax regulations, articles on taxes. I'd summarize stuff from *BusinessWeek,* the *New York Times,* the *Washington Post,* the *Wall Street Journal,* things like that. Then I did the same thing for two other magazines on insurance and tax-exempt organizations. But my heart wasn't in it.

ZZP: And you were writing while you were doing that?

EPJ: Off and on. I was never one to get up and do it every day. I suppose thinking of it should also be counted as working.

II. "PEOPLE ARE STILL PEOPLE. AND THEY NEVER IMPROVE."

ZZP: Even before reading *The Known World,* I feared for you because of the possible response; I feared other black readers would be upset by the premise of the novel. Were you ever fearful about such a backlash from black readers? Or providing ammunition for certain white readers?

EPJ: No, I suppose I was kind of blinded. I learned about the black slaveholders when I was in college. It's a known fact—well, a little-known fact—and I think that the fact that there were such people gave me license to create this fiction. If there were no black people in this country whatsoever that owned slaves, then I wouldn't have felt that I could write this. I never thought at all about people coming along and hating what I'd written because it was a fact. People have to live with what was factual and what was real. And that's what I would have thought if people had come along and said something [negative].

I didn't want to give ammunition to the antireparations people, and I did mention that in a letter to my editor—but in the end reparations is not based on a certain people giving to another people—the concept addresses the entire system—no matter who profited from it. This [*The Known World*] was just one more weapon in the hands of those people. But reparations addresses slavery [in general], not the fact that there were white people who owned black people.

ZZP: Did *The Known World* come about as a particular interest in an anomaly, or did it arise from an interest in the universality of what any slaveholder represents: a capitulation to a system in which humans are bought and sold?

EPJ: Yeah. I think I sort of started out with the intention of writing about the slaves who were owned by Henry Townsend; I was going to focus exclusively on those people. Because when you're a storyteller you're trying to come at the story from a different angle. So I decided to go at it from that angle. In all the novels that are written about slavery, all the writers that went up to the "house of slavery" went in the front door, which is black-and-white with no shades of gray in sight; and I just decided to go at it from the side, and open a door that hadn't really been opened very often, and that was the door involving black slaveholders.

Again, when you're a storyteller, you try to be different, fresh, even if ultimately, of course, we're all dealing with the same issues anyway. People in *The Known World* are doing the same things people said and did five thousand years ago. People are still people. And they never improve. [*Laughs*]

ZZP: I like what you're saying about going around through the side door; it does seem as though when we write historical novels, we feel as though we have to write the story that is going to validate the conditions of our ancestors. But writing more obliquely and less directly seems to be the project of fiction, to tell the ultimate truth rather than just the facts. And perhaps we're less likely to fall back on received wisdom—

EPJ: Yes. Henry Townsend says he's going to be a better master than any white master has ever been. But in the end, he's blind to the fact—the way all the white masters have been blind to the fact—that slavery affects everyone who participates in it. And it's important that he's black, but in the end it's the same old thing. The same old crime.

ZZP: The protagonist Henry grows in thrall to his white master and the power his master wields, but Moses, Henry's slave, never imagines that he could have a black master. Moses eventually begins to want to replace Henry, to be a black master as Henry was—to own slaves himself.

EPJ: The thing about Moses is that, chronologically, the first time you meet him he's radically different from the Moses you get at the end: he's been chained to this woman Betsy, and he's talking about them being one and them not being separated, and through the end he's gone through any number of things that make him the kind of man who throws his family away. He goes from being a man who believes in family to a man who feels he can get on top by throwing his family away.

ZZP: That loss of family seems to presage the destruction of the community at large. Is this deliberate?

EPJ: Yeah. My editor, Dawn Davis, came back with some very minor suggestions about the manuscript of *The Known World,* which allowed me to go back over the manuscript once again and do some other things.

In the second go-round, I was interested in how people had survived slavery, and I realized that one thing that helped people was that they had family—at the very center of that idea was Elias [one of Henry's slaves]. Here was a single-minded man who had one thought: to be free. He never intended to be close to any human being on that plantation; he wanted to run away and be free. But then, through circumstances, he falls in love with this woman who's crippled and cannot run [away with him]. Then, through his love for her and the family they create, he finds a different kind of freedom.

ZZP: So there are characters who have family, and they survive. What about the people who didn't have family?

EPJ: One of the characters, Stamford, doesn't have family, but he's redeemed because he begins to care about others being redeemed, and in a certain sense he finds a family, which is not what he'd been doing all his life when he was chasing after what I call "young stuff." So once he finds a family in a certain sense, the children—he has an affinity for children—he's redeemed. The people who have a family or develop one are the ones who're ultimately saved.

III. "ABOUT EVERY CHARACTER IN [*LOST IN THE CITY*] IS A GIRL OR A WOMAN, AND I ENVISIONED THE COLLECTION AS GOING FROM BIRTH TO OLD AGE. I WANTED TO GO FROM AN INFANT TO AN OLD WOMAN."

ZZP: Back to *Lost in the City*. In "The Girl Who Raised Pigeons," the father, Robert, finally comes home with his infant daughter after his wife's death. The kids playing on the street know enough to respect his grief. We see these little kids who are poor behaving with dignity and respect—reverence—something that seems missing from the images we see of blacks today. In your stories a number of people have that high level of consciousness despite their poverty.

EPJ: I lived on a street like that. An era when people talked about that maxim "It takes a village to raise a child." Adults looked out for kids who weren't even in their familes. And I was really conscious of how all that ended. When those people had to move out of that neighborhood. Because, as I show in the story, it obliterated the neighborhood.

And also, all the adults I knew growing up were born and raised in the South, and they came to the city with a sense of community, of looking out for each other when they came to the North. After one, two, three generations, it's gone. Nowadays you don't dare chastise some child out there in the street that's doing something wrong, but when I was growing up it was all right, some kid would do something wrong and get a spanking by somebody in the neighborhood, then when his parents came home and found out, he'd get another spanking. But all that went away. For some reason.

ZZP: For what reasons?

EPJ: Drugs. Even though the Civil Rights era came along, things didn't improve the way we needed them to improve. We didn't have any money, but it was just a nicer world.

ZZP: In "Marie," the eponymous character is part of that old community. I love the phrase Marie repeats to herself after she's slapped a rather saucy, ineffectual bureaucrat: "You whatn't raised that way." Though the story is contemporary, Marie herself absolutely harkens back to that pre–Civil Rights era.

EPJ: About every character in that collection is a girl or a woman, and I envisioned the collection as going from birth to old age. I wanted to go from an infant to an old woman.

ZZP: I thought it was really wonderful to show a range of women; I think a lot of men shy away from writing about women, as though it might be beneath them to write about the lives of women. I suspect many men wouldn't admit they thought that way, or even suspect they thought that way.

EPJ: Well, I don't know where they're living.

ZZP: Do you think the black community has gotten to the point where we can write about that loss of dignity you spoke of—abandoning the fairy-tale idea of always uplifting, but not, perhaps, recording reality? I'm thinking of Zora Neale Hurston, who wrote using folklore and anthropological observations and the Gulf dialect of Florida blacks—and then Richard Wright says blacks shouldn't write in dialect, that it doesn't uplift the "Negro community."

EPJ: People can write it, but whether or not anyone will ever get a chance to read it—given what publishers want to publish nowadays—is doubtful. And the fact that fewer and fewer people are reading. I mean, you can go forth to the typical black teenager nowadays and they might not be able to name five writers born before 1950, but you ask them about the history of some rap star and they know all about it.

Writers, of course, have always done whatever they wanted to do: the problem is that a lot of people have not wanted to publish them. The range is now so narrow. I don't know if I would be the kind of person I am now if that was all there was to read.

ZZP: I guess I'm saying that Wright's idea was that "Negro writing" had to uphold the race—

EPJ: You have an obligation to tell the truth. I remember when I was thinking about the girl who raised pigeons and her father, and I was writing during a time when more and more stuff was coming out about how bad black men were.

As the story develops, he remains with this child: he becomes a father—but I realize that if the story I was working out in my head had him look down in that carriage and walk away, then that's what I would have had to do as a storyteller. It's good to do things that uphold the race, but sometimes a storyteller has to go down a different path.

But the reaction of black people [to *The Known World*] has been 99 percent positive. Only one or two examples come to mind when that hasn't been the case. Any negative reaction is by people who haven't read the book. "You have to keep in mind that black families who owned slaves often bought their own families..." Well, if this cat had read the book, he would have known I'd written that in the first few pages.

A white woman in Fairfax, Virginia, said, "I've read Toni Morrison, and I wonder where you did the research on how people talk." Essentially she was saying the black people in the *The Known World* talk too intelligently. I didn't mention Jebediah, who's *I ain't dis, I ain't dere* all over the place; but he's smart enough to know how to get under the skin of Fern Elston, who thinks she knows more than anybody else.

A writer can't sit down and think about what everyone else is going to think—I never thought about what someone in Jackson, Mississippi, might think, or someone in Oakland, California. When I sat down to write *The Known World,* I had only one reader in mind: myself. I was trying to make it as good as I possibly could. So it's best not to sit down and anticipate the reaction down the line. You have to just tell the truth as you know it.

ZZP: Many of the reviews of *The Known World* remark that it is a difficult book to enter, but that once you get going, the reader becomes accustomed to your almost Biblical tone. I found it to be almost the opposite; we're lured in by beautifully written prose that at first appears to be third person, from Henry's slave Moses' point of view, but we soon find ourselves in a kind of naked, objective omniscience that's so unsettling because it's *so* objective, forcing the reader to provide her own moral yardstick. We have to confront ourselves and our own prejudices when we're reading this. Is that lack of commentary your way of forcing the reader to come to her own conclusions?

EPJ: No, I can't say I thought about that, actually. The one notion that I did have was that I was going to be writing such a horrendous story that had its own emotional charge that I didn't need to come along and provide what I often call "neon language." I mean, the thing that you write about in such novels is how people suffered in slavery. The grown folks. And the children, as well. Everyone, everyone [suffered]. The story itself was emotional enough that all I had to do was simply report.

I was influenced when I was in grad school—twenty-five years before I even thought about writing this book—by this Bible as Literature course. I'd never really read the Bible all the way through like that. The Bible we read was the Jerusalem Bible, which is the Catholic Bible. There was a lot of objective prose throughout that. I remember in particular the description of Jonah in the belly of the whale—it was just flat-out reporting, you know, a sense of "these are the facts." And your heart breaks for the man, without the writer ever injecting any sort of commentary whatsoever.

ZZP: That reportorial device strikes me as very Old Testament, where we get all those stories like those about Jeremiah and Jonah, as opposed to the New Testament, which becomes more parable-based.

EPJ: Yeah. Well, I knew the kind of story I would be telling and wanted to do that with straight flat prose. And I think I tend to do that with everything I do, simply because of the kinds of people I'm writing about. These are not people who go into an antique store and think that their lives are going to end because they don't find the right table. These are people with real problems.

ZZP: Fern, a black schoolteacher, and William Robbins, Henry's former master, inculcate in Henry certain ideas about what it means to be a property owner. Their characters seem to suggest that evil requires a model, that we perhaps need to visualize evil as normal before we can become primed to adopt a system like slavery. Were you thinking of these characters in these terms—as models?

EPJ: Henry's problem is that during his formative years, his only influence was William Robbins, because his parents could only come once a week, and there were many times when they weren't even allowed to see him, or times when Henry wouldn't show up when they came to visit.

And Fern, she realizes that her soul is doomed, but she's standing at the gate—and doing all she shouldn't be doing, nevertheless.

ZZP: I kept envisioning Fern as a Condoleezza Rice character.

EPJ: I was intrigued in the 1980s by all the black conservatives coming out of the woodwork, and they were parroting Reagan's line "It's morning in America," and that essentially racism was dead, and we all could be judged on what we do with our lives and not the color of our skin, but we know, day after day, that people are still being oppressed. Every other month, I read in the *Washington Post* how testers will go to apartment buildings and see if they'll be rented to, and you find out that black people are still being discriminated against.

Those are the kinds of people who—along with the rappers and all those violent sports players—who, if slavery were legal, would own slaves.

IV. "IF YOU CAN'T WRITE THE PROPAGANDA, THEN YOU AT LEAST SUPPLY THE SANDWICH FOR THE PERSON WHO WRITES THE PROPAGANDA. YOU CAN AT LEAST EMPTY THE TRASH CANS—WE ALL HAVE TO DO WHAT WE'RE ABLE."

ZZP: I remember reading an interview with E. Annie Proulx where she said that all of the books she'd written were like these parcels that had been delivered to her, wrapped in brown paper, and that all she had to do was unwrap them, so that essentially, when she sits down to write, it feels as though all she has to do is take dictation. Is that what it's like for you?

EPJ: Yeah. It felt that way. It's like taking dictation from yourself.

ZZP: That's sort of scary to me. I don't quite understand that.

EPJ: You've written it out in your head, so it's Annie Proulx taking dictation from Annie Proulx. I was afraid you were going to ask—what is it that people say? [*Begins talking in a whiny author Q&A voice*] "I just sit down and my characters take over…" I think that's such crap! My answer to that is, if all you have to do is let your characters take over, then I guess you can go out, watch three or four movies, then come back and the work is all done! The "characters" have done it.

ZZP: Well, I find that when I'm writing there's a back-and-forth process—I'll think, then I'll write some, then what I've written influences the next train of thought, and so on. It seems as though people like you and Annie Proulx are doing a lot of that back-and-forth work in your heads. Do you think that comes from having an extraordinarily analytical mind?

EPJ: I don't know what kind of mind I have, but I tell students that if you're driving (I don't drive) on the Baltimore–Washington Expressway, and if your plan is to end up in Baltimore, and you start off at twelve noon, you might see a road sign for a town you've never heard of, ever. And that is the detour in the writing. The final chapter will never change substantially, but there are detours before you get to that final chapter that are surprises. So you end up visiting this town and end up including something about it that you hadn't prepared for.

ZZP: I remember hearing Leon Uris talk about writing that way. He compared it to setting sail on the open seas, but having a destination port… have you written a story in which the destination was one place and the story ended up in a completely different place?

EPJ: No. Generally not. You're always learning how to do this writing stuff… you work it out—the beginning, the middle and the end—in your head, and you go over it. And that's what happened to me with *The Known World.* I went over it all those years in my head, trying to make sure one chapter led logically to the next chapter. So it was as well laid out as I could possibly get it. So when I actually wrote it, there weren't too many substantial changes. A few things here and there.

ZZP: At the end of "A Rich Man" Horace ends up on his apartment floor, going through all those records that have been smashed by the young people who started crashing at his retirement-home apartment. I love the ending, but it's very strange—it's just the names of all those albums: *I'm Gonna Pin a Medal on the Girl I Left Behind. Ragtime Soldier Man. Whose Little Heart Are You Breaking Now? The Syncopated Waltz.*

I was wondering, was it a matter of starting at the end, knowing here's a man who's going to arrive at this complete dissolution, or did you actually have an image, specifically, of those broken records?

EPJ: No. I think what had happened was that I could see these two people married for a long time, and they were living in this small space together, and yet they were living separate lives, and I just decided to provide what would happen before then and what was going to happen afterward.

I do remember actually listening to those records. The penultimate one [*Whose Little Heart Are You Breaking Now?*] said something directly about the entire story: the final one was vague like all the others were. One of the copy editors at the *New Yorker* wanted me to move that one to the end, but I didn't want that. I didn't want the very last one to say anything directly like that.

I tend to collect things. I have this great interest in stuff that's old and in the years before I was born; what records looked like, what the world looked like back then. Time-Life had a series where they did a decade of the twentieth century, and I was able to find this 1920s one. And I remember thinking, Which one should be first on the list and which one should be last?

ZZP: What kinds of things do you end up collecting?

EPJ: I have a great many 33 1/3 records that I've picked up since the late '60s. A lot of the things I've been interested in collecting have been speeches. I have Elijah Muhammad; I have a great one by Eldridge Cleaver. I think he's speaking extemporaneously at Syracuse University in 1968. It's just great. He engages the audience and he's funny a lot of the time.

I think I have Jesse Jackson, W. E. B. DuBois speaking sometime in the '50s, a couple of tapes by Lenny Bruce, Dick Gregory…

ZZP: You sort of remind me of James Alan McPherson, with his vast archive of speeches.

EPJ: He had lots. I wish I could get copies of what he has.

ZZP: I know he makes copies of tapes. He's always giving them to me. He'll give me a tape, and I'll ask if he wants them back and he'll say, "Keep it, keep it," but he'll lose one of the copies, and I end up sending them back to him.

EPJ: ...Angela Davis. I have this great one with James Baldwin talking, too—

ZZP: How long ago was that before his death?

EPJ: I think it may have been the '70s. I found it in a remainders bin. Brand-new when I got it. I think it was in Charlottesville. The ones from the '50s and '60s are just great. But that one from Cleaver is just wonderful. At that time I think Huey Newton was in jail and Cleaver's going through this whole thing about the political system, and Averell Harriman—Harriman was part of the Vietnam negotiations at that time in sixty-eight. [Cleaver would say,] "He's a liar, he's a liar..." When he comes out of the place where they're negotiating, he says, "Oh, they just won't talk right." And goes on: "He's a liar, he's a liar." Both sides of this album, he has this joke, then a standard line, "All power to the people, peace and freedom, power to the peace and freedom people. Black Panther Party, power to the Black Panther Party." It's just really moving in certain places. I was very enamored of the Black Panthers, the black power movement.

ZZP: Did you ever think you would join the Panthers?

EPJ: There wasn't a Panther office in Worcester. And I had so many other things to take care of.

You see these black people now, and they have their nice cars and their nice clothes and everything, but you can see a sort of emptiness. It reminds me of something Maya Angelou said, maybe twenty-five years ago, about people being "exiled to *things*."

ZZP: Yes. It's as though we can't escape naked materialism. People talk about America losing some sort of moral center, and politicians are taking advantage of that fear.

EPJ: I don't remember when the great force of the anti–Vietnam War movement started, but now we've got Iraq. By this time with Vietnam, there was a great movement out there already. Right now there are people protesting who are antiwar, but there's not the great force that there was with the Vietnam War—and these [Republican] politicians who come along and just out-and-out lie about the situation, coming out and calling the AARP pro-gay, and antisoldier—and no one will deign to call them on it!

ZZP: Perhaps people feel the need to get back to something basic, but it seems like those people aren't realizing that they're being told they can't dissent or criticize—

EPJ: If you even *look* in a particular direction, then you're accused of being on the wrong side. If they continue to get away with it, then before you know it, it's going to get worse and worse.

ZZP: Many writers suspect that being a [fiction] writer has nothing to do with the political world, that their writing isn't going to change anything. Do you ever feel that same sense of frustration?

EPJ: Of not doing enough?

ZZP: Yeah, or feeling that what you're doing as a writer doesn't directly address what's going on.

EPJ: Sometimes, but I know there's not very much that I can do. When I write fiction it's far removed from everyday events. But you are a certain kind of person: you believe in a certain kind of right, no matter what, so when you're writing, the everyday world is consciously on your mind, so what you know as being right seeps into the writing nevertheless.

ZZP: But do you think that ends up changing people?

EPJ: I don't know. I don't think anyone will read what I write and think, I should be more involved with the world around me. So you have to do what you can do in other ways. If you can't write the propaganda, then you at least supply the sandwich for the person who writes the propaganda. You can at least empty the trash cans—we all have to do what we're able.

I never set out to write an antislavery novel, even though of course I'm fiercely against it, but my beliefs come out in everything I'm writing.

V. "I DON'T HAVE ANYTHING TO SAY, SO I DON'T THINK PEOPLE SHOULD SPEND THEIR TIME TRYING TO GET ME TO SAY ANYTHING."

ZZP: One of those typical questions: do you have any particular writing routine?

EPJ: No, not really. I get up and fix coffee. I don't even really like coffee, but I've found that psychologically, I wake up more with it, just the smell. And I just start writing.

I have a bit of music that I always use. For about 95 percent of *The Known World* I used this tape—and again, this is the physical writing, not the mental—I had copied, six times in a row, Judy Collins singing, "That's No Way to Say Good-bye," then after that I taped the opening credits to Paul Newman's movie *The Life and Times of Judge Roy Bean.* They're both quite moving pieces and rather melancholy. There's something in listening to those pieces that helps me do what I have to do.

I was plagued—from 1999 until last year—by the people living above me who didn't put carpeting down, so my niece gave me a Walkman, and when I was up in the mornings, I had the headphones on, and the tape lasted for a half hour—first the Judy Collins was on for six times, then the movie music from *Judge Roy Bean,* then, when it was finished, I would get up and walk around while the tape rewound.

I paid a friend of mine to tape the movie on a cassette back and front and Judy Collins back and front, so now, rather than waiting about four minutes for the tape to rewind, I can just flip it over. [*Laughs*]

ZZP: I can't listen to songs with lyrics while I'm writing. Do you ever find that you get distracted by the words?

EPJ: The words don't bother me. They become a part of me.

ZZP: There's a song on a Branford Marsalis album, a chain gang song, "Berta, Berta," that I listen to while working on this novel. It might be from Albert Murray's *Train, Whistle Guitar.* Then again, I think it's August Wilson's *The Piano Lesson*—anyway, it completely makes the mood.

EPJ: Certain chords kind of transport you. Then all of a sudden, the scene you're working out is there. They may not be the songs the characters would listen to.

ZZP: I mentioned Albert Murray; did you read him at all, growing up? Who'd you end up reading?

EPJ: There's so many… I can remember reading McPherson when I was in college. I remember it was a black paperback and the letters *Hue and Cry* were in orange. And on the back he's there with a little picture, and he's in a peacoat. And I remember thinking, Wow, this guy looks like me! That's the sort of thing that gives you hope.

ZZP: I have an old *Hue and Cry* with that picture. It's a handsome picture.

EPJ: It was only a few years before that when I was reading *Invisible Man.* I was never thinking I would be a writer: I didn't grow up with that idea in my head, but I would be reading *Invisible Man,* and there was a picture of Ellison on the back, and I would come to a nice passage, turn the book over, and say, "You wrote that." Then I would turn back and go on with the story.

ZZP: Do you read any of your reviews? After a certain point do you stop reading them?

EPJ: Everything came in before this prize thing. Luckily nothing has been very mean.

ZZP: It seems as though writers are increasingly asked to be public figures, or a part of a scene—the conferences and the festivals and the parties—do you end up participating in any of that?

EPJ: I try to stick to the readings. I tell them I don't want to be at some faculty cocktail party; they insist on having those for some reason. I try to read student manuscripts. I read eight manuscripts at the University of Minnesota. I'll go to a class or hold individual conferences. I'll spend a half hour or more with each individual student.

ZZP: That's incredibly generous.

EPJ: I don't want to read and just leave. People invite you to read, and if you're raised a certain way, the least you can do is be a good guest. The last thing I like to do is go to these cocktail parties and schmooze around with a glass of wine or ginger ale and talk.

I'm much better in life when I have a script. You read. You answer questions. You read student manuscripts. You sit down and you talk with them and give them your opinion, however small it might be. But going to a cocktail party or somebody's house for dinner—there's no script there. I can't—I'm not comfortable living my life like that. I'm not much of a social person.

ZZP: Perhaps you'd be more comfortable if there were some sort of purpose to those parties besides the schools showing you off to the benefactors.

EPJ: Yeah, I don't have anything to say, so I don't think people should spend their time trying to get me to say anything.

ZZP: You were sued recently by a woman who claimed you'd shown up at her family reunion and stolen information from her to write *The Known World*.

EPJ: Well, I'm not a social enough person to go to anybody's reunion. The lawyer said she had some pamphlet about her ancestors, and she says I *leafed through it* and got all my ideas. Like "The ground was soaked with rain," and "the people talked all night and all day." Those are the quotes in my book that I supposedly got from her. [*Laughs*]

It's just so far off the wall. She's reluctant to produce whatever it is she's written.

ZZP: You're working on short stories now?

EPJ: About fourteen of them. I have about two or three left to do [for a collection]. So that's what I'll use the summer for. I've been thinking about them since the mid-'90s, thinking, thinking, thinking, and now I'm getting around to them.

ZZP: How long does it take once you finally decide you're going to write them?

EPJ: It could be weeks. I don't think I ever do anything in less than a week.

ZZP: Some people will take a whole year.

EPJ: If you're doing so many things—if you know you have to get up and go, like I've had to do for quite some time, you can't really relax. But when I can relax…

ZZP: Do you find that people treat you differently after your having won the Pulitzer?

EPJ: People ask if I'm happy about this and that, especially when they talk about the money. I am happy, but there's no car in the world I want—I don't want a car—there are places I want to go, but I'm not hungry to do world travel. There's no fancy house that I want.

I got some crabs the other week, twelve crabs, and that's a feast. That's wonderful. That makes me happy.

I was in graduate school, and I was rooming at this place the first year and we all shared the same bathroom. After I moved I wrote to this one friend of mine, "Finally I got a bathroom all to myself." He said I'd probably always be happy because there were small things that made me happy.

I remember when that basketball player Len Bias died of a cocaine overdose. Now, he's from Maryland, he should have gone right down to the crab-house, bought twelve crabs and an orange soda, and that would have fulfilled him. [*Both laugh*] Why didn't he do that? ✯

DAPHNE BEAL

TALKS WITH

JANET MALCOLM

"THE NARRATOR OF MY NONFICTION PIECES IS NOT THE SAME PERSON I AM— SHE IS A LOT MORE ARTICULATE AND THINKS OF MUCH CLEVERER THINGS TO SAY THAN I USUALLY DO."

Results are not guaranteed with:
Czech wit in translation
Emails
Photographs
Interviews
World War II–era recipes

very journalist who is not too stupid or too full of himself to notice what is going on knows that what he does is morally indefensible," Janet Malcolm writes at the opening of The Journalist and the Murderer *in the kind of fierce statement that has earned her a reputation as an unswerving truth-teller. Like many of Malcolm's other nonfiction works, this book, published in 1990, takes a specific event (a murderer suing a journalist) and unpacks it so extensively that the work illuminates a larger topic—in this case, the complex psychological dynamics at the heart of the art of journalism.*

Malcolm, who has been publishing pieces that seamlessly combine essay and reportage in the New Yorker *since the late '70s, has written eight books, spanning such topics as the politics and pitfalls of the field of psychoanalysis (*Psychoanalysis: The Impossible Profession, *1981), the problem of biography seen through the lens of Sylvia Plath (*The Silent Woman, *1994), and a meditation on the life and work of Chekhov (*Reading Chekhov, *2001). Others include* In the Freud Archives *(1984) and* The Crime of Sheila McGough *(1999), as well as two collections of essays,* The Purloined Clinic *(1992) and* Diana and Nikon *(1980, expanded in 1997). What grabs and regrabs the reader in her writing is its deft commingling of sleuthing and contemplation. Reading Malcolm, one has the sensation of being in the presence of a mind constantly in action on several levels, mediating between external reality (one most often consisting of facts that are at odds with one another) and her own consciousness. With the exception of* The Purloined Clinic, *none of her books is much more than two hundred pages, but the rigor of her writing gives them the quality of murals painted by a miniaturist.*

Malcolm can be unsparing in her portrayals of the people she comes across, but her extraordinary precision does not preclude compassion. Occasionally, Malcolm's subjects damn themselves, but more often they reveal the vanities, obsessions, and desires that we all share—if to a heightened degree.

Currently at work on a book about Gertrude Stein and Alice B. Toklas, Malcolm corresponded with me by email.

—Daphne Beal (Spring 2004)

DAPHNE BEAL: It's interesting that we're doing this interview by email, because one of the phrases that's long been in my head is your description from *The Silent Woman* of letters written today on computers as being "marmoreally cool and smooth," in contrast to letters from previous decades written on manual typewriters. Correspondence plays such a large role in almost all your books, not just the content and tone, but often the texture and feel of the letters' pages. Email seems to up that smoothness even further. Do you use it a lot yourself, or are "real" letters still a preferred form?

How do you think email has affected the way people communicate by the written word?

JANET MALCOLM: When I wrote *The Silent Woman,* email had not yet arrived—or was not yet in common use. I would not use the phrase "marmoreally cool and smooth" about email. I think of email as messy, both in appearance and in the character of the writing. Email encourages a kind of laxness, a letting down of hair. When I write a "real" letter, I care about how it looks. I will compulsively redo a letter if the indentations aren't uniform or if I've smudged the signature. With email, I don't know what the message will look like on the receiver's screen. I only know it will be surrounded by all kinds of stuff—titles, "headers," numbers, codes, etc.—that I had nothing to do with. So I take no trouble over the appearance of the message. I take some trouble over the message itself, but not as much as I would in a letter.

Doing this interview by email gives me a chance to think of answers to your questions. If we did it in person, I might just look at you in blank helplessness.

DB: Reading your work, it's hard to ever imagine you with such a look! I'm always amazed by the quick turns, the dips and dives through any given moment of interaction, especially when it comes to the psychological underpinnings of things. I read somewhere that your father was a psychiatrist. Did that mean you were very aware of psychology as a philosophy/art/science from an early age? Was that a field you ever seriously considered going into?

JM: No, I never considered becoming a psychiatrist or psychoanalyst, and while growing up I paid little attention to my father's work. He himself was not all that invested in it—for many years he was head psychiatrist of an outpatient clinic of the Veterans Administration. He loved nature, literature, and sports, and he was a gifted comic writer. Unfortunately, he wrote in Czech, and Czech wit does not translate well. This is not to say that he didn't excel in his work as a psychiatrist (and as a neurologist, his second specialty). He just wasn't pompous about it—as many psychiatrists were in those days. He had affectionate regard for his patients and no use for social workers. He was wonderfully satiric about them and their clipboards. A piece of writing of mine that is connected to my father is "The One-Way Mirror," about the family therapist Salvador Minuchin. Would you like me to tell you about that?

DB: Sure, I'm a sucker for anything about families and their influence.

JM: In the late '70s I gave up smoking and, naturally, couldn't write. I decided to do what the *New Yorker* called a long fact piece, which would require many months of reporting. I figured that by the time I finished the reporting I would be ready to try writing without smoking. I remembered something my father had told me about a remarkable man who cured anorectic girls in one session—at lunch with their families, at the end of which the girls would eat, the way cripples would walk at the end of faith-healing encounters. He had seen this man perform at a hospital near his clinic, and marveled at his powerful personality. I had never heard my father speak so enthusiastically about anyone in psychiatry, and decided to make that man, Minuchin, the subject of my piece.

For many months I took the train to Philadelphia, where Minuchin had a clinic, and watched him instruct a class of young psychiatrists in his kind of theatrical family therapy. When it was time to write, I found I could write without smoking. This was the first long fact piece I had ever done, and this kind of writing turned out to be congenial to me.

DB: How many years into your writing career were you when that happened? And did that process of choosing Minuchin for your subject matter become in any way a prototype for how you've chosen other topics?

JM: When I wrote "The One-Way Mirror," I had been writing for about ten years. I had done book reviews, essays on photography, and pieces about decorative art. But I had never done reportage. The way I stumbled on Minuchin as a subject is pretty much the way I stumble on all my journalistic subjects. I hear or read about someone, or someone writes to me. My book *The Crime of Sheila McGough* came out of a letter I received from its heroine, who thought I might be interested in her story of going to prison for a crime she didn't commit. Journalists get a lot of letters like that, but this one had an unusual atmosphere (and wasn't on yellow lined paper), so I wrote back. But why am I telling you this? Because you asked. One of the things that journalists come to understand after doing journalism for a while is the power of the question.

DB: I want to come back to Sheila McGough, but at the moment I'll make a kind of left turn if that's OK. Last fall you had an exhibit of your collages at the Lori Bookstein Gallery here in New York City, a medium (as I understand it) that you've been working in more privately for some time. How did you come to work in collage, and what kind of questions does the medium ask or answer that writing does not? Or is it more related to your writing than I'm supposing?

JM: To try to answer your question, let me quote from a piece I wrote about ten years ago about the artist David Salle:

> Writers have traditionally come to painters' ateliers in search of aesthetic succor. To the writer, the painter is a fortunate alter ego, an embodiment of the sensuality and exteriority that he has abjured to pursue his invisible, odorless calling. The writer comes to the places where traces of making can actually be seen and smelled and touched expecting to be inspired and enabled, possibly even cured. While I was interviewing the artist David Salle, I was coincidentally writing a book that was giving me trouble, and although I cannot pin it down exactly (and would not want to), I know that after each

> talk with Salle in his studio something clarifying and bracing did filter down to my enterprise.

Quoting this excerpt—apart from telling you something about my attitude toward artists—enacts what I do as a collagist. I have taken something from one place (the Salle piece) and put it into another (this interview). It also exemplifies what I do when I write. I do an enormous amount of quoting—of people and texts—in my books and articles. David Salle is a painter who does nothing but "quote" or "appropriate" in his paintings. But that is another subject. I guess what I have been trying to say is that, yes, collage is "more related to [my] writing than [you're] supposing."

DB: I remember reading about you showing your collages to Salle, but it seems like another thing altogether to show your work in a gallery. How, if at all, has exhibiting your work changed your relationship to it? For one thing, is it as fun?

JM: When I first started exhibiting I was ambivalent about the idea of people buying my collages. When you publish a book, the text remains in your possession, so to speak. When you sell a painting or drawing or collage, you lose it. It goes out of your life. At first, I wasn't ready to let go of my work. Now I am. I am happy when someone buys a collage. There are a lot of them now. I feel I can keep making them. But even as I say this, I feel a little stab of regret about the collages that are hanging on the walls of strangers, and that it is unlikely I will ever see again.

As for whether the work is as enjoyable as it was before I began to exhibit, the answer is no. I work harder. My standard of craftsmanship is higher and so is my idea of what is good enough to show.

DB: It does seem that while your writing and collage share certain qualities, the truth that collage is after is much more open-ended than writing's. I'm thinking in particular of your eloquent (that is, jaw-dropping) opening of *The Journalist and the Murderer,* about the inevitable betrayal by the journalist of the subject in the name of a higher truth.

The theme of betrayal is echoed in much of your writing—the biographer of the subject, the protégé of the mentor, the photographer of the subject (Diane Arbus especially comes to mind), Gertrude Stein of the Jews around her, etc. I wonder if you would comment on this recurring motif?

JM: I did not set out to write about betrayal, but by writing about journalism, biography, and photography, I kept bumping into it. In each of these genres the practitioner has an enormous amount of power over the subject. Apart from the practitioner's use or misuse of this power, the genres themselves have a built-in tendency to be unkind. It isn't only Diane Arbus who betrays the subjects of her photographs. Most people who have their picture taken hate the result. And most people who are the subjects of newspaper or magazine stories feel at least a little wronged if not outright betrayed. As for the illustrious dead…

DB: Being so thoroughly engaged in one of those inherently unkind professions, how do you reconcile the "not-niceness" (to borrow your description of the *Ariel* poems) of the finished piece with the process of asking your subject for his or her trust? Does that person occupy a different place in your thinking by the time you've finished writing than he or she did when you were in the thick of interviewing?

JM: In answer to your first question: You do not reconcile it. That is the moral problem of journalism. But journalists don't ask for the subject's trust—they don't have to. Subjects just give it. They are eager to tell their story and don't seem to realize that they are not invisible as they tell it. Incidentally, the final product of the inherently unkind professions isn't always not-nice. There are photographs in which the subject looks beautiful, and there are biographies and journalistic portraits from which the subject emerges as a great soul. I recently had the pleasure and privilege of writing about Anton Chekhov, about whom it is simply impossible to find anything seriously bad to say. Some of his biographers have tried—and failed.

I'm not sure I understand your second question. Could you put it more simply? (I'm reading Gertrude Stein's *The Making of Americans,* which may explain my difficulty in understanding a sentence that isn't simple and hasn't been repeated a hundred times.)

DB: I think what I'm really asking for is advice. In my own experience I find it incredibly difficult when writing about someone to transition from that human connection that happens in the most fruitful of interviews to the more critical stance I need to take afterward. Because Chekhov seems to be part of a very small minority of people, dead or alive, of whom one can say nothing bad, and because people's contradictions are among their most interesting qualities, the writer has to be able to step back from that intimate place of interviewing (or research)—where practically anyone's reality can seem like the truth for at least a moment—to a more objective point of view. This often feels like an almost painful betrayal to me.

What I wanted to find out (in my thickly veiled previous question) was how do you make the switch from supplicant or equal interviewer to authority writer?

Is this clearer? If not, we can just abandon this line of thinking. I also realize that *The Journalist and the Murderer* addresses this question in book-length form.

JM: I'm glad I asked. What you write is very eloquent. Yes, I wrote about this dilemma in *The Journalist and the Murderer,* but I did not exhaust the subject by any means. You bring something new into the discussion with your comment about the journalist's momentary identification with the subject. Since you are a novelist, you probably have more capacity for this kind of imaginative leap. I am incapable of writing fiction, so I am probably less empathic. But this doesn't seem to make any difference to the subject. He or she assumes your empathy—and then feels betrayed when what you write isn't like something he or she dictated to you.

I put it another way in *The Journalist and the Murderer* (if you'll forgive me for quoting from myself again): "The journalistic encounter seems to have the same regressive effect on a subject as the psychoanalytic encounter. The subject becomes a kind of child of the writer, regarding him as a permissive, all-accepting, all-forgiving mother, and expecting that the book will be written by her. Of course, the book is written by the strict, all-noticing, unforgiving father."

But getting back to your anxiety about the discontinuity between the coziness of the interview and the coldness of the act of writing—yes, it is a problem, and no, it can't be resolved. When you make the switch from "supplicant or equal interviewer to authority writer" you are, like every other journalist, committing some sort of moral misdemeanor.

DB: So maybe the adjustment I need to make is simply downgrading my transgression from felony to misdemeanor. I was thinking, too, about your reputation as a writer for being quite exacting toward, or even tough on, your subjects. The same rigor that thrills some of your readers seems to make others extremely uncomfortable. I wonder if you've ever felt that the reception to your work has been colored by the fact that you're a woman. Are women still meant to be "nicer" as writers, less difficult?

I ask because I think of my own interviewing style, at least in person, as incorporating some stereotypical feminine behavior: slightly low-status and deferential, punctuated by ready laughter, and driven by an accommodating attitude. Later, when I'm writing, I feel I've acted as something of a wolf in sheep's clothing.

I remember your description of your "more Japanese technique" in *The Journalist and the Murderer,* in contrast to the more flat-footed *Newsday* reporter's. I have a sense, of course, but wondered specifically what you meant by that?

JM: I really don't know whether the people who don't like my writing don't like it because of their perception of me as a tough, not-nice woman. It seems kind of ridiculous—I think of myself as a completely ordinary, harmless person—but what people think of your writing persona is out of your hands. The narrator of my nonfiction pieces is not the same person I am—she is a lot more articulate and thinks of much cleverer things to say than I usually do. I can imagine her coming across as a little insufferable sometimes. But she, too, is out of my hands—I may have invented her, but she is the person who insists on speaking for me.

As for the wolf in sheep's clothing question, perhaps the way to minimize one's feeling that one has not been as straightforward with the subject as one should have been is to be a little more straightforward. To swallow the too-nice thing one is about to say. To remember that the subject is going to say what he or she wants to say no matter what you say or don't say. You can't keep your mouth shut all the time, of course, but you do well to keep it shut a lot of the time. If silence falls, let the subject break it—even though that's a very hard thing to do. By the way, I don't think the "feminine behavior" you describe is limited to women journalists. Men journalists can be just as ingratiating, deferential, accommodating, and laughter-prone.

When you ask what I mean by the Japanese technique, you are not employing it.

DB: Your answer really made me chuckle. I can't say exactly why, except I think it has to do with the endless conundrum of writing—the fact that it *seems* so much in one's control (especially in contrast to, say, theater or visual art), and yet still there is that mystery of: who is this character who insists on speaking for me? The undeniable fact that in the end the work and its effect are out of one's hands.

Maybe then this is a good time to turn to the simultaneously charming and irascible Stein—speaking of being difficult. (I remember during my Midwestern childhood in the '70s confusing Gertrude Stein and Gloria Steinem, because, well, they were both considered impossible by local standards, but that's another story…)

How did you come to write about her and Toklas? Is that *New Yorker* piece being turned into a book, and have you finished it?

JM: You made me chuckle too with your wonderful mixing up of Gertrude and Gloria. Yes, I am continuing to write about Stein. No, I have not finished. It is an exceptionally beautiful day today, and I am reminded of what Stein wrote (or said she wrote) on an exam paper in a course at Radcliffe given by William James: "Dear Professor James, I am so sorry but really I do not feel a bit like a philosophy paper today." James (according to Stein) sent her a postcard saying: "Dear Miss Stein, I understand perfectly how you feel. I often feel like that myself," and gave her the highest grade in the class. There is reason to think that this didn't happen the way Stein said it did. But anyway, may I be excused from the examination today?

DB: Dear Miss Malcolm, I understand perfectly how you feel. I often feel like that myself. [And a week later…] Your response to the GS question left me unsure of whether you'd rather not talk about her at all right now, but my Malcolm-fan friends have been pressing me to ask why her, why now? I wondered if Stein's larger-than-life personality and work drew you initially to write about her, or if it was the question of her being Jewish and staying in France that began your investigation?

In contrast to Chekhov, she seems to be a more problematic literary figure and her writing arguably less universally loved than his. It made me wonder if the topic of your last book pushed you in a different direction for the next. Or, conversely, I was thinking about the continuity—if there is more pleasure in writing about the "illustrious dead" than living subjects at the moment?

JM: I told you earlier how I stumble on subjects for pieces. I stumbled on the Gertrude Stein–in–wartime piece when the *New Yorker* asked me to contribute to an issue on food. I decided to write about the Alice B. Toklas cookbook. While re-reading Toklas's chapter on what she cooked during the German occupation of France, I became curious about Stein and Toklas's wartime history. The longer piece followed my short piece about trying to cook a weird dish involving artichoke hearts and asparagus and calf brains. (The asparagus spears were somehow supposed to stand erect in a mush of calf brains and béchamel sauce.)

I'm planning to write more about Stein and Toklas, but I can't really say why right now. I may know when I've written the piece. As for whether it's more agreeable to write about the illustrious dead than about the living, I'd say it all depends on which dead and which living.

DB: I laughed again, mostly because I was afraid of what would happen if I thought too much about the idea of "a mush of calf brains."

Re: dead v. living subjects, how did the prolonged Masson suit affect your choice of subjects after that, if at all? I don't mean to belabor this question of choosing subject matter, but again I've been reflecting on how one knows what will make a good topic over a lengthy period of time—satisfying both the need for a certain meatiness and challenge, and for a pleasure in the task.

JM: Until this moment you were the first interviewer who did not bring Jeffrey Masson into the discussion. I guess that isn't possible after all. What you seem to be asking is whether being sued by him has made me leery of writing about people who are alive rather than safely dead. The answer is no. One of the reasons I refused to settle the Masson lawsuit (as the people he previously sued, Muriel Gardiner and Kurt Eissler, had done) was to leave no doubt in the minds of readers and future subjects that Masson's accusations of misquotation were untrue. As it turned out, a year after he lost his lawsuit at trial, my two-year-old granddaughter pulled a red notebook out of a bookcase, in which the things Masson said he didn't say were scribbled in my hand. The notes had been lost for ten years. The jury had decided to believe me anyway. But if the notebook hadn't got misplaced, there would have been no lawsuit.

Your reflections on your desire to find a subject that is meaty and challenging *and* pleasurable to write about interest me very much. They remind me of one experience I had of not taking pleasure in a subject. That was the subject—business crime—of my book *The Crime of Sheila McGough*. To master the intricacies of the con of a certain con man was very difficult for me. I may not have solved the problem of how not to bore the reader with what gave me enormous trouble to understand. The book was not popular. But I have a special fondness for it, though I may be wrong about its merits.

DB: Sorry to be so tiresome as to bring up Masson, just like the rest. I think it's impossible not to because it does sound like it was such an ordeal, and when I think about events or circumstances in my own life that affect my writing, it's hard not to be curious.

My final question is a two-parter.

First of all, I was intrigued by what you wrote about the Sheila McGough book, about your special fondness for it, and I wondered if you would say a bit more. It sounds like it gave you some trouble in the writing. Is that difficulty where the fondness springs from? (Sometimes I think I may have assigned too much value to pleasurability in the writing process…)

The second part is one of my reprise questions, and it has to do with email (just to complete the circle). In the course of our interview, I've often thought about your description of email as a letting down of one's hair and inherently messy, and tried to figure out if I agree. Messy, yes, but is it truly a letting down of one's hair, especially when the person on the other end isn't particularly known? I've often felt that email has a kind of conscious messiness (as in, "Well, this isn't perfectly articulated, but hopefully she'll know what I mean…"), whereas talk seems like the messiest form of communication of all, the way things slip out.

In short, my question is this: at the end of this interview, has your opinion of email changed any since your original answer, and is this the first interview you've done by email?

JM: To answer the first part of your question, about why I am specially fond of *The Crime of Sheila McGough*: I like its oddness. I think it may be the most original of my books. I like the second part where I travel to the South to interview various strange persons, and the coda where I go to Treasure Mountain, where Bob Bailes, the con man, was going to build a fantastic resort, and where I find a peaceful late summer landscape. I like the book's own late summer melancholy. And, of course, I like Sheila McGough, a most unusual and sad person. Finally, I was glad to use some of what being a defendant myself taught me about the law and lawyers. Without that knowledge, I would not have been able to write (or even been interested in writing) the book.

About email. Yes, this is my first email interview, and yes, talk is the messiest medium of all. Any transcript of a tape recording confirms that. Email lies somewhere between speech and proper writing. But I don't consider our interview a true example of email. Knowing that what I write will be published, I naturally take some trouble over it, and I assume you have done the same. No, so my opinion of email hasn't changed, because I haven't really availed myself here of its permission to write sloppily.

[*After reading the interview, Malcolm sent the following email.*]

JM: I read the interview in the way one looks at photographs of oneself, and, except for one place, I thought I came out looking OK. But the exception may be the most interesting part of the interview. I'm talking about the place where you ask me about the Masson lawsuit. Until that moment the atmosphere of the interview is friendly and collegial and almost conspiratorial. Now it turns icy. I make an unpleasant observation and then launch into an absurd defense of myself. In defense of my defensiveness, I can only say that for a long time I wrongly assumed everyone would know that the accusations against me weren't true. Now, having finally learned that accusations must be answered at once, I ridiculously answer accusations that, years later, no one is making.

But what is most interesting about this moment in our interview is the illustration it offers of a subject's feeling of betrayal when he or she realizes that the journalist is writing his or her own story. In my version of the story of my writing life, I wouldn't give Masson any role whatever. But your version—and any other good journalist's—would naturally give him a role. The lawsuit happened and my wish to deny its significance cannot cut any ice with you. My getting all huffy about your natural and not at all badly intentioned question just goes to show that even journalists are not immune to the vanity and self-deception that interviews bring out in their subjects and that journalists, like novelists, lie in wait for. ✯

ZADIE SMITH

TALKS WITH

IAN McEWAN

"I HAVE NOW REACHED THE STAGE WHERE AS SOON AS ANYONE SAYS LIFE MOVES AROUND A SINGLE ORGANIZING PRINCIPLE I STOP LISTENING TO THEM. I DON'T FEEL THAT LIFE ORGANIZES ITSELF AROUND ANY SINGLE PRINCIPLE. IT'S A RELIGIOUS IMPULSE TO ONLY GRASP AT ONE THING, ONE EXPLANATION."

Aspects of the "English novel" to avoid:
Polite, character-revealing dialogue
Stable, linear narrative
Lightly ironic ethical investigation
Excessive amounts of furniture

I have often thought Ian McEwan a writer as unlike me as it is possible to be. His prose is controlled, careful, and powerfully concise; he is eloquent on the subjects of sex and sexuality; he has a strong head for the narrative possibilities of science; his novels are no longer than is necessary; he would never write a sentence featuring this many semicolons. When I read him I am struck by metaphors I would never think to use, plots that don't occur to me, ideas I have never had. I love to read him for these reasons and also because, like his millions of readers, I feel myself to be in safe hands. Picking up a book by McEwan is to know, at the very least, that what you read therein will be beautifully written, well-crafted, and not an embarrassment, either for you or for him. This is a really big deal. Bad books happen less frequently to McEwan than they do to the rest of us. Since leaving the tutelage of Malcolm Bradbury and Angus Wilson on the now famous (because of McEwan) University of East Anglia creative writing course, McEwan has had one of the most consistently celebrated careers in English literature. We haven't got space for it all here, but among the prizes is the Somerset Maugham Award in 1976 for his first collection of short stories, First Love, Last Rites*; the Whitbread Novel Award (1987) and Prix Fémina Etranger (1993) for* The Child in Time*; he has been shortlisted for the Booker Prize three times, winning the award for* Amsterdam *in 1998. His novel* Atonement *received the WHSmith Literary Award (2002), the National Book Critics Circle Fiction Award (2002), the Los Angeles Times Book Prize for Fiction (2003), and the Santiago Prize for the European Novel (2004). He's written a lot of good books.*

Because of the posh university I attended, I first met McEwan many years ago, before I was published myself. I was nineteen, down from Cambridge for the holidays, and a girl I knew from college was going to Ian McEwan's wedding party. This was a fairly normal occurrence for her, coming from the family she did, but I had never clapped eyes on a writer in my life. She invited me along, knowing what it would mean to me. That was an unforgettable evening. I was so delighted to be there and yet so rigid with fear I could barely enjoy it. It was a party full of people from my bookshelves come to life. I can recall being introduced to Martin Amis (whom I was busy plagiarizing at the time) and being shown his new baby. Meeting Martin Amis for me, at nineteen, was like meeting God. I said: "Nice baby." This line, like all conversation, could not be rewritten. I remember feeling, like Joseph K., that the shame of it would outlive me.

I didn't get to speak with McEwan that night—I spent most of the party hiding from him. I assumed he was a little annoyed to find a random undergraduate he did not know at his own wedding party. But I had just read Black Dogs *(1992)—that brilliant, flinty little novel bursting with big ideas—and I was fascinated by the idea of an English novelist writing such serious, metaphysical, almost European prose as this. He was not like Amis and he was not like Rushdie or Barnes or Ishiguro or Kureishi or any of the other English and quasi-English men I was reading at the time. He was the odd man out. "Apparently," said my friend knowledgeably, as we watched McEwan swing his new wife around the dance floor, "he only writes fifteen words a day." This was an unfortunate piece of information to give an aspiring writer. I was terribly susceptible to the power of example. If I heard Borges ran three miles every morning and did a headstand in a bucket of water before sitting down to write, I felt I must try this myself. The specter of the fifteen-word limit stayed with me a long time. Three years later I remember writing* White Teeth *and thinking that all my problems stemmed from the excess of words I felt compelled to write each day. Fifteen words a day! Why can't* you *write just fifteen words a day?*

Ten years later, less gullible and a writer myself, it occurs to me that my friend may have fictionalized the situation a little herself. An interview with McEwan himself, like the one you are about to read, was of course the perfect opportunity to settle the matter, but it's only now, writing the introduction after the fact, that I remember the question. I do not know if Ian McEwan writes fifteen words a day. However, he was forthcoming on many other interesting matters. McEwan is one of those rare novelists who can speak with honest perspicacity about the experience of being a writer; it is a life he openly loves, and talking to him about it felt, to me, like talking with an author at the beginning of their career, not at its pinnacle. The fifteen-word thing may indeed be a red herring, but my friend had intuited a truth about McEwan: He is not a dilettante or even a natural, neither a fabulist nor a show-off. He is rather an artisan, always hard at work; refining, improving, engaged by and interested in every step in the process, like a scientist setting up a lab experiment.

We did this interview in McEwan's house, which is Dr. Henry Perowne's house in the novel Saturday *(2005). It is a lovely Georgian townhouse that sits in the shadow of London's BT Tower. From the balcony of this house Perowne sees a plane on a crash trajectory, its tail on fire. It is a perfect McEwanesque incident.* —*Zadie Smith (Spring 2005)*

I. "IT HAD BEEN A MALEVOLENT INTERVENTION..."

ZADIE SMITH: I'm not good at this. I interviewed Eminem a while ago and when I got home and transcribed it it was more like "An interview with Zadie Smith in which Eminem occasionally says yes and uh-huh." I talk too much. I'm going to get straight to my first question, which I guess is also the biggest one. I thought we could start there and maybe get small afterward. Because I read all the books so close together—

IAN McEWAN: What order did you read them in?

ZS: Basically chronological.

IM: OK.

ZS: Except *In Between the Sheets,* which I read only a few days ago. Anyway: there is a line in *The Child in Time* when you discuss the traumatic event in that novel, the abduction of a child: "it had been a malevolent intervention." And much of your past fiction has dealt with that idea, of a malevolent intervention. Then when you read this latest book, *Saturday,* which deals obliquely with 9/11, it becomes clear that something about the nature of what happened on that day was already a McEwanesque incident. Because the burst of the irrational into the rational was your modus operandi anyway. And so (this is a strange thing to say to the writer himself) when you see a writer moving into his strongest period, and staying there, or at least not losing his previous strength, then I always figure that either the age has come to meet him or he's come to meet the age. I think it's the previous case with you, and I remember thinking even before I read *Saturday* that if there were to be a 9/11 novel which was integrated and serious and soon—because it is quite soon—it was more likely to be written by you than anybody else. Because your fiction was already *about* the idea of a malevolent intervention. And I wondered whether you knew that consciously or whether you agree with that.

IM: The first thing I remember thinking was that it [9/11] was a heroic moment for journalism. That was my first sense. Perhaps it's because Annalena [Annalena McAfee, McEwan's wife] works in a newspaper I take an interest in the sort of *thingyness* of newspapers, but it happened two o'clock our time, London time. So front pages had to be clear and basically twenty-five pages set out, produced, and this much-hated profession had its sudden noble moment.

ZS: But it was a moment. You talked about that in the two articles you wrote about September 11 for the *Guardian*. The moment turns quickly and depressingly.

IM: But it was a moment that seemed first to demand accurate journalism before anything else. That was my first feeling. And the best things written about it have been journalism, not fiction. I read a lot of what came out and was impressed by it. Actually I think another instance of this on a much smaller scale was the Dunblane massacre. Hit the wires at about three-thirty in the afternoon. By the time of the London evening papers there were ten, fifteen pages. So my first instinct, my first reaction was that journalists rose to the bar that day, and when I wrote I just wanted to write in that public way, expressing my immediate reaction, the same honorable tide that everyone else was on. Not to write fiction. But even as I was doing that I was thinking the human way into it would take more than journalism, would be more intimate than that. The thought of so many of these people announcing their love down mobile phones…

ZS: There was a small paragraph—I think it was in the second article you wrote about it—where you say that if the terrorists had been able to empathize properly with these others, with the very *idea* of otherness, then they couldn't have done what they did. Now, that's something I do believe, and it's a belief I sort of "push" in my fiction—that real empathy makes cruelty an impossibility. But I always assumed when I read your fiction that that wasn't at all what you believed. Especially in the earlier work, the opposite, much darker truth seems to be being articulated: mainly, that even after empathy people still can and do perform the most terrible acts.

IM: I've always thought cruelty is a failure of imagination. And I know that I include within that the possibility that some people do empathize with their victims very much, in fact, that's the reason they harm them—they get some erotic charge out of harming what they love. But that's a special case. That's still about pleasuring the self and not heeding to the true terror of the child that's being tortured or whatever it might be.

At least since the early '80s, it's began to fill out for me as an idea in fiction that there's something very entwined about imagination and morals. That one of the great values of fiction was exactly this process of being able to enter other people's minds. Which is why I think cinema is a very inferior, unsophisticated medium.

ZS: Absolutely. Because you get surfaces only.

IM: Right. And with the novel we have happened to devise this form, this very elastic, mutable form that can allow us moments of real human investigation. Milan Kundera says very wise things in this context. He lays a lot of stress on the novel as a mode of investigation. It's an open-ended way of looking at our own image, in ways that science can't do, religion's not credible, metaphysics is too intellectually repellent on its surface—this is our best machine, as it were.

ZS: You use that machine quite differently from your peers. Yours are different English novels than the English novel as I was brought up to think about it.

After I read your back catalog I Googled you and I found this website for kids—because a lot of kids are studying you at the moment, you're on the A-level list. It was a message board of kids freaking out because they didn't know how to read you. It was very interesting. I think the barrier they kept coming across is that they come with their ideas of an English novel, the classic English novel, where character is revealed through dialogue for a greater part of the book, where action is laid out along a basically stable idea of linear time, where the tone is lightly ironic and your job as a reader is to perform a kind of ethical investigation. They particularly rely on a pretty muscular narrator to nudge them in the direction of correct judgement. So Austen never leaves us in any doubt that Mrs. Bennett is not a person to be respected, for example. But your books screw with time, they use very little dialogue, and the narration is ethically ambivalent. It's all a bit metaphysical when you're sixteen and you've got an essay crisis on. They were freaking out.

IM: Why are they freaking out? I don't understand. Because they're being told too much?

ZS: Well, let's take one of those aspects. Time in McEwan. Most of your contemporaries dealt with time in a pretty traditional fashion. If Rushdie was interested in it, if Amis was interested in it, if Barnes was, it was usually historical time. And partly politicized historical time in the case of Rushdie and when Amis spins time backward. Flashbacks and historical jumps are used to cast the present in a new, challenging light. But the idea of what does it really feel like to *be* in time, to exist in it—this is not something that English A-Level students have to face up to very often.

IM: Well, I don't have any conscious design on time, I don't think—except when I was thinking about it as a specific element of the novel, as with *The Child in Time.* But apart from that, if there's anything going on about time in my novels it's really a spin-off of some other concern. Something to do with the fine print of consciousness itself. I mean, I'm interested in how to represent, obviously in a very stylized way, what it's like to be thinking. Or what it's like to be conscious, or sentient, or, fatally, only half-sentient. And how difficult it is to see everything that's going on and understand everything at one time and how much our recollections can play into what we accept as reality—how much perception is distorted by will. That's something I find very interesting. The ways in which we convince ourselves, persuade ourselves of things, either to settle some notion of our own or an intellectual position. That's why I've liked the evolution of psychology, they talk a lot about self-persuasion… In my fiction I've tried to indicate my sense of how interestingly flawed we are in the ways in which we represent ourselves and "what we know" to each other. So if time gets fractured or refracted along the way, that's an offshoot. I don't do that consciously.

ZS: Maybe it's "the malevolent intervention" that messes with time. Like the car crash in *The Child in Time,* where a four-second moment seems to last forever. I thought when I read *Saturday* that your audience, through 9/11, now has a mass experience to mirror exactly that strange sensation, when time elongates. The towers fell in slow motion. Time was warped by this insane event, and we all felt that communally. Prior to that my only experience of time trauma was when I was fifteen and fell out of my bedroom window—timewise, that was a deeply surreal experience. I knew that privately but to share it with anybody was a bit—

IM: You fell out of your bedroom window?

ZS: Yeah.

IM: Sleepwalking?

ZS: No, no, no, trying to smoke a fag.

IM: Oh my God.

ZS: Yeah, comedy story. I almost died, but the point is, that fall and the slowness of it, literally the *days* of it—I couldn't find a way to talk about it without sounding a little loopy. But several times in your fiction that feeling is expressed, very accurately, I think.

IM: Yeah, but isn't it also something to do with demands of narrative—so let's say we're looking at a fifteen-year-old, balancing a buttock on a window ledge, doesn't want to breathe smoke back into the bedroom—

ZS: Yeah, that was it.

IM: Suddenly you're dividing the moment with much more intensity. Even in describing it you're slowing the movement. Because you think this is high-value, rich experience, therefore only two seconds are 1,200 words. And you've done it for the reader, already, without having any notion of time, you would have conveyed this slowing instinctively. And probably, one mistake I regret in *The Child in Time* was the way I harangue the reader, telling everybody that "TIME IS SLOW." You don't need to say that. The prose slows it down.

ZS: But I think in the car incident the two are quite well meshed, the description and the feeling, it's a pretty amazing passage.

IM: Yeah, all I need to do is cut away from the bits where it says "time slowed."

ZS: Now, what about repudiating previous work? I've been trying not to read the reviews of *Saturday* because I want to have my own feelings about it, but I presume a few people picked up on *The Child in Time* reference and also the magic-realism references in the book. You satirize that kind of writing, and also the magic realism in your earlier work. And actually, reading your back catalog, I realized there's quite a lot of it. More than I remembered.

IM: Yeah. I wouldn't do it now, I must say. And although I never really trusted any magic-realist literature, very far, I was at least able to—you know how it is, you give characters views you can't or wouldn't condone.

ZS: Yes, exactly. It's fun to do that. It makes you brave.

IM: Yes. But I suppose I do have a sneaking sympathy with the view that the real, the actual, is so demanding and rich, that magical realism is really a tedious evasion of some artistic responsibility.

ZS: Because the magic is *in* the real. I was trying to pick out some of my very favorite lines in *The Child in Time*—and there's the one about the neck. Do you remember this?

IM: No. Neck?

ZS: Yeah, it's a lady's neck: Emma Carew.

IM: Oh, right. "The fan of tendons round the neck of Emma Carew, a cheerful, anorexic headmistress, tightened like umbrella struts when her name was remembered and spoken aloud."

ZS: Exactly. Now, for me, that brings wonder already, there is no need for the rest. But was there a switch in your mind, a point where you decided to stop writing stories about women in relationships with monkeys, for example?

IM: Well, as I say, I never had much time for it.

ZS: The short stories have quite a bit of it, though.

IM: There's some.

ZS: There's a lot of different approaches: there's hyperrealism, there's allegory, there's the supernatural, the grotesque—there's a whole raft of techniques used to introduce the incredible.

IM: Yes, but those were short stories and I think they're great to try, to "put on," like trying on your parents' clothes. When people ask, "Is there any advice you'd give a young writer?" I say write short stories. They afford lots of failure. Pastiche is a great way to start. But I was never really a great one for that kind of extreme Angela Carter magic-realist stuff… although actually I got to know her and admire her and was kind of a neighbor in Clapham.

ZS: Oh, really?

IM: I liked her really on the basis of those stories she wrote in Japan. But then the further she got into fairy tales and then into *Nights at the Circus*—that wasn't for me.

It seemed to me such a narrowing down of all the possibilities. The real, the actual, they place heavy demands on a writer—how to invent it, how to confront it or pass it through the sieve of your own consciousness. So I was never a great Márquez person, I admired the *Tin Drum* but never really admired it the way I did Kundera, say. And it seems to me now that that style has become a bit like the international style in furniture, this sort of lingua franca that really defies the central notion of the novel, which is that the novel is local. It's regional, it's a bottom-up process, and somehow these international styles seem to have a top-down process. They are too similar to each other.

ZS: They have trademarks. One of their trademarks is a kind of kinetic energy. Energy at the expense of everything else.

IM: Yeah. It's tennis without the net. There's no fun.

ZS: Nothing at stake.

IM: Yes. But then I thought if I'm taking a sideswipe here at that kind of fiction [in *Saturday*], I'd better include myself!

II. "SOMEONE ONCE ASKED ME, 'IF YOUR LIFE COULD BE EXTENDED TO 150 AND YOU COULD START ANOTHER CAREER, WOULD YOU?' AND I SAID, 'NO, THANKS, I THINK I'LL STICK AT THIS.'"

ZS: I still feel this technical difference between you and the generation you came up with, not just in quality but in kind. I found a quote of yours: "What drove me was an impatience with the English fiction I read. It seemed like a polite talking shop of which I was no part," and I wanted to think about that in reference to dialogue, because I do think your dialogue is different and serves different purposes than, say, Amis's. There's a lot less of it, for starters.

IM: Well, Martin would have his roots more in Dickens, in a love of the absurd and caricature.

ZS: And dialect plays a more serious role with Amis, as it does for me. Less so with you.

IM: Yeah.

ZS: Only, recently there's more dialect in yours than there was before.

IM: Yeah. Martin used to sit around with his dad and take a lot of pleasure in looking, with some kind of hilarious scorn, at the way people spoke and how these phrases passed into the language, and he would come back with a fresh nugget and say, "Yeah, Kingsley and I were talking about the way people say"—whatever it was—and he'd be able to impersonate it exactly.

ZS: He still does that?

IM: Yeah. Wonderfully accurate, but there is some distancing going on there, too.

ZS: Well, there will always be a little difference in someone like Martin's comfort in the language, his kind of flippant freedom with it, and your own, possibly more hesitant, approach. You spoke a little bit about that in "Mother Tongue," and linked it with class.

IM: There is all that. My mother's hesitancy in language was a crucial element of my English class position. But like anything to do with English class, my exact position was complicated. My parents were working class but when I was fourteen my father was commissioned as an officer... He was one of the British army officers who've come up through the ranks; they're not Sandhurst, they don't have university degrees and they're not posh, and all his friends were similar people. And I know looking back that all the other officers sort of looked down on them. They respected them, too, because they knew an awful lot about the army. And when my father became an officer, we were immediately posted somewhere else, so we went from being part of the sergeants' mess world to the officers' mess world. And that was a kind of rootlessness right there, which was partly about language, the way we spoke and the way we did things.

ZS: It's like you had a kind of impersonality thrust upon you—and of course there's a lot of English criticism about that idea. That the less rigidly placed you are in this society the more conceptual space you have to write.

IM: It's the business of class but also, for me, a question of rootlessness in terms of location. I spent my first three years of life in Aldershot in a garrison town and then it was the Far East and then it was North Africa, so I know, even when people say, "Where do you come from?" well, I can say Aldershot, but I know that I'm not rooted in any particular place. And then I went to a strange boarding school, a state boarding school where the kids were largely working-class kids from central London from broken homes, they'd take a few kids from lower-middle-class parents like myself, an officer but not grand, not Sandhurst. The idea was to take those kids from central London, working-class kids, give them the kind of education they would have got at a public school and send them to university. And that's what they did. It was an old-fashioned, ameliorative view which is now long out of fashion. So that was another kind of rootlessness: I was with all these boys, there were three hundred of us in what was once a stately home on the Essex-Suffolk border, beautiful countryside. It was hilarious, a wonderful school in many ways. Everyone stayed in the sixth form, they sent a third of the sixth form to Oxbridge—

ZS: That's pretty impressive.

IM: Yeah, everyone went to university. And then I went to sort of a bright, plateglass-type university in Sussex and then another one in East Anglia.

ZS: Were you conscious of wanting to be a writer or of taking it seriously from that early stage? Your first stories are so unerringly confident.

IM: I think I was making a strength out of a kind of ignorance. I had no roots in anything and it was almost as if I had to invent a literature.

ZS: One of the other striking things about your stories is the absence of—I don't know what to call it—let's say a "judging consciousness." The narrator who guides your judgment as you read—that idea is completely evaporated. The reader is absolutely out on a limb. There's no help given, and English readers, like those kids on the internet, are used to at least being pointed in the direction of what they should disapprove of. And that's not there.

IM: I wanted to write without supports. I was very impressed by a quote from Flaubert:

> What seems beautiful to me, what I should like to write, is a book about nothing, a book dependent on nothing external, which would be held together by the strength of its style, just as the earth, suspended in the void, depends on nothing external for its support.

ZS: Christ. You need ambition for that.

IM: But I was writing tiny little stories, certainly not novels. Those kind of remarks impressed me, I liked them, and there still is an element of that remaining. At the beginning of *Saturday* it's there in the idea of the character getting naked out of bed and standing unencumbered in the dark. It's as if he's just being born.

ZS: It does have that form, of the whole day being made with nothing taken for granted, no quick flashes into the past, every single block of it is built, as if by hand. You go through the day with Henry.

That's an enormous amount of work, I would think, to write.

IM: Yeah. But to go back to this business of roots and stories and what I didn't like in fiction—

ZS: Right, because I thought you meant Iris Murdoch at first and that kind of conversational fiction, "chattering classes" or Hampstead fiction, or whatever.

IM: There are many of them still alive, like Margaret Drabble, and I actually was inclined to change my view later, because there's good stuff there… but at the time, in describing a world about which I knew nothing and had no interest, I was impatient. I thought writers ought to be hippies. I did have a rather romantic sense of what it should be. I got a bit hot under the collar about all the politeness and the overstuffed quality.

ZS: Furniture everywhere.

IM: Furniture. All of it described, you know, the names of everything. But it was exactly this: too much already taken for granted. It was a world and the reader was meant to have already filled in a lot of the colors, assuming a bond between writer and reader—a class bond, often—and I didn't share it. Whereas with people like Roth there seemed to be an energy about the prose. It had this wonderful self-invented, handmade, watermark quality, and that's why I liked both Roth and Updike. They've loomed over my writing life, even though nothing in my stories reveals that.

ZS: That intrigued me, too, these influences of yours that can't quite be detected, or at least not directly.

IM: But it's about reading something while you're working and your heart is just longing for your project, and the joy of reading this book by somebody else is actually what makes you turn up at the desk the next day in the broader sense, you see. If I can just generate the same feeling in the reader that this writer generated in me then I'll have succeeded. And that is probably the biggest influence.

ZS: What about some of the things that have been said about your progression as a writer? Usually the story is from good to bad to worse, but you've moved forward and consistently got stronger and stronger and I've heard a lot of quite lame dinner party suggestions as to why that might be so. But I wondered how you felt about it yourself. My feeling is that being slightly outside a privileged literary class tends to make you more artisan-minded, the way Keats was, the idea of working and working and working until it's right.

IM: I had a long apprenticeship. I started writing in about 1970. It was 1978 before I published a novel and even that was just sort of an extended short story. As was my second one.

ZS: But you have always been a writer—I mean, you're working life has been a writing one. And this is a subject which honestly concerns me, not a little, because it's my life and it's likely to be my life for a really long time. And I'm terrified by the stultifying effects of being a writer and staying a writer. But you don't seem to feel it, or not as strongly as I do.

IM: No, not at all. Someone once asked me, "If your life could be extended to 150 and you could start another career, would you?" And I said, "No, thanks, I think I'll stick at this." And the reason I gave, I quoted Henry James on fiction. He said that the concern of the novelist, the subject material, is all of it, all of experience. And you don't run out of experience by being a writer.

ZS: That's true. Sometimes it feels endless. But to me I have other days where I feel like it's a corrupt, intellectually finite, and stupid way to live, with nothing real in it—I can feel myself cannibalizing my own life and I think, How long can this go on for? There is a lot in *Saturday* of the details of your own existence.

IM: It is the first time I've really cannibalized my life.

ZS: It is the first time. And I wondered what happens next.

IM: Next, I will almost certainly have an entirely invented set of circumstances.

ZS: There's always a difference, though. Certainly I find the more I carry on at this lark the less I have time for imagined, physical detail. I just don't do it. If I need a sofa, I look across the room and there's a sofa. If I need a lamppost, there's a lamppost in the street. I can't conjure lampposts out of nothing. Maybe when I was fourteen. That's completely beyond me now.

IM: No, quite. And also how much furniture does one need anymore? In answer to your question, having cannibalized my life for this novel, it makes the next one easier. I'm left with everything that's not *this* [*points around the room*], and that's a hell of a lot. I have no idea what it will be. There's also all the past, which I've never really borrowed—my childhood. But I don't know. Naturally when people say, "You've got better," I get a bit pissed off and say, "Well, what was wrong with the others? What was I doing wrong before?"

ZS: Well, it's not that the earlier stuff was worse, but it's that the tools and machinery of this one work so very smoothly, one feels completely confident as a reader. You've no problem at all anymore with "making a novel." When I think of both my novels the second halves of both are rubbish because of basic, technical inability. When you're younger every page is still a struggle. And when I read *Saturday* I just felt: well, "making a novel" is the least of your bloody problems, mate. Same with Roth. There are other things that are being developed—ideas, themes, larger ambitions to do with a canon of work—but the "making a novel" bit feels like it's done effortlessly. Maybe that's not how it is at all. But I wondered whether the autobiographical stuff makes the composition process a slightly smoother process.

IM: I have to say I thought it would be. I made this decision, OK, I will blatantly use my life in this next novel so that will save me an awful lot of time. Actually it didn't. It was just as much a struggle. Even when I was actually using the internal layout of this house for the scenes, it rarely occurred to me as I walked about this house that this was the same house in the book. It's somehow a map of a parallel house.

ZS: Talking of parallels, there's a paragraph in *Saturday* about surgery, apparently, but it seems to me to be about writing.

IM: Oh, well done.

ZS: I read it and thought it can't be about anything else. You know the paragraph I mean? "For the past two hours he's been in a dream of absorption"—it's such an exact description of what it's like to write when it's going well. And my favorite line is when you talk about him feeling "calm and spacious, fully qualified to exist. It's a feeling of clarified emptiness, of deep, muted joy." The events you put next to it, as comparative experiences—the love-making and listening to Theo's song—are two human states which are often advertised as bringing similar pleasure: basically, personal relations and art. But the book seems to suggest that there is a deeper happiness that one can only find in work, or at least, creative work. And I felt that joy coming off the book in every direction. Joy at being a writer!

IM: I'm glad that you found that paragraph. I knew I wanted to write a major operation at the end but it would really be about writing, about making art. So it starts with him picking up a paintbrush. Or rather, I was *so* sure, when I went for the operation, that Neil Pritchard, the surgeon, when he paints the marks on the patient, was using a two-inch paintbrush. And when I sent him the last draft, just to check it one last time he said, "I don't use a paintbrush," and I said, "But surely surgeons do," and he said, "No, no." I was so disappointed personally. He dips the paintbrush in yellow paint and as the aria of the Goldberg Variations starts, he makes his first stroke and it is a moment of artistic engagement... But very, very reluctantly I had to replace it with a sponge on a flap.

ZS: The joy of the extended analogy is that it allows you to write about writing as work. Usually when you read books about being a novelist, all you really get is the character at lunches and his publishing routines, and that's nothing to do with the process of writing. It's so hard to sit down and write about that procedure, but I feel that metaphorically it's done here.

IM: The dream, surely, Zadie, that we all have, is to write this beautiful paragraph that actually is describing something but at the same time in another voice is writing a commentary on its own creation, without having to be a story about a writer.

III. "I'M NOT AGAINST RELIGION IN THE SENSE THAT I FEEL I CAN'T TOLERATE IT, BUT I THINK WRITTEN INTO THE RUBRIC OF RELIGION IS THE CERTAINTY OF ITS OWN TRUTH. AND SINCE THERE ARE SIX THOUSAND RELIGIONS CURRENTLY ON THE FACE OF THE EARTH, THEY CAN'T ALL BE RIGHT."

ZS: I want to ask you about the optimism in *Saturday.* There's this recognizably Updikean enjoyment in the book, which I love; you seem to relish the things of the world. And you're right; it *is* an amazing thing to be able to go and get a glass of fresh orange juice in England—these supposedly normal things that would have been revolutionary even sixty-odd years ago. But surely one of the problems we have with all this progress is that it has been at the expense of foreign places and foreign people who do not partake of the progress, and that's kind of exactly the reason we're in this shitstorm/"war-without-end" nightmare scenario right now. So I found it hard to celebrate with Henry Perowne, knowing what his privileges are based on.

IM: Yeah. Well, I guess this is writing against the current in as far as I would take your view to be one of the conventions of liberal intellectual anxiety, one of the spectral opponents of the pleasures of life in the West. Perowne has these, too. He has all these marvelous advantages and yet he finds himself in a state of anxiety—we have all the pleasures and yet we're looking behind our back. And the reason I wanted to make Perowne a wealthy man is because, actually, that's what the first world is.

ZS: But by any comparison, he's pretty damn wealthy.

IM: The fact that he's wealthier than some but not all journalists…

ZS: You knew you were going to be set up by that. Some people were always going to find the descriptions of Perowne's luxurious life distasteful.

IM: Yeah. That doesn't touch me at all. Because I know that these journalists are wealthy by any planetary standard. That's precisely why I had him gazing at the locks on his door, thinking about the bad people, the drug dealers who want to get in—there's an embattlement. They're on the other side. You block these people out of your world picture. It's a kind of framing. You cease to see a patient on the table because you only see the little square, the mole—

ZS: Exactly. But then you are saying that happiness is based on unreality or a bubble of unreality.

IM: It's a kind of framing, yes. But great things are achieved within that frame.

ZS: The other thing about championing progress is the danger that we go too far in the "celebration of all things Western" direction. I'm reading articles by Rushdie recently which rigorously defend Western thought, and because I've just re-read *Black Dogs* (in which the character Bernard is a great defender of the principle of "rationality"), it did strike me that Rusdhie has become Bernard Extraordinaire. He's defending the Enlightenment against all comers now, bravely and viciously, but very strongly. I understand his emotion, exactly. But it's strange when you consider where we were fifteen years ago when some of the more confident Enlightenment assumptions, the quasireligious worship of the rational, for example, were being radically questioned. And now we're at this point where it's three cheers for Descartes because we've got these madmen in their planes. It's like we've all become radicalized in response to that.

IM: When the Enlightenment was being sort of undermined by the theorists in the academies, that was done with a general sense of security about the ultimate cultural victory of Enlightenment values, and now I think that victory is a lot less assured.

ZS: And so would you say you've lost patience, if you've ever had any patience, with the idea of religion?

IM: Absolutely. I agree with Salman about that. I have no patience whatsoever.

ZS: I suppose I feel the same, but I feel strange about feeling it.

IM: I'm not against religion in the sense that I feel I can't tolerate it, but I think written into the rubric of religion is the certainty of its own truth. And since there are six thousand religions currently on the face of the earth, they can't all be right. And only the secular spirit can guarantee those freedoms, and it's the secular spirit that they contest.

ZS: You were asked once what you believe, truly believe though you can't prove it, and you said: the absolute belief that there's nothing after consciousness. But something about *Saturday* and its joy in the world and, again, that kind of Updikean pleasure, made me wonder whether you'd ever imagined yourself moving in that vaguely Christian direction…

IM: No.

ZS: Never? No change as you've got older, no inching fears or hopes…

IM: No. I don't see any paradox in that which celebrates all things within the context of the extremely brief gift of consciousness.

ZS: See, for a lot of writers even the phrase "brief gift of consciousness" is enough to send them into a fit, and I'm one of them. As a breed, we tend to harbor quite severe death fears.

IM: And *gift,* by the way, is a metaphor because—

ZS: Nobody gives.

IM: Indeed, there's nobody there.

ZS: But I think amongst English writers it's quite unusual to have such a solid, nondeath fear.

IM: I have an absolute death fear! I don't want this thing to end. [Philip] Larkin expresses that feeling so beautifully.

ZS: But I think with Larkin, he's the kind of man who would have taken any religion that seemed even vaguely convincing, he wasn't fussy. He'd take anything—he didn't believe in being brave… but as it happened everything was too stupid to be acceptable to him. Anyway: enough about death.

IM: Yes.

IV. "THE EROTIC IMAGINATION DOES NOT NECESSARILY NEED CRITICAL MANIFESTOS… IT CAN'T BE GOVERNED IN THAT WAY."

ZS: I want to talk to you about sex and women. You said something once about *The Female Eunuch* being revelatory. I think that about that book a lot as well—as weird as it is to talk about that now, given all that's happened in the past six months. [Germaine Greer appeared as a contestant on Britain's *Big Brother* TV show.]

IM: Yeah. Is that the same Germaine?

ZS: It's hard to imagine. Anyway, I wasn't there in seventy-five to see the first book come out, but I would imagine the word *femi-*

nist was not one often used much in the context of your short stories. But the women in them and the care and concern with women all the way through your fiction is really interesting to me. And there's a lot of honesty about the deep, masculine hatred for women.

IM: "About it." That's the key.

ZS: Right. Almost every dimension of it is looked at. Silent women, damaged women, sexually vulnerable women, little girls, everything.

IM: I got a good kicking over all that. I was trying to write about the very things that I felt the feminist discussion was involved in, and also to have some fun writing about them. The first story you get is of a man who falls for a shopwindow dummy and then I just let this man project every fantasy onto her, just see what happens.

ZS: There's an idea in those stories that sex is where things can go most right and most wrong. That seems to be a very McEwan idea. It'll save you and also completely destroy you.

IM: But also it seemed to me at the time, in the '70s, that there needed to be a huge realignment in the way men and women would talk to each other. And I'm absolutely certain if you were to get into some time machine and go back to the early '60s, the condescension and also the apartheid would completely amaze you.

ZS: It's like when I'm reading Kingsley Amis. Whatever the attitude is to women is not really the interesting thing, it's that the women are so *other*. It's as if they've come off a different planet. There's no communication at all. You want to say, "Go on, Kingsley, poke her with your finger, she's *real*!"

IM: There was no game about it, either. People lived it. I used to talk to Martin Amis about thinking of girls as real people and then he married Antonia and I think then he got it, he suddenly saw something he hadn't seen before, and actually his books have changed. Meanwhile I was going in the other direction. I remember going to a conference on the erotic, I don't know why I'd been invited, it was a time when the left, they were tough cookies, there were many separatists. Anyway, I gave a very good talk and what I was trying to say was the erotic imagination does not necessarily need critical manifestos, that it can't be governed in that way. The erotic imagination can be very interested in unkindness, for example. In sadism. I was booed offstage. I said, until you take that onboard, then your picture of this is not accurate. I said, let's talk about masochism, for example, male *and* female masochism.

ZS: That's the basis of *The Comfort of Strangers.*

IM: Yeah. So that's what I then went on to write. I felt: Oh, well, there must be other terms for discussion about what takes place between a man and woman beyond sociology and critical manifestos. What about the sort of thrilling notion that you could test love, test trust, that you could experiment with un-freeing yourself?

ZS: So the stories are news in a way, news from the male consciousness. And the news is: male consciousness ain't always the happiest place to be. And it's news unattached to dogma, which in 1985 I would imagine was a pretty out-there thing to do.

IM: 1981.

ZS: Oops.

IM: But, yes, and actually within a year or two there were American feminists writing about the erotic in ways that were really much closer to what I was trying to write about. British feminism is very rooted in Marxism, so it was very much about wages and matters of real concern, but it sat very uneasily in any discussion about the erotic.

ZS: Certainly in the past ten years feminism has become much more willing to talk dirty. There's a kind of cheap, fetishized version that you get in the women's magazines, trumpeting women who are able to say, "Yes, I am a feminist, but I still quite like being tied to a doorknob for three days." It's easy to satirize that stuff, but I feel you really believe in the underlying argument that there's no point in feminism ignoring the female instinct for the perverse. And then you get the other side of the argument, typified by my husband, who believes masochism and sadism will always be found to have its root cause in some kind of emotional damage, that there's no other reason.

IM: No, he's absolutely wrong. Madonna famously said being tied down gave her the thrill and comfort of being strapped into a car seat when she was three. I thought, Ah! She's said it.

ZS: The quote at the end of *The Comfort of Strangers:* "She was going to tell him her theory, tentative at this stage, of course, which explained how the imagination, the sexual imagination, men's ancient dreams of hurting and women's of being hurt, embodied and declares a powerful single organizing principle, which distorted all relations, all truth."

I'm a writer who never writes about sex. It's so far from my own fictional world, and it unnerves me when you say "powerful single, organizing principle." You mean that sex is the pole that everything else moves around—in which case, I'm really missing a trick. That seems to be what you were saying in 1982. And I wonder if you still feel that.

IM: No, I don't.

ZS: Because it's a very big thing to say.

IM: That's a very big thing to say especially in a tiny novel. But it's something that someone who had just gone through what the character had gone through might well feel. But no, I have now reached the stage where as soon as anyone says life moves around a single organizing principle I stop listening to them. I don't feel that life organizes itself around any single principle. It's a religious impulse to only grasp at one thing, one explanation.

ZS: I understand.

IM: That's interesting, though… I don't know where things stand now in the sexual debate. I've just started reading *Villages* [John Updike's new novel]… plenty of sex in there.

ZS: I know. It's unbelievable. I don't know how he stays interested. I find it amazing, not just purely technically, but the virility of the man, the continued interest.

IM: The virility of the man!

ZS: You know what I mean. He's still bothered. He loves women and he says, somewhere in that book, that he can't believe that women "tend to us" or "care for us at all" or something like that. As if to say: what a miracle it is. He doesn't seem to have ever gotten over the idea that women don't mind making love to men.

IM: I like the bit at the beginning when he's being shaved, the hero, and it's like: The girls all worship us but of course they don't have enough intellect to be able to worship us. *If only they knew how vast our consciousness is…* But seriously, it still remains difficult, more difficult now than it was, to understand what the true relation is between men and women. Back then everything was being stirred up, it was a blizzard, it was an argument you had to get involved in. Now it all seems to have slowed and settled. A sort of muffled silence.

ZS: In a lot of the chick lit, depicting women slightly older than me, the sexual maturity is that of a nine-year-old, maybe. The sex is just this giggly and ridiculous activity one is subjected to in order to make a man stay in your house and marry you. There's no honest expression of female sexual desire, the kind you find even in those old cheesy feminist manuals like *Our Bodies, Ourselves.* We've gone backward. I mean, if you had a daughter who believed this stuff they're printing now, you'd be devastated.

IM: I keep hearing that song "Too Drunk to Fuck"—have you heard that?

ZS: Yeah. Things have not gone well in the past ten years.

IM: What a shame.

ZS: What about your two boys? Are you conscious of bringing up different kinds of men from the ones I had to date?

IM: Yeah, I think so. They're both very rapid in their development. When they got to the age of about sixteen or seventeen, they had their first girlfriends, and stayed with them for two or three years. I think it was enormously healthy. And they remained friends with them afterward. And now Will is in his second long relationship and Greg has just finished his first, but they still meet and it's very touching. Three-hour phone conversations still go on and they seemed to have had lots of sex. Far more sex than I'd *ever* imagined at the same age. I find it deeply enviable.

ZS: One of the critical standards I remember being levied at all your generation of male writers was: *Does he write women well? Can he write a convincing bird?* Do you think about that still? Does it concern you? Do you think you've improved?

IM: I think I'm sort of gender-blind on this. I think it was Fay Weldon who said that a man could never write a woman properly, which I thought was ludicrous. Taken to its logical extension, novelists could only write about themselves; you couldn't write about an old person, a young person, a person you didn't know. Henry James said that in the contract between writer and reader one thing we must accept as given is the subject matter. I accept that wholly. It's a great contract. There's nowhere you'll not let your imagination go.

V. "AS YOU GET OLDER YOU FEEL THE NEED TO MAKE YOURSELF CLEAR..."

ZS: Ah—I wanted to talk about the places you let your imagination go. Dark places. The most striking thing in *Saturday,* I think, is the final scene, in particular the sadism of it. Now, either I'm an idiot or—well, I just didn't expect it, I was caught out completely. I was having a lovely time in a lovely world with lovely people and I went upstairs to read the last hundred pages—Nick [Nick Laird, Smith's husband] was downstairs watching TV with friends—and was sitting alone with this book feeling like I was being attacked. My scalp was prickly, I was sweating, I kept wanting to shout downstairs but then there's no point trying to explain what's happened in a book if somebody's not reading it... I felt physically assailed. And maybe there's a lot of fiction which does that and I just don't read it. I'm always reading this flowery literary fiction. But I'd never had that feeling before. And I never expect that response from my readers, I never expect anything physical from them. I know I can't make them cry and I can't make them go [*sharp intake of breath*] like I was doing with your book, yesterday. So I wonder if you sit down and aim for that response and how you can possibly pace a novel, bargaining on that result? Because what if it didn't happen? What if I just read that scene and went, "Uh, yeah," and moved on?

IM: I knew what I wanted to get, I had no idea exactly how I was going to get it. I leave blanks in my planning, and there are bits it's best not to think about till you get there. I didn't know whether he had a knife nor did I know what he wanted. I had to write it to find out what was going to happen. I mean, I knew that he would end up being thrown down the stairs, and that the operation would happen but I was looking for my... well, to go back to where we started this conversation, to 9/11, and the sense of invasion, one can only do it on a private scale. If you say the airliner hit the side of the building, a thousand people died, nothing happens to your scalp. So I, in a sense, tried to find the private scale of that feeling.

ZS: But what advice would you give regarding how a writer might *earn* that moment? Because when I finished reading I thought you'd done exactly what you needed to do to earn that moment. I didn't feel that you'd tried to scare me in a cheap way or you'd taken a back door. More could have happened in that scene, in fact. I was interested, in my mind, as to how far you could have gone with that narrative before I was angry with you for a manipulation. All the narrative decisions you make in a scene like that are ethical decisions, and also aesthetic, and you have to make them, they're serious. And someone who can't write makes them very badly.

IM: Especially if you're going to have a young woman with no clothes on, being looked at in that way. How long you dwell on it is key. And I felt I was taking a risk having Daisy naked. And the risk was—well, first I got it completely wrong, I didn't make it frightening enough and the reason I didn't make it frightening was I didn't want to humiliate her. But then it was unreal. So I had to go back and I made her defiant. But it just didn't stand up.

ZS: I would never be defiant in that situation.

IM: There's no way anyone could be defiant with this man holding a knife to your mother's neck. But again the question of the amount of time one dwells on the nakedness. And I thought if I was Updike now Perowne's gaze would be relentless and we would have to have Daisy's body described. And I thought: There Perowne cannot go. So I went to fear and fear did what I thought a brother and father would have to do in an emergency. Look to the floor, think of a way of attacking. And in a sense so did I, I looked to the floor. Apart from the swell of her pregnancy. The whole thing is four pages. It's narrative time enough but not particularly long to dwell.

ZS: In the past you worked more on the complicit nature of the reader-writer relationship. That story about the father with the two little girls, "In Between the Sheets," makes you complicit by constantly allowing—without authorial comment—these descriptions in which the father makes the children sound older than they are. Several times they're described as looking older, speaking like women, moving like women. This makes the reader complicit in the pedophile's idea, or potential pedophile's idea, that these girls could be his. And that's an incredibly uncomfortable experience as a reader.

IM: Yeah. I was very keen on making readers uncomfortable. I think I've lost that ambition now, it doesn't interest me so much as a project.

ZS: It's a kind of cruelty.

IM: Yeah. Leading the reader into siding with the murderous pedophile or rapist. It's not so interesting.

ZS: Or offering the reader an extreme, antihumanist perspective on a human being. In the story "Homemade" you describe a young boy running a race as a "tiny amoebic blob across the field… staggering determinedly in its pointless effort to reach the flags—just life, just faceless, self-renewing life…"

IM: Yeah. I was trying to be funny. Because he comes home thirteenth.

ZS: But the reader is also being forced to see people from perspectives the novel as a form doesn't usually encourage.

IM: Absolutely.

ZS: Do you think your taste for that has lessened a little?

IM: It has lessened a little. Because I think death anxiety or numbers-of-days-left anxiety make me keen to make sense of the human, rather than to distort it. I think there's a wonderful recklessness you have in your twenties and thirties as a writer, you can do terrible things because although intellectually you know your time will end, you don't yet feel it in your blood, in your gut. It's a recklessness I think one should really enjoy, relax into it, spread out. As you get older you feel the need to make yourself clear.

ZS: Right.

IM: There are a couple of things. One is you have children, and as you age, there's some growing sense of wanting the human project to succeed. Not fail. Or you no longer wish to dwell quite so much on the possibility of it all going wonderfully, horribly wrong. You begin to wish it would go right.

ZS: So, in conclusion: what are you going to do about your mellowing coinciding with the world's hard-core radicalization and madness? That's a strange mix. You feel it in *Saturday.* The collision of somebody in that moment of their life where they're feeling satisfied and fulfilled and unfortunately that moment's happening on a planet that's losing the bloody plot entirely.

IM: Yeah, it is an extraordinary moment. It's like we've engaged ourselves in some medieval struggle. We had our Diderot and Voltaire and now you'd hope we'd at least now investigate the structure of DNA, and the origins of the universe, and the possibility of understanding more about ourselves with a new metaphysics—but that's not the focus right now. The struggle is a medieval one between faiths.

ZS: Yeah. It's all gone wrong. When I was in America around all these classic left-wing intellectuals, the feeling was one of literal despair. They just run through the streets screaming. That's basically their only reaction to the moment they're in, as if this moment were unprecedented. But that's the interesting thing—it's nowhere near unprecedented. I liked the fact that in *Saturday* you seemed to be saying, instead, what we were getting here is a madness that, in truth, has always accompanied progress.

IM: You know, twenty-five years ago or twenty years ago, all we talked about was the possibility that the Soviet Union and the United States were going to have a global conflict and do it in Europe. That was the unprecedented moment.

ZS: You wrote your own apocalypse story at the time as well.

IM: It felt like a real possibility. And we got very indignant, caught between two empires, we thought we might all die. Martin Amis famously said that if the war started he would drive home, shoot his wife, and then shoot his children.

ZS: He doesn't do things by halves.

IM: As a humane act. So the liberal Left went around saying, "Dear sir, in your interview, you said you'd shoot your wife and children. Do you really think that's an appropriate response?" But anyway, it was on our minds. And madness was in the air.

ZS: In *Saturday,* Henry Perowne wonders whether the madness and trauma of 9/11 will take a hundred years to resolve itself. Do you believe that?

IM: At the end of *Saturday,* I think of a figure like Perowne but a hundred years earlier, 1904, and of what terror lay ahead then. We've almost forgot the First World War, Stalin, and then the Second, the Holocaust—if we had a fraction of that we'd be very fortunate. At least we know what we're capable of. But the moment is not unprecedented.

ZS: Maybe everything takes a hundred years or more to play itself out. Look at the bloody Treaty of Versailles. Now: next question is utterly unrelated.

IM: Good.

ZS: I read your back catalog over a month or so and I felt very satisfied merely having "read all of McEwan." And then I thought, Fuck, imagine *having written all of McEwan*. So I was wondering what it feels like to look at your own bookshelves and see this nice little backlog of work. This little stack. I don't know what that would feel like. Amazing, I would think.

IM: It's not amazing, because you get there by very slow increments. If you think of Updike—*that's* amazing. Updike's "Also by" page is now a few pages long in itself. An insane amount of books.

ZS: That is insane. He has a condition, I think. It's a disease with him—he can't stop.

IM: Graphomania. Well, it would be easier to dismiss if it wasn't so good.

ZS: Does it give you pleasure, though?

IM: It's like a family album, the consciousness of your own past—well, you must find this already. I certainly find it. People say what were you doing in such and such year, and I know exactly what I was doing. I know I was publishing a particular book, or halfway through one. These books are the spoonfuls with which I've measured my existence. ✯

SEAN WILSEY

TALKS WITH

HARUKI MURAKAMI

"WHAT THE NOVELIST NEEDS IS NOT DIVERSE OPINIONS BUT A PERSONAL SYSTEM OF STORYTELLING UPON WHICH HIS OPINIONS CAN TAKE A FIRM STAND."

Interests that would seem to cancel each other out:
Kafka, baseball
Chandler, drinking in moderation
Dostoyevsky, browsing used-record stores

Haruki Murakami has published thirteen books in English, of which the majority are great, and two are better—that is, deeper, funnier, lonelier, more life-affirming and breath-taking and sleep-depriving—than anything I've ever read.

A rough sketch of Murakami's pre-writing years goes like this: born in 1949, in Kyoto, his self-described uneventful suburban childhood was enlivened by voracious reading of Dostoyevsky and Raymond Chandler (the latter in paperbacks left behind by American sailors). A few years as a middling university student in Tokyo introduced him to the two loves of his life, jazz music and his wife, Yōko; he married and opened a jazz club, called Peter Cat (cats being a third love), which was such a success that Murakami's life seemed set on its course—comfortable, bohemian—until, as he told an audience in 1992, "Suddenly one day in April 1978, I felt like writing a novel... I was at a baseball game... in the outfield stands, drinking beer... My favorite team was the Yakult Swallows. They were playing the Hiroshima Carps. The Swallows' first batter in the bottom of the first inning was an American, Dave Hilton. You've probably never heard of him. He never made a name for himself in the States, so he came to play ball in Japan. I'm pretty sure he was the leading hitter that year. Anyhow, he sent the first ball pitched to him that day into left field for a double. And that's when the idea struck me: I could write a novel."

So he wrote a novel. Every night after closing Peter Cat, Murakami sat at his kitchen table, drank beer, and in six months produced the short, Vonnegut-like Hear the Wind Sing *(1979). He submitted the novel for a literary award, and when it won Murakami went to get Dave Hilton's autograph—"I feel he was a lucky charm for me"—then went back to the kitchen table and wrote another novel,* Pinball, 1973 *(1980). This book (coupled with a movie deal on the first) was successful enough to allow him to sell the jazz club and become a full-time writer at age thirty-two.*

Established, Murakami moved back to the suburbs and began work on A Wild Sheep Chase *(1982), technically the final book in a trilogy that began with the first two—the trilogy of the rat—though he considers it his first novel because it's where he found his voice. (An unfortunate footnote to this success story is that neither* Hear the Wind Sing *nor* Pinball, 1973 *will ever be available in the United States because, as Murakami bluntly told* Publishers Weekly *in 1991, they are "weak.")*

Style found, weakness behind him, lifestyle then changed. Murakami began exercising religiously, running marathons, eating meticulously, drinking moderately—living with a Shinto purity in order to maintain the rigorous work habits that have permitted him to be so consistently productive. He also began translating, mostly American writers, dividing his days between his own writing and the rendering into Japanese of Americans'. With his regime in place Murakami produced some astounding books, beginning with the hyperexperimental Hard-Boiled Wonderland and the End of the World *(1985, and still his personal favorite), and then, in pursuit of a wider audience, changing course to write what he described to* Publishers Weekly *as a "totally realistic, very straight" story, its title aimed directly at the mainstream:* Norwegian Wood *(1987). The novel was so huge that he fled Japan to escape the unprecedented pop-star scale of his success. On the lam he wrote* Dance Dance Dance *(1988), a rollicking sequel to* A Wild Sheep Chase *(making a two-thirds-suppressed trilogy into a half-suppressed quadrilogy) and* South of the Border, West of the Sun *(1992), an elegiac version of* Norwegian Wood*—quieter and more mature.*

Then, working as a professor in the United States, he began his masterpiece, The Wind-up Bird Chronicle *(1994–1995), in which he took the best of his experimental and realistic voices, plus a new sense of history and morality, and closed in on what makes a writer immortal.* The Wind-up Bird Chronicle *was published in Japan in three volumes in 1994–1995, and in the U.S. in 1997 in a single abridged edition. Since then Murakami has returned to Japan. Short stories have always come naturally, and he has written some of his best in the past few years, collecting them in the two-hundred-page tour de force* After the Quake *(2002). He's also written a nonfiction book,* Underground *(2000), about the poison gas attacks on the Tokyo subway, and two more novels,* Sputnik Sweetheart *(1999) and* Kafka on the Shore *(2005).*

For this interview we communicated by email; I wrote questions in English, and he responded in Japanese. Jay Rubin, translator of The Wind-up Bird Chronicle *and author of the indispensable biography* Haruki Murakami and the Music of Words *(2002), translated the answers into English.*

As an interviewee Murakami does not open up the deepest recess of his heart and soul. As a writer he opens up yours.

—Sean Wilsey (Summer/Fall 2004)

SEAN WILSEY: It occurs to me that the most malevolent figure in your work is a sort of professional interviewee (Noboru Wataya in *The Wind-up Bird Chronicle*); and you equate his facility with the media (and the slipperiness of his opinions) with his evil and soullessness. You seem to be saying if a person is too good at opening his mouth in public he's empty inside. Then again, one of the most illuminating interviews I've ever read with anyone on any subject was the *New York Times*'s interview with you on the subject of 9/11, and its similarities to the Tokyo subway gas attacks. There you said, speaking of cult leaders and their relationship with their followers, "If you have questions, there is always someone to provide the answers. In a way, things are very easy and clear, and you are happy as long as you believe." How does one speak publicly without becoming a professional/Noboru Wataya, or stopping people from thinking for themselves?

HARUKI MURAKAMI: I often get calls from newspapers asking my opinion on some news event or other—for example, "What do you think about Japan's decision to dispatch Self-Defense Force troops to Iraq?" or "What's your view of the twelve-year-old girl who cut her classmate's throat?" and such.

I do of course have my own reasonably clear personal opinions about such events. But there is a definite difference between my having an opinion as an individual and "novelist Haruki Murakami"'s having an opinion. Still, it goes without saying that any personal opinion of mine appearing in the newspaper will be read by the public as the opinion of novelist Haruki Murakami. And so I make it a rule never to respond to questions from the media.

I am not, of course, saying that novelists must not express their personal opinions. It is my belief, however, that, rather than expressing his views on a number of diverse matters, the role of the novelist would seem most properly to lie in his depicting as precisely as possible (as Kafka described his execution machine in chillingly minute detail) the personal biases and environmental forces that give rise to those views. To put it in a more extreme manner, what the novelist needs is not diverse opinions but a personal system of storytelling upon which his opinions can take a firm stand.

In that sense, Noboru Wataya's stance is, as you suggest, shallow and superficial. Precisely because his opinions are shallow and superficial, they communicate with great speed, and they have great practical impact. What I wanted to convey to the reader through my portrait of Noboru Wataya was the dangerous influence that contemporary media gladiators, who use such rhetoric as a weapon, exert on our society and our minds: the special cruelty they deploy below the surface. We are practically surrounded by such people in our daily lives. Often, the opinions we assume to be our own turn out on closer inspection to be nothing but the parroting of theirs. It is chilling to think that in many instances we view the world through the media and speak to each other in the words of the media.

The only thing we can do sometimes to avoid straying into such a sealed labyrinth, is to go down alone into a deep well the way the protagonist Watanabe does: to recover one's own point of view, one's own language. This is not an easy thing to do, of course, and sometimes it involves danger. The job of the novelist, perhaps, is to act as a seasoned guide to such dangerous journeys. And, in some cases, in the story we can simulate for the reader the experience of undertaking such a task of self-exploration. For me, the story is a powerful vehicle that performs many such functions.

What Shoko Asahara, the founder of the Aum Shinrikyo [the cult that released poison gas on the Tokyo subway], did was to undertake the deliberate abuse—and misuse—of such functions of the story. The circuit of the story he offered was oppressive and firmly closed off from external input. By contrast, the circuit of a genuine story must be fundamentally spontaneous and always open to the outside. We must reject all things Wataya-like and Asahara-like. This may well be the marrow of the story I am trying to write.

I responded to the *New York Times*'s request for an interview because I wanted to speak about my general view of the world and of the novel, not to give my personal opinions or to play rhetorical games. There is a major difference here. Wouldn't you say that

Noboru Wataya is less an interviewee than a commentator?

SW: Let me ask novelist Haruki Murakami about writing. You've talked about loving and being influenced by Carver, Chandler, Dostoyevsky, and Kafka. I love Dostoyevsky (*The Possessed* is one of my favorite novels), and I have always found him very funny; do these writers also make you laugh?

HM: I agree that *The Possessed* is one of Dostoyevsky's funniest novels. Carver and Chandler, too, have wonderful senses of humor. Kafka's novels and stories are weirdly comical in their very structure. Humor plays a big role in my fiction, too. I suspect that you can't have genuine seriousness without an element of humor.

SW: What do you think about cuteness? Modern Japan, or at least the Japan we see over here, at its most extreme, seems like a nation swinging between its obsessions with either the extremely cute, or the extremely efficient (Hello Kitty; Honda Civic).

You've said that violence is the key to Japan. *The Wind-up Bird Chronicle* is the book in which you wrestle most directly and harrowingly with Japan's history of violence, and the character you use to wrestle with it is called Cinnamon—a very cute name. What are you saying about cuteness? Is Japan's obsession with cuteness a means of wrestling with the violence of its recent history?

HM: I myself am not much interested in the cute and the efficient, so I can't really answer your questions. The commodification of the cute and the efficient is not something unique to Japan. Mickey Mouse is cute, after all, and the Swiss Army Knife is efficient. And nations are violent systems by definition. I feel it can be dangerous to explain whole cultures with buzzwords.

SW: The Japanese artist I most closely identify you with is Hayao Miyazaki, whose (sometimes cute) characters have to struggle with tragedy or loneliness or loss. As artists you both seem to know loss and deal with it in somewhat similar ways. Do you like or identify with Miyazaki?

HM: I have never seen any of Miyazaki's films. I don't know why, but I have never been much interested in *anime*. I like to keep a sharp division between things that interest me and things that don't in order to use the limited time allotted to me in life most economically, and anime just happens to belong to the category of things that don't interest me.

SW: I've noticed that female musicians in your work tend to be classically trained, and somewhat cursed (Reiko from *Norwegian Wood;* Miu from *Sputnik Sweetheart*), while the men are happy cads who play jazz, like Tony Takitani's dad [from the short story "Tony Takitani"]. Reiko and Miu possess great skill and dedication, but insufficient emotion, and, ultimately, following deeply scarring emotional incidents, which they are each incapable of translating into art, they give up on music. As someone who used to run a jazz club, and who has said in numerous interviews that "concentration" is the most important tool a writer can possess (rather than emotion), what are you saying about the creative process? Is music really that different from writing? (There's a great deal of music in your sentences.) Why do your female musicians always have such a hard time?

HM: Women often act as mediums in my novels. They guide the protagonist to "places out of the ordinary," and they make the story move. As you know, music (along with dance) is the art most deeply imbued with ritualism. In that sense, a woman with musical ambitions may be an important presence in my work. Both Reiko and Miu might be said to be "mediums who have been abandoned by the gods." For them, their having given music up (their having been forced to give music up) is equivalent to their having severed a special tie with the world. (Now, don't forget this is entirely my personal opinion, not the opinion of novelist Haruki Murakami.)

I believe that concentration plays an equally central role in both music and the creation of a novel. Only the outward appearance of that "concentration" is different. The performance itself is usually the final expressive form in the case of music, and so the appearance of that concentration inevitably turns out to be more short-term, more expressive, more tangible. In the case of the creation of a novel, the concentration has to be more long-term, more introspective, more enduring. The way I see it, emotion is more an ordinary part of everyday life. It exists in everyone. Human beings devoid of emotion simply don't exist (do they?). In order to get a firm grasp on an emotion and express it with precision in an objective medium, however, what is required is strong enough powers of concentration to bring time to a temporary standstill. And for that what you need is the physical strength and stamina to maintain that concentration as long as possible. This is not something available to just anyone.

At the same time, I think that having made my living through most of my twenties as the owner of a jazz club taught me a lot about music and played an important role in my writing of novels. It might be true to say that I imported my methodology as-is into my novels—the importance of rhythm, for example, the joy of improvisation, the importance of establishing empathy with an audience. This is not a metaphor. For me, writing and the performance of music (though I don't actually perform music) have a direct and literal link in the air.

SW: Your male narrators are often unemployed, or unconventionally employed, but they always make it clear that money is a non-issue. There are some meditations on money in your early books, but the subject dropped out of your fiction quite quickly. Why doesn't money interest you?

HM: For no special reason. I suppose I'm just more interested in other things. I grew up in a family that was neither oversupplied with money nor troubled by a shortage of money, so, for better or worse, I probably never had to think seriously about it. As an adult, of course, I had to start dealing with money problems as a practical matter, but I suspect that one's childhood experience plays a big role in these things.

SW: You get up early in the morning and write on a set schedule every day. How much note-taking do you do outside of this schedule? Does the writing part of your brain turn off when you finish writing, or are you always writing?

HM: As a rule, I don't think too much about my fiction when I'm not sitting at my desk. If anything, I try hard to think about something else (or about nothing at all)—to switch gears in my head by doing sports or listening to music or reading or cooking. Maybe, in some remote corner of my mind, I'm thinking about my novel. Not even I know how my brain works.

SW: Do you ever just decide to take a break and not write?

HM: For me, writing is like breathing. I'm always writing something. When it's not fiction, I'm translating or writing essays and stuff like that. Writing is like training for an athlete or practice for a musician. If you stop entirely, it takes a long time to get your pace back.

SW: But in your periods of less intensely sustained labor, how do you fill your time?

HM: I'm happiest when I'm making the rounds of the used-record stores.

SW: You wrote your first novel at a table drinking beer, and there's a lot of beer in it. (In fact, by my informal count, there are an average of three beers consumed on each page of your first two books.) Do you still drink beer? Do you have a favorite beer?

HM: I still like beer and often have a drink. I like Bass Ale and Samuel Adams. I'm not a big drinker, though. I like a bottle or two in the evening, maybe with a little whiskey or wine afterward.

SW: In addition to your medium-like women, your books often contain a cursed place or thing—in *Dance Dance Dance* it's the

Dolphin Hotel and the Maserati ("the curse of the Maserati"). In *The Wind-up Bird Chronicle* it's the abandoned house. Where do these things come from?

HM: I don't know, maybe those places (or places like them) exist inside me. I really can't say much more than that writing about such places is entirely natural for me. Unnatural things occur quite naturally there.

SW: Can you talk a bit about where you might be going next? I've noticed that you seem to be writing in new ways, about both younger and older characters.

HM: What I want to do is write about lots of different characters in lots of different situations, and that way to create stories with greater breadth. New character types are beginning to appear in my books because I know now how to write them. ✯

NELL FREUDENBERGER

TALKS WITH

GRACE PALEY

"THE WRONG WORD IS LIKE A LIE JAMMED INSIDE THE STORY."

Locations of seats that inspired stories:
By the front window
At the American Academy of Arts and Letters ceremony
On the steps of the library
In front of a military parade

I first met Grace Paley in 1996 in Prague, where she was the writer-in-residence at a summer fiction workshop. She was staying in a baroque apartment building near the university, where each student got to meet her; I remember especially the wide stone stairs and massive double doors. I think I first approached Paley's stories the same way I climbed those stairs: a little too reverently. I remember being surprised by the tremendous warmth and humor of her prose.

Paley is a writer whose authority, both literary and moral, has put her firmly in the American canon—a funny position for a person whose politics and habit of speaking the truth as she sees it have gotten her into trouble with the establishment again and again. The week we met, in May of

2005, she attended a ceremony of the American Academy of Arts and Letters, where she is a fiction fellow and where, in the same grand auditorium in Harlem, in 1970, she had accepted an award for her short stories with an incendiary speech about the U.S. bombing of Cambodia and Laos. In 1969, she traveled to Vietnam as a representative of the peace movement, to bring back American P.O.W.s; five years later she went to Moscow as a delegate to the World Peace Congress.

"Two ears, one for literature, one for home, are useful for writers," Paley has written: a kind of explanation for stories that don't sound like anybody else's. Paley was born in 1922 to Russian immigrant parents in the Bronx, but her literary ear was tuned first and primarily to poets. I think it must be their precision, as much as her Russian-Yiddish-English childhood, that makes her storytelling voice so distinctive. Although she started as a poet, today she's best known for her stories, a fact that probably says more about contemporary American literary culture than it does about Paley. In a way she's tricked us, though: her stories are as demanding as poems. She reads aloud as she writes, refusing to accept the almost-right word, and her work requires a similar level of attention from the reader.

Paley has published three collections of stories, The Little Disturbances of Man *(1959),* Enormous Changes at the Last Minute *(1974), and* Later the Same Day *(1985), two books of poems, and one book of poems and prose pieces,* Long Walks and Intimate Talks *(1991). Her essays, reports, speeches, and notes about writing are collected in* Just as I Thought *(1998). People often bemoan or wonder at the fact that Paley hasn't written more; maybe what they mean is that she hasn't made more of a fuss about what she has published. Her friend and neighbor Donald Barthelme, famously had to come across the street and encourage her to go through her files in order to find the material for her second story collection, published fifteen years after the first one.*

Today Paley lives primarily in Vermont with her husband, the writer Robert Nichols, but complains that she spends most of her income traveling back and forth to New York. She still keeps the apartment on West Eleventh Street where her children grew up; we conducted this interview in the kitchen, over tea with sugar that she'd "stolen" from a restaurant around the corner. Afterward, she took me to the living room to show me the window where the "wild old woman" in "One Day I Made Up a Story" leans on her elbows and yells out at the street. Paley admired a lush gingko tree growing just outside the window. "It wasn't here when we moved in," she explained. "At that time there were no trees, except in the fanciest neighborhoods. The city was worried that the roots might crack the pavement or something." She laughed: "Look at it now."

—Nell Freudenberger (Spring 2005)

I. MEANING

NELL FREUDENBERGER: In the short essay "Jobs," you say, "The whole meaning of my life, which was jammed until midnight with fifteen different jobs and places, was writing." When did you first know that?

GRACE PALEY: I think I always sort of knew that's what I was doing, because I made no effort to do anything else. Except have children.

NF: Well, and all the other work you did—the peace work.

GP: Yeah, well, that was just natural. That was part of how my family lived, and how I lived and stuff like that. I mean, I said that, but actually: what is the meaning of my life?—it's stupid. It's a very stupid remark, to tell you the truth, because to say at whatever age I was then, What is the meaning of my life?—you don't know what the meaning of your life is until you're just about done. You didn't come to hear Stanley Kunitz last night, did you?

NF: No.

GP: Well, everybody who ever wrote a poem in the world was there. It was at the Bronx Community College Auditorium, which is enormous, and utterly packed. And I thought of all these people going home and writing a poem...

NF: I've heard you talk about how your first stories were published, by your friend's husband Ken McCormick at Doubleday.

GP: Yes. That's what happened. One of the great accidents. People always—you know, when I do readings—always ask about it, and I say, "It's just luck. I mean, I'm embarrassed by the luck of it all."

NF: Was that simply a good experience, or was there any anxiety about publishing them?

GP: Well, no, what happened—what happened was a very good thing, because if that hadn't happened, I would've written another story when I got around to it... and another story when I got around to it. You know, I would've been much slower—even slower than I am. But I was not slow in getting that book together. He said, "I want seven more stories, and then I'll publish the book. I had, actually, another one or two very small ones, and then, inside of two years, I finished the other stories. But if that hadn't happened, I would not have done it. I would never have written "In Time Which Made a Monkey of Us All," which is this long story, you know? Which I just read recently up at Dartmouth.

NF: It's a great story.

GP: Reading it aloud surprised me. There's stuff in it I would've thought that nobody would've gotten. Anyway, the point is, I never would've gotten to write that story. And probably not either the one or two before. So it was really just the luck of it. Because I'd been writing poems anyway, and never sending them out. I sent them out once, when Jess [Paley, her first husband] came home from the army. I was about twenty, twenty-one then. And I published three poems in a magazine called *Experiment*—they took them. But then the war ended, and life got very thick, and we had to find a place to live, and it was very exciting—a young couple—well, you know that. So, that was good, but I don't know if I ever would've reached that point of experience in writing that I would've taken certain risks and stuff like that.

NF: You've said that the First Amendment has been useful to our country, and that "it has made our literature one of the most lively and most useless in the world." Do you think American literature, and fiction in particular, can be useful?

GP: Well, all of art is useful, isn't it, in that sense? You couldn't grow up and live without art. I mean, you couldn't live without storytelling, couldn't live without painting. It's just eternal. It's very old, it's a hundred thousand years old, at least, and you draw pictures in caves, and tell stories, and write the Bible—write all sorts of things. It's not helpful; it's not not-helpful. It exists, just like we exist.

NF: In the introduction to *Just as I Thought,* you make fun of Americans a little for their obsession with hunting down their ancestors. Why do you think Americans are so interested in genealogy, but not very interested in history?

GP: I think probably everybody is interested in genealogy to some extent. I mean, there are some cultures where the great-great-grandparents are like gods. Their bones are kept in an altar; all cultures are different in that respect. I think there really is a kind of normal curiosity, eventually, about where you come from. I mean, my parents didn't talk very much about it. And nowadays, with the tape recorder and all, young people are extracting stories like anything from their parents. They're not letting them sit there like a log and saying, "Nothing happened. Oh well, that was nothing." [*Laughs*] "So why did you leave Daddy?" "Ah, well, we were just fighting, didn't know what to do—I thought I ought to get a job..."

But I think it's true that the technology exists, and that's one of the reasons that it's happening.

NF: You've said you used to worry your stories were "too personal." That they weren't about the kinds of things people would want to read about.

GP: No, I didn't say that. I said because they were about women's lives. But not personal. I never even thought about that. I just thought of how women I knew were living, and nobody was interested in that. It was after the war, after all—not too long after the war. Ten years or so. It was a men's literature. Simple as that.

II. EDUCATION

NF: The other day at the American Academy of Arts and Letters ceremony in Harlem, we heard Roger Wilkins talk about the progress we *haven't* made in American education since Brown v. Board of Education. Did you agree with him?

GP: Well, I'm not here. But I know that even where we live, in Vermont—as you can see [*Paley passed me two digitally printed photos of her grandchildren at the beach*] my grandchildren are African American children—my daughter was working with a group of people to get an antiracist statement from the school. There aren't more than five, six, seven kids, but still, as she said, it was about educating the white children. And she had a lot of trouble getting the word *antiracist* in. The school board kept saying, "That's too strong." [*Laughs*] "Say 'diversity.'" You say "diversity" and you sound like you had an iron and you smoothed everything out. As soon as I heard that word, I knew that it was going to be a warm iron that could just go over all the wrinkles. So even there where I'm living, the governor—who's not a bad guy, you know, he's a Republican, but the Republicans of Vermont, they're very relaxed mostly—he just didn't reappoint to the human rights commission the one black guy who was on it. So it's all white guys. It's as if you were talking about women's lives or something, and you only had men. So even there, in a place like Vermont, the lesson hasn't come through.

It's interesting, you know, if you look at television, they really have a lot of black people on television nowadays. That was a shock—since I don't have television—when I come here, I look at it. I'm astonished, really. But the black fathers all have very light wives. I mean, if I was a black person myself, personally, I would really be in a rage about that. Look at it sometime, you'll see.

Wasn't it *Cosby*? The men are black, you can see that. But the women are very light.

NF: You've said you're an optimist by nature. Have you maintained that optimism about American public education?

GP: No, I'm not optimistic in that sense. I think it's a characteristic rather than a thought-through position of any kind. It's a disposition almost—I have that kind of disposition.

NF: Well, you're friendly. It's nice.

GP: Well, I'm friendly to the world, yeah. I feel as long as people are acting in the world, there's hope. In areas like, say, the election: It didn't come out good. But the number of young people especially, who went door to door, who learned some political things. It was quite remarkable. I mean, those young people aren't going to disappear… yet.

NF: Do you have an opinion about single-sex education for women?

GP: Well, I think in general I don't like single-sex education. I think it's worse for boys than for girls, though. I think boys should not be corroborated at every turn. I taught at Sarah Lawrence for twenty-two years, so I watched it change. And the women—some of them were very powerful, and some of them were not—and some of them were aggressive and some were not—some of them were wonderful writers, strong and all that, and some were not. They ran the whole spectrum. Then the boys came. Well, the first thing that happened, in the theater: the boys began to be directors, and the girls were actors. Then the boys took over the paper for a while—I mean, whatever happened, the boys stepped in. On the other hand, there were very few, so they were in a state of constant embarrassment. But I saw that they were able to do that, and it really took a couple of years for the women to get back their power. But they did get it back. I mean, they got back a certain degree of their power.

III. VIETNAM AND CHINA

NF: Where was the "Women's House of Detention," where you were in prison for six days during the war in Vietnam?

GP: Oh, everybody knows it. It's right where the park is now.

NF: Do you remember what you did to get sentenced?

GP: We sat down in front of a military parade. I think that's what I did—I'm not sure.

NF: Were your kids curious about it?

GP: They were all for me. I have a photograph of Nora, when they're all about eleven years old or something like that. Her class from P.S. 41 right here. They all had banners of some kind—they were very into things.

NF: Writing about your trip to North Vietnam in 1969, where you went with other representatives of the peace movement to bring back prisoners of war, you say, "Of course, when you go to a foreign country where you don't know the language, you certainly can't see or hear too much 'for yourself.'" But then you say, "So if my understanding of Vietnam was imperfect, my understanding of my own country was growing daily."

GP: Oh, I said that? That was smart. [*Laughs*]

NF: I know that trip confirmed a lot of what you already thought about the American involvement in Vietnam. Were there also some surprises?

GP: You know—we don't know war. So any aspect of that is a shock. It's a great shock to see whole villages decimated. Just the sight of the women, cleaning up afterward… those things were great shocks. It really gave me such a view of these P.O.W.s, because they were all officers and they were all pilots. They were all bombers. All these P.O.W.s had really committed terrible acts.

NF: And it seemed to you that they hadn't been treated very badly, once they'd been captured?

GP: Well, I shouldn't say that, because they said that to us. They sort of described what had happened when they were captured. There were people about to tear them apart, because they'd destroyed their village. The young militia stepped in between. The anger of the people—I couldn't understand why they didn't tear them apart. Look—if it was me, if it was my little corner here of Eleventh Street, I don't know what I'd do. The reason I say that is I'm sure in many cases they succeeded in really harming those guys. The ones that I talked to described the anger of the people, but then said that people stepped in.

But what happened in prison, I don't know. If you went down and met the prisoners, and the guards, the sight was so scary because our guys were all so big. And if they were starving to death, they didn't look it. They didn't look fat—they were thin—but standing beside them were these small people, also very thin. So a thin, small person and a thin, big person, look—at one point I thought, They should have *two* small, thin people watching one big, thin person.

NF: And a lot of those guys ended up going back to flying after they were released?

GP: Well, that's what we heard, yeah. Or teaching flying. Very important things were happening that year, sixty-nine. In sixty-nine, as we were leaving, a reporter came and said, "When you go home, tell everybody that Cambodia and Laos are being bombed." And we did, but nobody listened. And then it was 1970 that I got this award from the American Academy of Arts and Letters, and a couple of guys who were getting art awards, painters, came to this very house to talk to me, and said, "You know, we have to do something. We have to speak up. We can't just sit and let them give us this stuff. We have to say something." And I said, "Yeah, I agree with you." Well, it turns out—I'm the writer, right? Well, I had to write the statement, and I had to take the statement [to the Academy]. So I was scared to death. You saw that place, right? And you saw the way it's all set up. I just remember coming in, and there was Muriel Rukeyser…

NF: I don't know her.

GP: One of the great American poets. You must read her, darling, you must. And she was sitting there, and I said, "Muriel, I'm going to say this thing." And she said, "Good!" And so I got up there, and they gave me—I forgot the name—a very lovely guy gave me this thing, a very important man, gave me this and made a statement. And I made this talk: I said, "You know, at some point institutions will have to take a position on this. Meanwhile, I understand that you can't do that right now, but certainly I can and many of the people here can." And I got such a lot of applause. And I got *such* abuse. Both. From the front, I got a lot of applause. From the seated—great men, you know—one of the guys, he actually taught at Sarah Lawrence, was screaming out, "Inappropriate! Get her off! Inappropriate!"

And they did get me off—I mean, they didn't push me or anything. They said thank you, and I walked off. But I had said it. I said thank you, and got off. And Norman Mailer in writing the history of what happened omitted that. And I felt really washed out, especially since he said that the guy who gave me the award he thought was so brave.

NF: Brave for what?

GP: After I spoke—trembling and terrified—he said, "Yes, it's true: we must not be doing this." Which is, I mean, great—it's lovely that he did it. Anyway, that's funny. Funny story.

NF: I love the story "Somewhere Else"—twenty-two Americans visit China "with politics in mind, if not in total command." You said you went to China in the '70s, right?

GP: We were invited there by China. We were called political activists, so we had a goodly number of Reds among us, you know. The one thing that neither the Chinese nor the Americans knew was that there were people with tremendous political splits in our group. I mean, they were forced to talk to each other, and never would have. There were real China guys, real Maoists a couple of them, and a couple of real Russia supporters.

And Barbara Ehrenreich was with us. She was the best. I understood what a reporter does. I mean, that was long ago—she hadn't written these books yet. She went around and she asked questions. I watched her; I was so impressed by the way she didn't let anybody off the hook. She would keep asking them these questions: "Why do you think Zhou Enlai has ruined your daily work with his political position," and so on and so forth. "In what way?" She really showed her very fine self.

NF: In that story, the characters are still "in love with the revolution and Mao Zedong"; by the time you wrote the story, would they have known more about the Cultural Revolution and everything that had happened?

GP: Well, we had to know more. I remember I went to Iowa to do a reading, and I met all these old poets who had just been released. They had been sent down to the country [during the Cultural Revolution]. And I met this guy, Wang Meng, who was very interesting, also a writer. I know him the best because I flew back in the airplane with him. He later became a cultural ambassador of some kind. He was very interested in the Uigur people; he'd been sent among them. And he became a translator with them. I just read about them now; they suddenly appeared in the newspapers, after not thinking about them at all for twenty years. But the old poets, they said, "It was all right; it was OK. We found out how the peasants lived, you know." That was their answer. But there are wonderful novels that show how terrible it was for people, to be sent down to work with peasants who didn't really want them.

NF: Did you start out with the idea that the story would happen both in China and the Bronx?

GP: No, that just happened. I just felt that I had to write about it. You know—the thing is this: if I just wrote about China, it would be a report, more or less. You have to have two stories to have a story. That's what I've been teaching my classes. You need two stories, at least. And for a novel, of course, you probably need more. I couldn't find the other story. I mean, I wasn't conscious of this; my idea that you need two stories came long after I wrote everything. I said, "Oh, that's what I was doing."

NF: You went to the Soviet Union and Vietnam in connection with your work for peace. Have you traveled much without a political task to do?

GP: [*Laughs*] Well, it's more for literary tasks now. I go to England, and Ireland—I had to read—and to France, Germany, Italy, you know.

NF: I know the stories have been published all over the world, but was there one country where you felt they gave you special attention?

GP: Well, I've been told that they love me in Japan, but they didn't invite me to come, so I feel bad. But I've done better with royalties in Japan than almost anywhere. My books do all right abroad; if I paid more attention and went over there more, it would probably be better. I should've gone to Germany not too long ago. They were studying my stuff, and I really should've gone. Even just to sell books, but…

IV. DESCRIPTION

NF: New York City is everywhere in your stories. But you don't describe it physically very much. Why?

GP: I'm not a describer. I don't know why. I just feel like it's so described—they don't need me to describe it. There are so many books with descriptions of this street or that street. Every now and then I talk about the trees on Eleventh Street, but apart from that, I really don't.

NF: You've said that the difference between a story and a novel is "the amount of space and time any decade can allow a subject and a group of characters. All this clear only in retrospect. Therefore: Be risky."

GP: OK, I'll stand by that. Whatever it means. [*Laughs*] Read it to me again!

NF: What did you mean by that in terms of your own work? Was there something about the time you started writing that made stories more natural to you than novels?

GP: Well, basically, in terms of my own work, I worked as a poet first before I wrote stories. And the short story is very close to poetry.

NF: Yours are.

GP: No, but in general, it's closer to poetry than it is to the novel. When it's too close to the novel, it's not very good. It means it's being overdeveloped or something. That's what I think. But it seemed almost natural for me to begin to write short stories after writing poems. And I tried to write a novel, and couldn't—I really couldn't stay interested in those people, and every fucking thing they did, you know? It's a very different thing, and a lot of novelists can write good short stories, but a lot of them really can't, because they can't pick the thing up. It's like poems, you just sort of pick them up in your hand… and there it is.

NF: Does it have something to do with the "wild old woman" in "One Day I Made Up a Story?" She leans out the window to shout at the street, and then closes the window to play the piano for a while. And then she opens it again.

GP: Yeah, I'm a little bit like her. I sit at the front window. Exactly—there's the piano and there's the window.

NF: Is there a conflict between writing and worrying about the world, or are those two activities complimentary?

GP: Well, they are complimentary, but you're pulled at different times. People always say, "Well, how did you balance"—you know, I didn't balance *one thing.* I mean, everything was out of balance. Totally. But sometimes the kids were the most important thing. Sometimes the writing was the most important thing, and sometimes the politics. But at the same time they were all important, and sometimes I had to go to a demonstration, or I had to write a preface—that pulls you away. And there are writers that wouldn't be pulled away, I have to admit. My husband is a writer, and he works from five-thirty until eight-thirty in the morning, every morning, and he just finished his last novel. I think it's a masculine thing, basically—he won't let anything pull him away from that. I'm glad I didn't have children with him. [*Laughs*] I mean, I'm glad I met him later.

NF: What's it like being married to another writer?

GP: I've been married to him for thirty-five years, so… hell, I like him a whole lot. I mean, I like him with my whole heart. He's published mostly by New Directions and by Johns Hopkins Press. And his short stories are so different than most people's.

NF: Are his stories pretty short?

GP: Oh—no. Not particularly. I don't think he'd do a two- or three-page story. I don't think he'd find it worthwhile. [*Laughs*]

NF: I love "Wants." I think that's my favorite of your stories.

GP: Is that the library one? That one I wrote sitting over there. [*Points in the direction of Sixth Avenue*] I mean, I was sitting on the steps of the library, and I saw this guy, and I thought he was Jess.

But he wasn't. So… I was thinking about it. I just walked home. I had that story pretty much in my head for several days, and I just sat down and wrote it.

NF: It sounds so good out loud.

GP: I love to read out loud, anytime, anywhere—anytime anyone asks me.

NF: And do you read your stuff out loud while you're working?

GP: Yes. I do. I went through a period when I didn't, and it showed.

NF: Did you make a conscious decision to switch to the first person to write "Faith in a Tree?"

GP: No. I had the first couple lines of that "Faith in a Tree" and I was thinking about it in the park—which they're now going to fuck up totally. Millions of dollars to move the circle so that it lines up with the arch. It's horrible—they want to take down the mounds, which kids loved.

NF: In "Faith in a Tree," she has a kind of political awakening on the playground, and she begins to "think more and more and every day about the world." Did you have a moment like that, or was it more gradual?

GP: It was more gradual for me. I'm not her, really. But she could be a friend of mine. I always say she works for me.

V. DEBTS

NF: You've said that you don't write your stories *to* anyone, but sometimes you write *for* someone. I think you mean telling someone else's story, in order to understand it. Is that right?

GP: Well, I think when I said that, it was early. I have a story called "Debts" and with "Debts" I felt I owed a story to my friend Lucia. I tried to be as accurate as possible, which made it very convoluted. Other stories I've written for people—my friend who was dying—a story called "Friends." I wrote it for them, not to them. Everybody thinks that they went with me to visit her, but they didn't. In "Friends," she's dying, and three friends come to visit her by train. We didn't all go together at all—but now people think we did.

NF: Your stories use very colloquial language, but they send me to the dictionary pretty often, too.

GP: Oh, really?

NF: Is there something about that combination of plain and fancy words that's important to you?

GP: Well, I love words—I love the language. It comes from poetry: every word is special. Which is hard to do in a novel, I know. But I feel that way. The wrong word is like a lie jammed inside the story.

NF: Are there some writers you've admired your whole life?

GP: I mean, my whole life… [*Laughs*]

NF: You talk about loving Eliot, and then growing not to love him—are there some others like that?

GP: Oh, I never liked him that much. I loved him less than I loved other people—much less.

NF: You loved Auden.

GP: I loved Auden, I loved Robinson Jeffers. I loved these very strange men. This work—very different from a Bronx kid. But when I was quite young I loved those insane Robinson Jeffers poems about the West Coast, you know, quite crazy.

I loved Edna St. Vincent Millay. I loved all the poets, I mean, in general. I didn't get to love Whitman for a long time. I didn't need him until much later. But then I did get to love him, too. But as for books, the wonderful books you read when you're young and they stay with you forever. When I was about eighteen or nineteen all we read was *Ulysses* by Joyce. We'd walk up and down, saying it, saying those words. But I haven't read it in a long time; I don't know if I ever will again. But I know those were important language things for me.

NF: What about Virginia Woolf?

GP: I didn't love Virginia Woolf when I was very young. I don't think I loved her until I got to be middle-aged. I didn't have a feeling for her until I was in my forties and fifties. I mean, I loved "Three Guineas"—I loved some of her political things, before I loved the novels. I loved the Russians, because they were around the house all the time. I didn't love Dostoyevsky.

NF: But Tolstoy?

GP: I loved Tolstoy. I loved Chekhov, Turgenev. I loved all of those guys. Mostly, as time went on, it was Isaac Babel I loved the best.

NF: A character in one of your stories asks his father, "If you had it all to do over again, what would you do different? Any real hot tips?" Can I ask you that?

GP: Any hot tips? [*Laughs*] The only thing you should have to do is find work you love to do. And I can't imagine living without having loved a person. A man, in my case. It could be a woman, but whatever. I think, what I always tell kids when they get out of class and ask, "What should I do now?" I always say, "Keep a low overhead. You're not going to make a lot of money." And the next thing I say: "Don't live with a person who doesn't respect your work." That's the most important thing—that's more important than the money thing. I think those two things are very valuable pieces of information. ✯

ALEXANDRA ROCKINGHAM

TALKS WITH

ORHAN PAMUK

"GOD ONLY WHISPERS TO REAL POETS, GENUINELY POSSESSED. I WAITED AND WAITED AND WAITED. NOTHING CAME. OK, HE'S NOT TELLING ME ANYTHING. LET ME IMAGINE, WHAT WOULD HE TELL ME IF HE WHISPERED?"

Characters in Orhan Pamuk novels:
An Italian scholar who becomes a slave
A blind miniaturist painter in sixteenth-century Turkey
A poet murdered, possibly, by a political extremist
A biographer attempting to woo the ex-girlfriend of a poet murdered, possibly, by a political extremist

Orhan Pamuk is the author of nine books—to date, six have been translated into English: The White Castle, The New Life, The Black Book, My Name Is Red, Snow, *and, most recently,* Istanbul. *His novels address the nature of faith, God, representation and image-making, the politics of Turkey, nationalism, and love. Perhaps most notable, though, is his exploration of sensitive and pressing questions surrounding Islam and the conflation of "East" and "West." Nowhere else than Turkey are these questions so manifest in everyday life, and now, thanks to Pamuk, they are alive not only in the literature but in the public discourse as well. In an interview with a Swiss newspaper in February*

2005, he uttered a single phrase, "One million Armenians had been killed in these lands and hardly anyone ever talks about it except me." Pamuk was charged under Penal Code Article 301/1 for "publicly denigrating Turkish identity," which usually carries a penalty of imprisonment of six months to three years; because the statement was made in a foreign country, if he were convicted, his prison term would be increased by one-third.

The trial of Orhan Pamuk in Istanbul on December 16, 2005, was bedlam: "marked by constant shouting and scuffling, turning violent at times," PEN observers reported. It was packed with foreign diplomats, representatives of the European Parliament, Turkish intelligentsia, and international observers from various freedom-of-expression groups. Confrontations and heckling were commonplace both inside and outside the courtroom. Nationalists lining the streets hurled insults at attendees as they left the building, and Pamuk's car was pelted with eggs.

The government eventually dropped the case, citing a legal technicality. But it is assumed by most observers the charges against Pamuk were dismissed in order not to undermine Turkey's chances of accession to the European Union. Although he is only one of more than a dozen writers, journalists, and publishers currently being prosecuted in Turkey (in the past year PEN has monitored more than sixty such cases) it's startling that a single freedom-of-expression trial could have such a profound effect.

I met Pamuk at his office in Cihangir, two months before he uttered the infamous phrase. High on the fourth floor, his desk heaved with papers and books. The rounded dome of a mosque loomed just outside the window, its Turkish crescent a cardboard cutout on the distant backdrop of the Bosporus.

—Alexandra Rockingham (Winter 2005)

I. BLINDNESS

ALEXANDRA ROCKINGHAM: I read in a May 1997 *New York Times* interview that you take off your glasses to write. Is that still true?

ORHAN PAMUK: I think now I have… bipolar, they say?

AR: Um… bifocal.

OP: Yes, bifocal, I'm sorry. Bifocal glasses... but most of the time, yes, as I write, I take them off because the habit has stayed with me, and in fact, without glasses, my face can get closer to the paper—which is a nice feeling.

AR: So when your face gets closer to the paper—

OP: That means the outside world is closed. You follow what your hand is doing, you are reading and re-reading, and even if I raise my eyes from the page, the rest of the world is blurry—which is good. Then after a while, I put on my glasses, and that's why they're broken. [*He gestures to the joint where the arm meets the lenses*] Because I do this most of the time. [*Laughs as he pulls off his glasses with a twisting motion*]

AR: When I read that you took your glasses off to write I thought it had to do with the fact that, in your books, there's always something describing art-making where, for example, in *My Name Is Red* [an ersatz murder mystery set in the sixteenth-century court of the Ottoman sultan], the best painters, the best of the master miniaturists, are the blind ones.

OP: Yes, OK. But for me the eternal joy of being in this world may be best represented in the joys of seeing. In all my childhood I was terrorized by the idea of going blind. I don't think this is a unique fear, but whenever I saw a blind man in the street I would try to put myself in his place. Ninety percent of the time they were men, because blind men were at least allowed to go out into the street to beg. In my childhood I saw lots of begging men in the street—whether really blind or not, it didn't matter.

But also, to be bored in life was, for me, to have nothing interesting to see. I remember going to my mother's barber, and she told me: "Just sit here for half an hour, OK?" And you just look around and there's nothing to find. You want to see something, but it's all empty walls. You just want to commit suicide.

Movies are about seeing for me, not about stories. Sometimes as I watch a movie I forget the story. This used to happen with my wife, who later realized that I'm not an idiot; I just follow the image and then follow my own story, you know, just staring [*his jaw hanging open*], not necessarily because the film is boring or slow. And then occasionally I would say, "So what's happening?" And she would say, "Don't you understand?" [*Laughs*]

AR: I know exactly what you're talking about. But then that's very interesting because—in *Snow,* for example, there's a phrase where you say, "a poem has arrived," and it's like a mystical experience, or it comes from God—

OP: Whatever. Hmm. God or Coleridge. [*Laughs*] Yeah.

AR: And making art, writing or painting, in your books, seems to be something that has to come from outside of a person. Like the way, in *Snow,* the main character, Ka, returns from exile in Frankfurt. He travels to Kars, in eastern Turkey, to research the suicide of the Islamist head-scarf girls, and he is beset by poems. And being blind and having painted for fifty years, the miniaturists in *My Name Is Red* are now able to do really good work. It's not that they're able to paint an earthly, normal horse well, but that they're able to paint what God intended when he created the horse. Is it that you believe that, in order to make good work, an artist needs to be somehow blinded?

OP: No. No. In fact, as you say, behind that blindness lies so many years of labor. Those painters in *My Name Is Red* are able to draw when they're blind because, now that they have given thirty years to drawing the same horse, without their will or decision or their personal intended energy, even their hands have now memorized the beautiful thing. They can do it almost without any self-involvement. The implication is that art is also about craftsmanship, learning the technique, lots of repetition, and mastering an image. The time they have devoted to mastering just one line or one figure is so great that even if they don't see, they are now gifted with God's vision. Now that they are masters they can turn out their vision inside their heads.

And the relation of this with, say, Ka, is that he spent so much frustrating time not being able to write poetry, which was also a sort of a refining of his soul or his intellect. When it finally comes, it's not something that he acquired for nothing. When God's grace, so to speak, fell on him, it was because he gave—again, just like my painters—so much time and so much spiritual energy and agony to be a good poet. So I don't think it's essentially about blindness. Blindness is perhaps a stage, or a situation that may refer to perfection. But at first you have to give your labor, or your time, your devotion to art. That is essential. That is what I think.

AR: But when Ka's poems come to him there's mockery in your tone.

OP: Yes.

AR: Mockery of the inspired moment.

OP: I am aware that the reader will be aware that, just as you say, nothing of this sort can ever happen. No poem will come as it is described by Coleridge, which, we can guess, is probably a lie. But I don't trust my own authority to convince the reader, so I refer back to Coleridge. This mannerism is not mine but Coleridge's—it lies at the heart of Western Romantic poetry—that you're almost possessed by the poem, then it comes, and if you make a mistake it disappears—so fragile, so graceful, and so wonderful. So Ka is doing a bit of a mechanical reproduction of Coleridge's more genuine act, because in Coleridge there is something genuine. Even inventing that lie—it is an elegant lie—is as important as the poem itself. A sort of frame for the poet which says, "God talked to me."

II. A BOYISH RIVALRY

AR: Your books often examine the interaction between the realm of art and ideas and the realm of action. For example, in *Snow,* a murderous coup staged by a theater troup during a live broadcast of their politically inflammatory play—a coup de theatre, as you call it—is undermined by the absurdity of the situation. Even to use the term *coup de theatre* says a great deal, probably, about your opinion of Turkish politics and the various coups that have occurred here over the last several decades, and possibly about political action or even action in general. Is there something you can say about how action and ideas—

OP: Well, I just want to interrupt you and say I'm a bookish person. To make a point about these references you're making, my bookishness should be admitted. I should confess it. And then the Cartesian distinction between life and mind, between the perceiving and seeing and categorizing mind and the rest of human experience, and creating a strong boundary between them, which lies at the heart of positivistic Cartesian post-Renaissance Western thought beginning from, say, the seventeenth century, is, of course, another strong bookish invention. Bookish people feel comfortable when there is a boundary line between the life of the mind and the life of the body, whether obviously or in a hidden way, which is, of course, artificial. I may be that kind of person.

AR: In the end it does seem that you give the last word to art.

OP: Yes. Of course. We are in the world of the text. When you're writing a book or when you're producing a painting, you're addressing people who've chosen that work. And you know that it's a minority—no matter how popular your books are, you belong to a sort of… almost a sort of a religious minority. And in the long run we all go there, to books, for a sort of a consolation, along with some joy. We need books or paintings—I never refer to music because I'm stupid in that—because we need to be consoled. And of course, the fact that we go to the imaginary is also related to the fact that this real world—maybe the distinction is also false—is not satisfying enough.

AR: And art usually, or often, prefigures something which happens in the world of the book. In your books life often imitates art.

OP: Not all the time.

AR: But quite often.

OP: I can't make that kind of generalization about my books, you know. If you make them, I am titillated and turned around by your observations. But if you continue to make these kinds of general statements about my work, I'm a bit disturbed. I don't want to say yes or no, because that's not what I do for myself.

AR: *Snow* is almost like a Platonic dialogue about the nature of faith, God, political action, Islam…

OP: *Snow* is also about the distinction between being a poet, and a novelist or prose writer. The tradition here in Turkey is that the poet is the person through whom God speaks. *That* is the art. *That* is the thing that you should be inborn with. That *is* the prestigious and glorious thing. While fiction writing—at least it used to be, maybe it's changing—was seen as more of a sort of journalism or craftsmanship. Most of the Ottoman statesmen, and some of the sultans and rulers, one out of three, would be poets. They would create their collection of poetry in order to prove that they were a distinguished person, educated. So in *Snow,* there is a sort of rivalry between the poet and the prose writer. Of course, a very boyish rivalry. Good friends, Ka and Orhan, the poet and the prose writer…

AR: Because Orhan turns up in *Snow.* Orhan is a character writing a book about his friend, the poet Ka, who is murdered, possibly by a political Islamist. So Orhan, we learn, has followed in Ka's footsteps to try to research the book about him. Even going so far as to try to fall in love with Ipek, the woman with whom Ka was determined to fall in love—

OP: Yes. Orhan, who I sometimes jokingly say has his revenge on his character, the poet Ka, who is dead. Orhan even attempts to get his girl! [*Laughing*] A very bad guy! My Kurdish, old-fashioned, pre-modern friends, after they read *Snow,* say, "Orhan, how can you flirt with your dead friend's girlfriend, or make a pass at your dead friend's girlfriend? How can you?!" [*Laughing more*] They seriously said this. Suspicious of me! [*Laughing really hard*]

But anyway, there is that kind of boyish rivalry there. In fact, my joke about poetry is a sort of a defense, an idea that runs between the lines of *Snow*—that I also wanted to write poetry but God did not whisper anything to me. God only whispers to real poets, genuinely possessed. I waited and waited and waited. Nothing came. OK, he's not telling me anything. Let me imagine, what would he tell me if he whispered? So I begin to imagine. And the things that I imagined and wrote down are my novels. [*Laughing still*] God's not whispering anything, but at least I'm *imagining* that he is whispering, and writing *that* down. This is what he would have told me if he whispered. Here it is, sir. Here are my novels. Read them. [*Laughter*]

AR: In *My Name Is Red,* Black takes off to the east of Anatolia, as a young man, and comes back ready to begin his story. Even in your book, which is—well, Turkey is "East" in my worldview—but even in your book set in Turkey, "the East" functions as the wilderness, as the place where the characters go to find themselves and endure suffering—

OP: I'll tell you something. I have just come back from Japan, China, Hong Kong, Taipei. And you know what they say? This is very peculiar... No one thinks his country is completely East. In China, they say, "Yes, Mr. Pamuk, we have the same East/West question here." They think that they are also torn between the East and the West, the way we are here in Turkey. They don't consider themselves in China or in Tokyo completely "East." They think that they have some part of the "West" and "East," you see? No one, except some few British, and some Americans—maybe some

French—think that they are totally Western. [*Laughs*] And no one—this is maybe more surprising—thinks of themselves as thoroughly Eastern. Where is West in China? Or Tokyo? They have an abundance of West in themselves. And they will tell you this, and then they will smile—knowing the strangeness of it. There is no place, perhaps, in humanity, where the subject considers himself completely Eastern.

AR: That's very interesting. What does that tell us?

OP: I don't know. I don't want to go into it. Let me enjoy the poetry of this—the strangeness of it—first. Let's not try to understand it.

III. "THE DESIRE TO COMMUNICATE KILLS MY SPIRIT."

AR: What about doppelgangers? I love the way you articulate it in *Snow,* as somebody who thinks your own thoughts.

OP: Yes, yes… or thinks the same thing at the same time.

AR: The relationship between the two young political Islamists, the two boys, Necip and Fazil, who thought the same thing at the same time, was very touching. And actually, in *The White Castle,* the relationship between the two main characters, Hoja, the master, and the Italian scholar, who is captured and becomes his slave—that relationship, surprisingly, becomes very moving. They become so intimate that their identities merge and are finally exchanged. Master and slave. And it's—

OP: Almost, sometimes, implying bordering homosexuality, right?

AR: No, I don't…

OP: Good. I'm pleased that you're not saying that. All the male readers say: "Well, you know, Orhan, are you gay?" They love this kind of approach. I'm pleased that you're not focusing on the eroticism… But probably the boyish wishfulness as I wrote these things is this: the delight or fantasy of effortless, cheap communication. I have never, in my life, managed to have a good, fully developed intellectual friendship with anyone, I confess.

AR: Oh no…

OP: Don't say, "Oh no." I don't think many people achieve that either. [*Both laugh*] When I was twenty I read André Gide's journal. Maybe I'll bring… [*Pamuk leaves the office for the other small library room in the flat. His voice grows fainter and fainter as he goes down the hallway.*] I'm sorry! I'm coming… [*He returns a moment later with the book.*] This is selections from his… someplace, I think at the beginning, should have… [*Searching for the passage*] He says something: "I should not talk with the others… the desire to communicate kills my spirit." [*Long pause*] "I destroy my best thoughts trying to communicate and share them with others, when I tell them in conversation." [*Long pause*] These are things that stayed with me from the early journals of André Gide. Wait… here it comes…

AR: What?

[*Pamuk sits gripping his armchair in silence. Suddenly the call to prayer blasts out of the minarets just outside his window, blaring so loudly it's not possible to speak. We listen to the entire call to prayer, which ends eventually with the screeching click of the speakers being turned off.*]

AR: It's strange… I wanted to ask if there was anything you had written in *Snow* which might be dangerous or cause trouble for you… It deals so deeply with Islam… But now, I don't think I will.

OP: Good. ✯

ALEC MICHOD

TALKS WITH

RICHARD POWERS

"THE BRAIN IS THE ULTIMATE STORYTELLING MACHINE, AND CONSCIOUSNESS IS THE ULTIMATE STORY."

The uses of narrative:
The sensuous derangement of familiarity
Escape from the straightjacket of the self
The rearrangement of one's viscera
Deliverance from certainty
Good medicine

The enigmatic and prodigious brainiac novelist Richard Powers tries to avoid flying, so when it comes time to visit his mother in Arizona, as he does at least once a year, he sometimes drives, normally overnight, from his home in central Illinois. Making his annual trek seven years ago, Powers was driving through central Nebraska near sunset when he became captivated not by another Gas 'n Go roadside attraction, but by a carpet of sandhill cranes, three feet tall, spreading in all directions over a barren field alongside Interstate 80. "I thought I was hallucinating from highway hypnosis," he says now, "and I almost drove off the road."

The Echo Maker, *which won the 2006 National Book Award, tells the story of Mark Schluter, a twenty-seven-year-old meatpacker whose truck careers off an "arrow-straight" Nebraskan country road into a ditch on the banks of the Platte River. Mark recovers slowly from a fourteen-day coma only to learn later that he suffers from Capgras syndrome, a rare neurological disorder that leads him to believe that the woman who visits him every day in his hospital room claiming to be his sister Karin is, in fact, an impostor. The only person Mark seems to believe, for a while at least, is the famous neurologist and best-selling author Gerald Weber, whom Karin convinces to fly to the flatland to examine her brother. As Mark (kind of) gets better, Weber begins to disintegrate. It's highly intricate and complex, but Powers juggles his manifold narrative threads with ease—as much a philosophical meditation on the mysteries of the brain as an emotional plea about the environment. Best of all,* The Echo Maker*'s a page-turner that finds its forty-nine-year-old creator as comfortable in the trenches of neuroscience as he's previously been writing about molecular biology (in* The Gold Bug Variations*), artificial intelligence (in* Galatea 2.2*), and virtual reality (in* Plowing the Dark*).*

I first met Richard Powers in the summer of 1998 at a bookstore in Oak Park, Illinois, which happens to be the hometown of Ernest Hemingway and not far from where Powers was born. At the time, he was on the first book tour of his career, in support of his novel Gain*. Though never a recluse in the Pynchon vein, Powers hadn't done much press and rarely granted interviews for his first five novels. (In fact, after the publication of his debut novel,* Three Farmers on Their Way to a Dance*, he moved to the Netherlands to write his next two books; his fourth book was written while in residence at the University of Cambridge.) I don't know what I expected, but it probably had something to do with disheveled clothing and unkempt hair—and almost certainly a stammer. The real Richard Powers, however, was a charming and amiable, smartly dressed fellow who spoke in person as he wrote in prose—in beautiful, intricate sentences, paragraphs at a time.*

These days, Powers is a professor at his alma mater, the University of Illinois. Because of his academic commitments—or maybe because he's newly married and perfectly at home in Champaign-Urbana—Powers didn't tour in support of The Echo Maker, *so this interview was conducted almost entirely via email, one question at a time, starting in mid-July. Which, after all, seems appropriate, since Powers wrote* The Echo Maker *on a tablet PC using voice recognition software. "I've always wanted the freedom to be completely disembodied when I'm writing," he has said, "to feel as if I'm in a pure compositional state."*

—Alec Michod (Winter 2006)

ALEC MICHOD: The first thing that struck me reading *The Echo Maker* was that it's filled with a lot of high-level neuroscience, yet the sentences never feel overburdened by the science behind the story. How did you resist the urge to cram the book with all your research?

RICHARD POWERS: Since *The Echo Maker* is about the intuitive and emotional foundation of cognition, I'm especially pleased to hear that the book's intellect and emotion felt fused to you. We often assume that novels of ideas and novels of character are mutually exclusive. My entire writing life, I've wanted to suggest that all novels are to some degree both and that some novels try to erase that artificial boundary in order to show the links between thinking and feeling. We're all driven by hosts of urges, some chaotic and Dionysian, some formal and Apollonian. The need for knowledge is as passionate as any other human obsession. And the wildest of obsessions has its hidden structure. Our theories about the world are deeply emotional, to us. Voiced idea *is* character.

My books have all tried to explore different ways of connecting past and present, fact and fiction, induction and intuition, essay and narrative. Each book has tried to hybridize those disparate elements in different ways. *The Gold Bug Variations,* with its themes of pattern-making and pattern-breaking, was necessarily a highly structured, idea-crazy book, although hopped-up with sexual desire. *The Time of Our Singing,* on the other hand, with its concerns of race, cultural ownership, and individual identity, was necessarily more character- and story-driven, although underpinned by a formal, musical structure.

From the start, *The Echo Maker* was a departure for me, with regard to storytelling. The gist of the plot hit me long before I sensed the general theme: a twenty-seven-year-old slaughterhouse worker suffers an accident and descends into a world of doublings, imposture, and estrangement. This plot slowly broadened into a story of how the brain cobbles up a highly provisional and improvised sense of self, one that, completely makeshift, still feels solid and continuous from "inside," even when we are completely dismantled by outside experience. One part of this story needed to dramatize a glimpse of all the new, accelerating discoveries in neuroscience about how the brain works. But even more importantly, from the viewpoint of its protagonists, the story itself had to unfold *inside* the maelstrom of what Antonio Damasio calls "the feeling of what happens." Such a plunge from the empirical to the emotional felt exactly right, given the deep, tangled networks of primitive processes that consciousness floats on.

My solution was to make the book itself a tangled network, to make every theory about the self—from sophisticated neuropsychology to old folk descriptions—part of some distinct character's arsenal for surviving the world and keeping his or her own precarious sense of self intact. So all the scientific material that I researched for a couple of years—the endlessly bizarre and frightening neuropathology that initially structures the story—became just one jumping-off point for treating the characters' private hopes, terrors, and beliefs. Brain science launched the book's plot events, provided material causes, and shaped the characters' conscious understanding of their crises. But neurology is just the start of those narratives that collide against each other in the larger narrative arc. Most of the resulting story (like most of the brain) is really subterranean.

The hardest part about doing the research for this book was hitting on an appropriate way to bury it. It takes 100 billion interconnected cells to conjure up a coherent story of the world. But if neuroscience concludes anything, it's that sensing and feeling and thinking and perceiving and hundreds of other seemingly separate processes are all conjoined in a huge, dynamic, and continuously revised narrative network. The brain is the ultimate storytelling machine, and consciousness is the ultimate story. Our neurons tell our selves into being. So any novel on the subject clearly had to tuck that insight back into a similar, self-narrating network.

For the first year of working on this book, I read as much about neural impairment and deficit as I could find, sometimes venturing downward into neuronal and synaptic chemistry, sometimes rising into higher speculations about integrated consciousness. A lot of the reading revolved around case histories. At the same time as I read the technical material, I began to develop a very intuitive, primal sense of my central characters. During the second year of work, I composed scenes and unfolded a plot, while continuing to read a lot of associated neurological material, although that reading was much more directed now by the specific needs of my characters and their actions. The research continued for the following eighteen months as I revised the initial drafts. Only now, I was reading the science not only to continue refining and verifying details but also because I'd become addicted.

In this way, I stumbled toward a form that would embody all the processes at the core of the brain's story-making. Mark Schluter suffers an accident that disastrously unhinges his cognitive processes from his emotional intelligence. At the same time, Dr. Gerald Weber, the cognitive neurologist who comes out to study Mark, begins to sense things with his emotional intelligence that his cognitive processes have previously hidden from him. Ultimately, the science gets absorbed into the stories the characters desperately tell about themselves and each other…

AM: If *The Echo Maker* has a guiding spirit, it's the cranes—cranes haunt the characters in your novel, but they also are woven into the structure of the story. What about the Nebraskan cranes appealed to you? Do they figure prominently in the neuropsychological literature or something?

RP: In fact, "echo maker" is the Ojibwa-Anishinabe name for the sandhill crane. My obsession with the primitive processes that underpin cognition began when I discovered these birds. I wasn't able to tell a sandhill from a stork until spring, seven years ago. I was making the long drive from Illinois to Arizona, where my mother lives. I'd been driving for a full day and was passing through central Nebraska near sunset, when I looked out into a barren field along the side of Interstate 80 and saw this carpet of birds, three feet tall, spreading in all directions. I thought I was hallucinating from highway hypnosis, and I almost drove off the road.

The sight was absolutely thrilling, partly because I didn't know what I was looking at and partly because the gathering was just so primordial. They really did look like some prehistoric remnant, something absolutely indifferent to human time.

I pulled off at the next town—Kearney—and got a room at a motel along the interstate. Asking around, I discovered that half a million birds—80 percent of every migratory crane in North America—staged on this short section of the Platte every March, like clockwork, as part of a migration that could cover thousands of miles. I got up before dawn the next morning to watch the morning ritual—the city of birds dispersing for a day of foraging. The experience was as spiritual as anything I've ever felt: these huge bipeds dancing and singing in an enormous, weirdly intelligent, communal act.

I began reading everything I could about the birds. It's a long and haunting literature, with lots of great prose by writers from Peter Matthiessen and Aldo Leopold all the way back to the ancient Greeks. I learned that cranes mate for life, that a crane will sacrifice itself for its young, that they learn by example how to fly across an entire continent, that they navigate the route by very particular local landmarks, and that they are largely solitary, until this annual gathering. I began traveling to see them—up to Wisconsin and over to the Jasper-Pulaski preserve in Indiana, where greater sandhills will stop in the late fall on their way south.

And I began seeing representations of cranes everywhere I traveled, from Central Europe to Japan.

Cranes became eerily human to me, and at the same time, totally alien. I wasn't surprised to discover stories in different folk literatures about cranes and people turning back and forth into each other. Later, when I first heard about Capgras syndrome, and how its sufferers fail to recognize only those people closest to them (while having no trouble at all recognizing everyone else), something clicked, some story about familiarity and strangeness, and the book started to take shape in me.

By then, I had become an amateur birder, learning basic identification and starting a life list. I began thinking completely differently about other species, and began paying attention to creatures that had been largely invisible to me. And in one of those confirming coincidences, as I read deeper into contemporary brain research, I learned just how smart birds really are. Apparently, for a long time, science has greatly underestimated the intelligence of birds, partly because the cerebral cortex of birds is relatively small. But it turns out that birds use an entirely different part of their brain as the seat of their intelligence, and the brain-to-body ratio of the most intelligent birds is comparable to higher primates'. Birds have elaborate social behavior, and they display lots of discriminating intelligence about clans and pecking orders. Hunting birds can cooperate with each other. Birds can even be deliberately deceptive—in other words, they are smart enough to be able to lie. Recent work on bird calls suggests something like grammatical structure. Alex, the famous blue parrot, seems able to make simple but meaningful and appropriate sentences. There's an astonishing short film that you can hunt down on the web of this New Caledonian crow, Betty, who actually creates a hook by bending a straight piece of wire, then uses the hook to lift a cup of food out of a hole. That's true toolmaking, something we used to think only primates did.

So here we are, sharing the planet with these creatures who are weirdly intelligent, smart in an alien way that we're not quite smart enough to see. And yet, the core parts of their brains are still contained in ours. Our estrangement from them, then, struck me as somehow analogous to our estrangement from our own subcortical selves. Setting the story in this little town in the middle of nowhere, whose central claim to fame was this annual massing of birds, gave me a way to open up the story to all kinds of neurological and ecological traces.

AM: Landscape too plays a huge part in *The Echo Maker*—more, perhaps, than it has in any of your other books, with the possible exception of *Gain*. Yet it's not just "this little town in the middle of nowhere" and its environs—it's not just the Nebraskan prairie—but, more importantly, the imperfect labyrinth of consciousness against which Mark and Karin and Dr. Weber are all graphed. Can you talk about the role "place"—be it the Midwest or the medial cortex—plays in your work, particularly in this book?

RP: Place has been important to me before in other stories, but never quite like it was for this one. I think you've put your finger on the reason: the book is about memory and recognition, but those mental skills are themselves deeply linked to the brain's spatial abilities. The hippocampus—that portion of the brain that orchestrates the formation of new memories—seems to have developed in large part as a way of mastering place. Animals with the greatest navigational requirements also have the most developed memory. If I can return to my bird obsession for a moment: a Clark's nutcracker, which possesses a well-developed hippocampus, can remember more than five thousand separate places where it hid seeds the year before. Remember that the next time you can't find your car keys.

Some neuroscientists have even proposed that the hippocampus may have originated as a processor of relations in space, a "spatial cognition machine," as it's been called. In some strange way, our capacity to form and retrieve memories—and with it, our ability to shape stories and construct a sense of self—may be a happy by-product of our sense of orientation. (Think of all the mnemonic systems that involve fortifying memories by placing items in an imaginary "memory walk.") Social intelligence—our ability to calculate and analyze complex interpersonal relations—may also be related to our spatial sense. Even our social vocabulary reflects that connection, when we talk about who's in and who's out, who's up and who's down, who's at the center and who's marginalized. For that matter, our vocabulary for the elements of storytelling itself is also highly spatial: exposition, situation, plot, reverse, arrival...

If stories about recognition and memory rightfully begin as stories of place, my story about Capgras quickly homed in on one particular spot out of the entire possible map. Kearney, Nebraska, is close to the geographical center of the United States, although it's probably close to the edges of terra incognita in many readers' mental landscapes. More importantly for my story, the town sits right on the crosshairs of two intersecting migratory corridors. On one axis, it lies on or near the great historical American east-to-west routes: Oregon Trail, Mormon Trail, Pony Express, transcontinental railroad, Lincoln Highway, Interstate 80. And on the other, it lies on the choke point of the Central Flyway, that continent-size hourglass used by hundreds of millions of migratory birds, with its narrow waist lying along a sixty-mile stretch of the Platte.

So all of these creatures who are navigating north and south through the changing seasons cross paths with humans—the animal perpendicular to everything—in this town of thirty thousand people. This town has completely shaped the mental imagination of Mark Schluter as well as his sister Karin, who has spent her entire life trying to escape it. Kearney is also the complete antithesis of the New York of Dr. Gerald Weber, the cognitive neurologist who comes out to examine Mark, only to discover, in this colossal emptiness—the Great American Desert—a foil for his own geographical estrangement, post-9/11.

I worked much more visually for this book than I ordinarily do, and I had great pleasure visiting the landscape of central

Nebraska, and inhabiting it again later, in memory. I even took to sketching scenes and situations, mapping out their locales—trying to come closer to a spatial sense of the story's secret, internal logic. In fact, the mystery elements of the plot—what actually happens to Mark on the night of his accident—depend on a working out of very local, specific events in time and space, and that kind of physical triangulation and cartography was something entirely new for me.

Geography may be destiny, but Kearney and the Platte, like every place else on earth, have been virtualized—completely transformed by broadband and its networked bits. The book explores that derangement too: the total defamiliarization of place in the digital age. Beyond that, the story also circles around the underpinning ecological question of who owns this long river that flows through three separate arid states. What happens when faraway, upstream water use forever changes life downstream? Who gets to drink from the limited flow? Do other creatures merit a share?

For me, the prairie-crossroads setting of the book ultimately became a material emblem for the provisional, distributed, improvised, even fictive nature of the self. If space is the field for memory, and if memory is the basis of our narrative self-invention, then we must live in some seam between inside and outside, some corridor between the place we make and the place that makes us. That's why I went to this crossroads, the empty, remote center of the Great American Desert.

AM: I want to ask about the place of the novelist in today's "Great American Desert"—where does this "seam between inside and outside" exist with respect to the novelist, post-9/11? I'm thinking particularly about the loosely Oliver Sacks–ian character of Dr. Gerald Weber, who undergoes profound transformations once he starts "treating" Mark. There's a huge mystery here—maybe even the mystery of the entire book—and I'm wondering if it has more to do with what it means to be a writer than it might at first seem.

RP: If Weber is like Sacks (or Ramachandran, Feinberg, Damasio, Broks, Gazzaniga, or any of the other outstanding writers of narrative neuropsychology), it's only in his attempt to locate, inside empirical clinical description, the same kind of empathetic leap that lies at the heart of fiction. Story is the mind's way of molding a seeming whole from out of the messiness of the distributed, modular brain. At the same time, shared stories are the only way anyone has for escaping the straightjacket of self. Good medicine has always depended on listening to histories. So any attempt to comprehend the injured mind naturally inclines toward all the devices of classic storytelling. Neurological case histories exist in a hybrid place between descriptive science and reflective art, a halfway place much like the narrated self's.

Many brain-injured people suffer from anosognosia—the total lack of awareness of any symptoms. When Weber comes to examine Mark, that's just what he finds: a man completely unable to see how his accident has changed him, who insists, rather, that something has changed in everyone around him, something that no one will tell him about. But Weber's examination occurs just at the moment in his own career when readers of his work have begun to accuse him of exploitation. The public has begun to claim that Weber has failed in precisely the kind of compassion that he has always prided himself on and that his work has always professed. And in his scrupulous attempt to understand Mark without turning the man into a self-serving story, Weber makes a frightening empathetic leap: if Mark still feels familiar to himself inside, despite all outward evidence to the contrary, how reliable is Gerald Weber's own sense of internal consistency and decency, in the face of the chorus of outside reappraisal?

Once you lose the bias that exempts you from the shortfalls you can see so easily in others, you also lose any internal authority for restoring your sense of solidity. After years of trying to see others from the inside, Weber at last commits to seeing himself from the outside. The effect on the neuroscientist is as totally estranging as Mark's brain damage. Emotional kinship—true empathy—is a bottomless well.

But weirdly, that act of bottomless, estranging kinship is probably the main goal of reading and writing novels. We read to escape ourselves and become someone else, at least for a little while. Fiction is one long, sensuous derangement of familiarity through altered point of view. How would you recognize your world if it wasn't yours? What might you look and feel like if you weren't you? We can survive the disorientation; we even love immersing ourselves in it, so long as the trip is controllable and we can return to our own lives when the book ends. Fiction plays on that overlap between self-composure and total, alien bewilderment, and it navigates by estrangement. As the pioneer neuropsychologist A. R. Luria once wrote, "To find the soul it is necessary to lose it." To read another's story, you have to lose yours.

The prevailing explanation for Capgras posits some kind of disconnect between high-level, cognitive recognition and low-level, emotional ratification: *She looks and acts and talks and behaves like my sister, but I'm just not getting that sister* feel *from her.* (Perhaps that explains why sufferers fail to affirm only those from whom they expect a deep sense of connection.) And simply by caring for Mark, Weber suffers that same estranging disconnection. In effect, you could say he contracts contagious Capgras.

Estrangement seems to have become the baseline condition for life in terrorized America. After November 2000, after September 2001, after the PATRIOT Act and the detainee bill, after Gitmo and Abu Ghraib, our stories—public and private—keep scrambling to keep America whole, continuous, and coherent, to *place* it. The basic outline of life here still looks familiar. But for a lot of people, the place no longer feels recognizable.

It seems to me that evil—the word of the hour, again—might be the willful destruction of empathy. Evil is the refusal to see oneself in others.

I truly don't know what role the novelist can play in a time of rising self-righteousness and escalating evil. Any story novelists create to reflect life accurately will now have to be improvised, provisional, and bewildered. But I do know that when I read a particularly moving and achieved work of fiction, I feel myself succumbing to all kinds of contagious rearrangement. Only inhabiting another's story can deliver us from certainty.

AM: The stories you inhabit have been packaged as novels, yet many novelists of your generation also publish essay collections or memoirs. I find that interesting. Is there a reason you haven't published a nonfiction book? What does fiction do that other kinds of writing can't?

RP: I've published a handful of nonfiction shorter pieces over the years, not to mention a trilogy of Borges-like fictitious essays (factitious stories?) that are neither fish nor fowl. I suppose I have a small volume's worth of short pieces by now, but these days, when existing print and digital versions of everything circulate so freely, collating and publishing these pieces as a separate volume (a form they weren't really conceived for) seems superfluous. I do have a topic for a contribution to Norton's terrific Great Discoveries series that I'd love to get to before I die. I have several ideas for volume-length meditations (for instance, an aesthetic and narratological look at computer coding), but the impulse to write fiction has never abated long enough for me to consider any of these nonfiction projects seriously. Memoir? That would require way too much imagination for me!

Neuroscience has recently turned up evidence for these extraordinary circuits in the brain populated with "mirror neurons." These things fire both when we perform an action and when we merely see someone else perform the same action. Other experiments suggest astonishing evidence that doing and imagining share the same circuitry. The primary visual cortex requires more blood when we merely imagine a scene than when we actually see it. Heart rates rise in subjects told to imagine running. Subjects who merely visualize physical exercise over an extended period can gain two thirds as much muscle strength as those who actually perform the same exercises. So fiction may be a far more potent thing than we think. Natural selection must have favored a love for fiction. Clearly, it has some survival value! Life is a complex and dangerous enterprise. Of course we're going to love taking the thing out for a spin on a completely safe practice track where we can try out any threatening or thrilling maneuver whatsoever, without any consequence except experience.

But our need for fiction also betrays a desire for kinds of knowing that nonfiction can't easily reach. Nonfiction can assert; fiction can show asserters, and show what happens when assertions crash. Fiction can focalize and situate worldviews, pitching different perspectives and agendas against each other, linking beliefs to their believers, reflecting facts through their interpreters and interpreters through their facts. Fiction is a spreading, polysemous, relational network that captures the way that we and our worlds create each other. Whenever the best nonfiction really needs to persuade or clarify, it resorts to story.

A chemist can say how atoms bond. A molecular biologist can say how a mutagen disrupts a chemical bond and causes a mutation. A geneticist can identify a mutation and develop a working screen for it. Clergy and ethicists can debate the social consequences of preimplantation genetic diagnosis. A journalist can interview two parents in a Chicago suburb who are wrestling with their faith while seeking to bear a child free of inheritable disease. But only a novelist can put all these actors and dozens more into the shared story they all tell, and make that story rearrange some readers' viscera.

Something truly interesting is happening in many basic sciences, a real revolution in human knowing. For a long time—centuries—empiricism has tried to understand the whole in terms of its isolated parts, and then to write out precise and simple rules about the controlled behavior of those parts in isolation. In recent decades, with the explosion of the life sciences and with a new appreciation in physics and chemistry of emergent and complex systems, a new kind of holism has emerged. Researchers, coming up against the limits of old-style reductionism while studying large, dynamic systems, have found that the whole can sometimes best be understood in terms of the whole. New attempts to describe richly interacting real-world phenomena have turned increasingly to complex models and simulations as valid scientific tools.

But that's the way that fiction has known things for a long time: through complex, connected models. Through massive simulation.

AM: Since the beginning of your career, you've garnered a lot of critical praise, and you have a passionate, possibly even cultish fan base, to be sure. Then *The Echo Maker,* deservedly so, received the National Book Award this past year. I'm wondering, for someone who has always blazed his own literary trail, so to speak, how such a mainstream accolade—and the increased attention it will place on you—might change your writing, if at all.

RP: Since the award was announced only two weeks ago, I'm not really sure what effect it will have on the reception of my books. I'm grateful for whatever increased reader interest such a prize might generate, and delighted that a somewhat offbeat book has been brought into a broader public conversation. As for my own writing life and process, I have always treated prizes less as certifications of the past than as licenses for the future. To paraphrase Larry Bird: scoring earns you the right to miss from anywhere on the court. All in all, the award is just a wonderful encouragement to forget about winning and, in Beckett's words, to "fail better."

AM: So what happens now? What's your next simulation?

RP: I'm embarked on a novel about whether the human race can have a happy ending. ✯

CORNELIA NIXON

TALKS WITH

MARILYNNE ROBINSON

"A LOT OF HIGH-QUALITY INTELLIGENCE AND SENSITIVITY IS MISSPENT OR UNDERUTILIZED BECAUSE WE HAVE BEEN ACCULTURATED TO BELIEVE, BY THIS GREAT VOICE AROUND US, THAT WE ARE TRIVIAL PEOPLE WHO WILL NOT SAY ANYTHING THAT REALLY MATTERS."

Things Americans refuse to believe about England:
English people can do dumb things
It is not all green and pleasant
English companies dump toxic waste too
In England, you can be sued for hurting people's feelings

What first drew me to Marilynne Robinson's work was the beauty of her sentences. It is a rare kind of beauty that is clear and simple and intelligent, restrained and tentative as it tries to tell the truth, always aware of irony and how near tragedy can be to comedy. It does not strive for musical effects, but it is like the best lyric poetry, in that it questions itself and tries to get things right, often failing and trying again. It can be precise as anything by Hemingway, as in this sentence from the first chapter of Housekeeping *(1980): "When they got the Ford back to the road she thanked them, gave them her purse, rolled down the rear windows, started the car, turned the wheel as far to the right as it would go, and roared, swerving and sliding across the meadow, until she sailed off the edge of the cliff." This sentence asks nothing of you except to see what has occurred, the way things happen in life, though it is the narrator's mother who is killing herself here. This event is too unexplained and too ordinary to decorate with music. Instead the prose regards it with a distracted wonder that remains open to metaphysical nuance.*

Marilynne Robinson was born in Sandpoint, Idaho, graduated from Brown University in 1966, and received a Ph.D. in English from the University of Washington in 1977. Her first novel, Housekeeping, *was published in 1980 and received the PEN/Hemingway Award. Her next book,* Mother Country: Britain, the Welfare State and Nuclear Pollution *(1989), was a finalist for the National Book Award in nonfiction and was followed by a collection of essays,* The Death of Adam: Essays on Modern Thought *(1998). Her second novel,* Gilead, *was published in 2004 and has so far been awarded both the National Book Critics Circle Award and the Pulitzer Prize.*

On May 2, 2005, I had the following conversation with Robinson in her living room in Iowa City. It helped me to see how all her works cohere around the complexity of human consciousness and her humane, democratic Calvinism. Listening to the tapes, I am struck by how much time we spent laughing together. *—Cornelia Nixon (Spring 2005)*

I. GILEAD

CORNELIA NIXON: Both your novels so far have been generational, focused on two twentieth-century generations but with time given to several earlier ancestors. The narrator of *Gilead,* Reverend John Ames, is seventy-six and writing to his seven-year-old young son in 1956. The timing allows for Ames's family memories to extend back to the Civil War, John Brown, abolitionist fervor, and the war in Kansas over whether it would be a slave state or free, as well as two world wars and the Great Depression. Meanwhile, the story is told at the start of the civil rights movement, and the final plot turn concerns the racism of the 1950s. Was that a late inspiration, or the reason for the choice of the narrator's age and the time setting?

MARILYNNE ROBINSON: Basically, it grows out of my interest in the history of the Middle West, which is in a very great degree in its early stages a history of abolitionism, which is a very much forgotten history, and the fact of its being forgotten is, was, concomitant with the loss of the cause itself. Oddly enough, the South is called the Lost Cause, but I think the North could have been called the Lost Cause also over the course of time.

CN: Abolition you think is a lost cause? I mean, slavery was abolished.

MR: Slavery was abolished, but these people had much more in mind than the abolition of slavery. They developed very integrated institutions. They created colleges where blacks were admitted on the same basis as whites, and it was very hard to tell unless they could confirm it otherwise that a student was black in one of these colleges, because they did nothing to signify the race of the student.

One of the things that is an important myth is that because the abolitionists were Northerners, New Englanders, they had very little experience with black people or with the institution of slavery, but in fact of course they had what you could call the only normal contact with black people that probably any white person in the world was having at that time, because black people were actually their students and their fellow students, and so on. These reformers felt very strongly, most of them did, and this is something else that's misrepresented, that the races certainly were equal, and they believed it on the basis of experience which would allow this to be seen as true. That's all forgotten.

CN: Do you think we have not accomplished the aims of the nineteenth-century abolitionists?

MR: I think to a certain extent we have. I'm not sure that we really have, because there was the long intervening period of Jim Crow and what was called Scientific Racism, which was the use that was made of Agassiz and Darwin during that period, in which there was a very strong quote-unquote "eugenic argument" against the equality of races, which is the same argument that led to the extermination of Jews and Gypsies and so on in Europe. It's exactly the same literature.

It's very pervasive, it's very transatlantic. There's a mid-nineteenth-century book, *The Inequality of Human Races,* by a French writer, and though the South published almost nothing, they did publish annotated editions of that. So it was very influential in prewar Southern thought. It was also at the same time extremely influential in the emerging racist thought in Europe.

CN: I am amazed by how well you channel John Ames, the preacher, born in 1880. How easy was it for you to inhabit him and his voice? How close is it to your own? Are his thoughts on the Bible and Christian doctrine the same as your own?

MR: Frankly, the book became possible because it suddenly seemed to me as if I knew that man, and it was a pleasure to write from that point of view, because writing a book is normally a kind of lonely misery sort of thing. But I would feel even after I've had a difficult day, I can go home and be with this old man. [*Both laugh*]

As far as his thoughts on the Bible and theology, he's within the same tradition that is my tradition. I would not have felt confident to try to write from another perspective. But at the same time, his religious thought is highly specific to his circumstance, and his circumstance is not mine. So, given his character and given his circumstance, I felt as if it were his thinking, in effect, you know? It was a strange experience. There were things that I absolutely knew about him, like he loved baseball. I've sort of been perfectly respectful of baseball, but I've never paid that much attention to it. And besides that, since he was so much older than anyone I've ever known, I had to find out what he would have known. So I hired a graduate student, Earle McCartney, the one who's credited in the book, and so he researched baseball for me. So, for example, Bud Fowler is an actual player.

CN: The great black player in the book? John Ames says he lost track of him after they started up the Negro Leagues, which I guess sort of sent him to obscurity. So that's another piece fitting together. I didn't realize that was where the book was going, but it's all about racism. Did you watch baseball when you were writing it?

MR: No. [*Both laugh*] I feel as though I've gotten as much of the idea of baseball as I'm likely to get in this life. [*Laughter*]

CN: I heard you say that you were inspired to write John Ames when you were writing a poem.

MR: I was actually working on another fiction, and the fiction had a character in it who, frankly, did nothing but sit on a bench. I mean, he was probably two pages of character. But he was a minister. Who knows where he was going. But he had written a poem, and a fragment of the poem—about "open the scroll of conch" [*Gilead,* pp. 45–46]—it was his poem, and it seemed appropriate, and also I felt as if I had to keep that acknowledgment of this other character, who had died aborning and for some reason vanished himself and left John Ames in his place.

CN: Do you write poems? Or was it just because of that character?

MR: It was just that character.

CN: Sometimes I realize that something I'm writing is just holding the place of something else that is going to have to be better. I love the character of the narrator's grandfather, the first of the three ministers named Reverend Ames. He lost an eye in the Civil War, fought beside John Brown in Kansas, and came back to live with his son (the second Reverend Ames, of whom he more or less disapproves) and his wife and child (the narrator). He believes in giving away whatever is of value and steals items from his son's house and distributes them around the neighborhood, to whomever has need of them. Near the end, John Ames says, "I think he was a kind of saint," and I tend to agree. Was he based on anyone in particular, any real person?

MR: In a certain sense. See that picture up there, that little framed photograph?

CN: [*Fetches the photo, of a historical marker in front of a farmhouse. Reads the plaque, about a nineteenth-century abolitionist minister in Iowa named John Todd*] So is he John Todd?

MR: There were a surprising number of people more or less like him, radical clergy, often New England Congregationalists and Presbyterians, who came out and did that sort of thing. He was a graduate of Oberlin, and the people that originally settled that town were from Oberlin. A lot of them came from the old Divinity School. That was a very big headwater for the religious side of the abolitionist movement, which was most of the abolitionist movement. In any case, they were amazing people. The things they did were just astonishing.

These people founded a college in Tabor that for a long time sent women—they educated women and men, as these places typically did—and they sent women graduates to Turkey and Korea and all sorts of places, where they started schools for educating women, and in many places they were the first schools to educate women in that country. And so they had this huge, I mean, really big ambition for creating enlightenment and equality and all the rest of it. And that's characteristic through the Middle West. Grinnell was founded in the same way, and Knox College, and Carleton College. You can just go on and on. It's a very beautiful tradition. These people were so enlightened and infinitely energetic, and they had beautiful prose styles, and they had magnificent educations. They all knew Greek and Hebrew and Latin and all the rest of it. The Congregationalists, after the Civil War, founded five hundred schools for educating black people in the South. They had this idea and they didn't stop. And then it's like they go *whap* into a wall. This huge kind of cultural overturning like an iceberg rolling over. And everything just gets lost and goes into abeyance. They get treated as fanatics.

You find this same rhetoric in H. L. Mencken, who thought they were ridiculous for trying to establish the equality of women and the equality of black people. It's one of the most powerful lessons that American history contains, that so much could be done so insistently and patiently by people of great idealism, and it can all be lost. One of the things that is most painful about it, and I think one of the reasons it was most effective, the turnover, is because it started from the top down, because racial theory, which is what evolution primarily was when it entered the country, came in through the universities. They would have their little charts, and it would show the ape, and the gorilla, and the black guy—

CN: And then the white guy—

MR: Yeah, and with a few other guys in between and no women at all. They had no role in evolution at all, you know. [*Both laugh*] You still can't find any women in those little charts. And then it was, well, look here, we have science to prove that you're utterly naïve to think these things can be accomplished. And because it was an intellectual culture that tried to establish equality, it was particularly vulnerable to this kind of supposed scientific rebuttal. I think it's not at all unusual in a war for the loser to win, in effect.

It's like the old paradox about the Romans defeating Greece and becoming completely subservient to Greek culture. There was the romance of the elitism of Walter Scott and so on. The racial hierarchy was very much reinforced from reactionary movements in Europe, which were also nostalgia for aristocracy. You find it in T. S. Eliot. You find it in those people that published *I'll Take My Stand,* Southern poets, Robert Penn Warren. It's like the French

Revolution and nostalgia for the beauty that was lost and the culture that was lost. And these people who were the first wave of abolitionists were as cultured as anybody this country has ever produced, but it doesn't matter.

CN: Like the first Reverend Ames and his Greek Bible.

MR: Exactly. And because they were who they were, he had hard hands and a Greek Bible, you see. And these things cancel each other out. [*Chuckles*]

CN: In both your novels, you work often in the narrator's interior, rather than in scenes, especially in the new book. Both are in the first person, and *Gilead* is one long letter, and though it does include scenes, much of it is summarized with direct statements that might not come up in dialogue. John Ames reflects philosophically as he ponders scripture, religious doubt, arguments to counter doubt. He does reveal things he may be unaware of, like his naïveté and long-standing prejudice against his best friend's son that at times seems to verge on sexual jealousy. But his blind spots are subtle, and some readers may miss them, while no one can miss the direct statements. How do you feel about the creative-writing dictum "Show, don't tell?"

MR: Oh, I think that dicta in general are to be eyed with suspicion. [*Laughs*] It's so strange. That one has such power, and even more we're told all the time that the problem with creative writing programs is that they conventionalize. I think this is not true, but when it is, it's because people are told things like "Show, don't tell." It depends absolutely what your character is, what your situation is, what your subject is.

I think, frankly, it's a little bit like behaviorism or something. I really wonder how much it carries over from science, I mean really crude science as understood in the late nineteenth century and the early twentieth century—that there's something illusory about thought, and that in fact it's behavior that counts, and only behavior, when in fact people's brains are buzzing all the time. People are to an incredible degree constituted of what they never say, perhaps never consciously think. Behavior is conventionalized and circumstantial. In many cases, the behavior that in fact would express what someone thinks or feels is frustrated, cannot occur. Here we are, basically organized to carry this big brain around, and [*laughing*] it's absolutely bizarre to act as if what goes on in there is not part of the story.

CN: I wouldn't believe in him as a minister if he weren't extremely thoughtful in presenting his thoughts fully flowered sometimes, and thinking them through again, right there on paper.

MR: I think of him as somebody who is very much in the habit of thinking on paper. I get a lot of mail from ministers. I may be the darling of the American clergy right at the moment. [*Both laugh*] But this mulling over is one of the things that they very, very much identify with.

II. HOUSEKEEPING

CN: Part of the phenomenal success of *Housekeeping,* published in 1980, was due to the contemporaneous burgeoning of feminist literary theory and the creation of Women's Studies programs, which embraced the book as a feminist statement about women's generational influences on each other and women's spirituality, which often is seen as including pantheist elements rather than conforming to any conventional church doctrine.

Now you have written a great second novel that in some ways parallels it, as a generational exploration of men's lives. *Gilead,* however, has no detectable feminist elements. Its main emphasis is on matters of faith, in terms identifiable with recognizable church doctrines, and on last things, the need to summarize a life and take account of it. Would you say your views have changed since *Housekeeping*? Or was your faith as well defined then as now and merely less recognized by critics then?

MR: I had less vocabulary for my faith, I suppose, because, frankly, I've read a lot of theology in the intervening years. I'm fairly firmly persuaded that the human species is made up of two genders and that they are more interesting in their aspect as human beings than they are in their aspect as either feminine or masculine. I think that the degree to which they are seen as different is highly suspect. The idea, for example, that at the level of what we might call mind, they are very different, is the thing that my dear abolitionists were trying to overcome by demonstrating that women were absolutely as intellectually competent as men were, and I think that what they accomplished is another thing that we've forgotten.

There were very great women in the nineteenth century, and I'm afraid it would be hard to come up with their equivalent in this enlightened time, which is a frightening thought. But they were women who were well and optimistically educated with the assumption that they certainly could be great. Which I think is not really by any means characteristic now. Instead I think that women are very largely being educated, frankly, to plead a case against the world at large, as if what they have to do is be fascinated by what has happened that ought to disturb or anger them, rather than being fascinated by the possibility of doing something else. They're not making the space that other women I think in another two generations will want to occupy. I'm even afraid that categories like pantheist are anti-intellectual. And I don't think that men are—the whole Romantic tradition is "pantheist." I think that things are being ascribed to gender that are not gender-determined, and it's tending toward limiting distinctions in the same way that people were doing in 1810.

CN: The emphasis on women being different from men does sound to me like the literature of the late nineteenth century, some of it by ministers, arguing that women will damage their uteruses if they are educated, that it's physically bad for them and beyond their capabilities, and that they should be treated as children, essentially.

MR: Exactly. And I really do think that too much of that has been internalized and so that there is an infantilization of women's intellectual life now. It's very regrettable. One of those painful ironies, another iceberg turning over. My idea of feminism is that the world can be seen deeply and seriously through a woman's eyes, which does not mean only a woman's eyes. I wrote *Housekeeping* the way I did, because, frankly, whenever I tried to put a male character in, he didn't fit, so I took him back out again.

CN: [*Laughing*] There is a brief appearance by a Mr. Fisher, Sylvie's husband, but he doesn't ever quite come onstage. And the grandfather is there but not for long.

MR: [*Laughing*] In any case, I consider myself an excellent feminist, but I don't consider myself an ideological feminist. When I was writing *Gilead,* something of the same kind happened, in the sense that I felt that it was generational in the way that meant that certain cultural things were passed down through the male line, in the same way that in *Housekeeping* certain things pass down through the female line, the whole issue of nurturing and so on. You feel terrible pointing out things about your own novel. But an enormous number of the decisions in *Gilead* are made by the wife. She's the one who says he's writing the boy's begats, and she in a sense shapes the project from the beginning. She proposes to him, and he always defers to her, and she gets mad at him when she thinks he has not been fair to Jack [his best friend's son], which he has not been.

I just don't think that anybody ought to accept a restrictive definition of herself or himself, or certainly not encourage it in other people either. When you consider what a complex thing a human being is, and what a complex experience any human being has, you're going to come up with a new roll of the dice every time. This country is as diverse as any population has ever been, and why do we need these stupid generalizations? Everything tends toward a party platform these days. I do want to say that *Housekeeping* was at least as well received by men as by women. There are lots of papers and so on written by men, which are perfectly fine things.

CN: I think it was a man who first told me to read *Housekeeping.*

III. MOBY-DICK

MR: You know, I've always admired *Moby-Dick* very much, and I was sort of disturbed by the implications I heard from feminists that I ought not to like this book because it has only male characters. And so when I was writing *Housekeeping* and noticing that men kept going over the side every time I tried to write one, that if I could write a book that had only female characters that men understood and liked, then I had every right to like *Moby-Dick.*

CN: I've noticed that. More and more as I read *Housekeeping,* I am struck by the parallels to *Moby-Dick,* which you signal in the very first line, which is roughly "Call me Ruth." I was pleased last year to hear that you were teaching a whole graduate seminar at the Iowa Writers' Workshop on *Moby-Dick,* right when I was telling my students that there is a certain Romantic view of nature in *Moby-Dick* that I was catching echoes of in *Housekeeping.* Were you conscious of the influence of Melville and other writers from that period, transcendentalists, American Revival writers, when you were writing it?

MR: I was very aware of it, actually. I wrote *Housekeeping* and basically I didn't expect it to be published, but I was very interested in the extended metaphor. The extended metaphors that really interested me were nineteenth-century American, and like so much of the nineteenth-century American world, it seemed to me that the experiment they were making ended before it was finished. And so I was sort of demonstrating to myself what I understood to be their mode of consciousness. They being Emerson and Thoreau and Dickinson, but above all, Melville. There is a transformative character in metaphor, when something is perceived and articulated in terms of what it suggests, how it might fit into a fabric of speculation, when you move through perception to idea. Not to say a closed idea, but an open idea that makes you realize what you have not thought before.

The method of Melville is just opening, opening, opening. He sees something, he transforms it metaphorically, he in a sense takes in from it what can be comprehended, what the fabric has allowed him, and then he feels the insufficiency of the thought. So the process begins again. That's interested me very much. One of the things that it does is make demands on language that language is almost uncannily capable of meeting, demands that are almost never made under other circumstances.

CN: So the white whale is a metaphor he's using to get at something he's trying to understand?

MR: The white whale is the mystery that makes every intervening mystery seem as if it could give evidence about the ultimate mystery. All the sorts of things he does—the mapmaking and the coffin for Queequeg, and when they do the sperm thing and he talks about the angels—the rise of the giant squid—just over and over, these beautiful images. He has the metaphor of the masthead, when the sailor goes up there and begins thinking great transcendentalist thoughts. It's the encapsulation of consciousness that is also the enlargement of consciousness. The analogy for it even historically is scientific method, which proceeds from the assumption that something is wrong with even the most brilliant idea. It can always be taken further, or it needs to be modified or rejected, and there is something beyond it, something beyond.

CN: I've re-read *Housekeeping* a dozen times in order to teach it, with that special sort of attention you give a book when you know you have to come up with something to say about it the next day, or at least ask the right questions. The biggest reason I love it is what I see you saying in some passages, that there is what I call a sort of permeable membrane between life and death, through which living beings or their souls may pass back and forth.

The lake is identified with death early on, when the grandfather's train slides into it. It's called Fingerbone, clearly skeletal, not Finger, and the girls' mother drives her car into it to kill herself. Ruth says that if the dead apple trees in her grandmother's orchard were to burst into bloom, "It should be no great wonder," only "a small change." People see and hear dead children who are cold and hungry all around them, begging for food. When the lake rises and swamps their house, a kind of darkness seems to come in with it and open Ruth to a clearer perception of their aunt Sylvie, who may have learned to pass through the membrane. She seems impervious to cold, and her version of housekeeping readies the place for bats, dead leaves.

It seems to me that Sylvie challenges the distinction between living and dead, and Ruth gets closer to her during the very dark night she spends out by the lake with Lucille, while Lucille recoils from it and moves in with her Home Ec teacher, whose housekeeping is conventional. Ruth eventually leaves with Sylvie to wander through realms that may be postmortal, since they burn down the house on their way out and may be run over by a train on the railroad bridge across the lake. That's what the local paper believes, and the final pages include ambiguous, ironic, almost funny statements about "after our death," and Ruth turns the coffee cold as a waitress in a coffee shop. My question is, am I right? Is that what you meant?

MR: [*Laughing*] Oh, I can't answer a question like that! I think that people, depending on their circumstance, live in a much larger continuum of experience than conventionally we allow ourselves to acknowledge. Part of it of course is the experience of loss that is simply the result of the passage of time, and we know that we are mortal, we found that out when we were very young children. I don't consider *Housekeeping* a realist novel in quite the way that some people do. One of the lines that was on my mind when I was writing it—all kinds of things were on my mind—it was much more allusive than I would have dared to be if I thought anybody would ever read it. [*Both laugh*]

I remember that line from the Yeats poem, "like a long-legged fly upon the stream / her mind moves upon silence," and that's a very lovely image, of the creature suspended on the surface of water. I consider the book a sort of poem about the mind moving. The mind moving in the ambiguities, the tides of memory and being, and time. I've said before, you probably know I've said this before—I don't think of these people as opposed. I think of them as arrayed—that one feels a yearning for darkness and woods and perhaps even death itself.

And then one also feels the yearning for the warm house, the lighted house. If you choose or are helped into the warm house—the benevolence of society sees to that—you never stop feeling I think the attraction of the other, if you've ever felt it. So that it's not as if you are simple, in the sense that you have made one choice or the other. One of the things that I think I say in the book, and that I wanted to say, is that the town itself understands this, but part of its sort of huddled quality is precisely the fact that it knows the attractions of dispersal—and entropy, call it that.

CN: Dissolution...

MR: Yes, exactly that! Part of the reason I wrote this book the way that I did was because, when I went to Brown, where I went to college, I was a curiosity, coming from Idaho. Anybody else was less rare. People considered Idaho just empty, like they'd been through and there was just nothing there. [*Laughs*]

In my own growing up I had always felt this intense, plangent emotional density about forests and mountains, hidden places and forgotten places. I wanted to evoke that sense of the landscape, which I think people often recognize as something they feel also. I think people that live in the Northwest understand what it is that I have tried to evoke. The myth of the West is so stupid, with all these cowhands and lumberjacks and so on, and my family actually homesteaded there, and I am the fourth generation to live there. So, the narratives I heard from my family were vastly different from that, which is another thing I wanted to evoke.

CN: I agree that it's not a realist novel. And yet it is also. It's a realist novel about consciousness and perception.

MR: Yes, exactly. Which is, like, 90 percent of reality. [*Both laugh*]

CN: *Housekeeping* has passages that remind me very much of Romantic poetry, especially Wordsworth's "Ode: Intimations of Immortality," about how we come from another world, trailing clouds of glory that we soon forget, and how sleeping, fainting, slipping away even toward death gets us back closer to the glory. There's been a lot said about dissolution in Romanticism, the attraction to dissolving, coming apart like something in water, including in Romantic fiction like *Moby-Dick*. But while water is important in both your novels, it is associated with death, dissolution, spirituality, and liberation in *Housekeeping,* and in *Gilead* it seems more recognizably Christian, since Reverend Ames calls it the purest liquid and therefore appropriate for blessing and baptism. This strikes me as a step toward doctrinal Christian thought and away from what feels like pantheism or the spirituality of the Romantic poets, perhaps. What do you think?

MR: I think they're on a continuum. Reverend Ames would have been a later representative of exactly the same religious tradition that produced people like Melville and Dickinson, certainly Dickinson, and also Thoreau and also Bronson Alcott and a lot of them. So they're analogous traditions. The minister, because he's thought about these things in these terms his whole life, expresses them in terms that are specifically religious.

But the passage you quoted is from a famous atheist. That's Feuerbach. So he's stepping outside of that kind of language when he says that. You know, water is what makes this planet. Without water, forget it. It happens that there is a huge lake by Fingerbone, as there was by the town that I grew up in. In the Middle West, water is a big deal because we don't have enough of it often, which makes you aware of rain. And water is extraordinarily beautiful. I don't think anyone has ever thought otherwise. As Feuerbach would say, I don't think it's an accident that it is so strongly associated with ideas of the sacred.

CN: I've often thought that technique implies worldview, that writers' technical choices indicate assumptions about reality that they may not even know they have. In *Housekeeping* you use what I call provisional narration when you allow Ruth to imagine conversations and events she did not see or hear. This works with poignance in the last three pages ("after our death"), where Ruth says that in the future Lucille's "thoughts are thronged by our absence" and she "does not watch, does not listen, does not hope, and always for Sylvie and me." This seems like a sophisticated spiritual statement, in a section that begins, "All this is fact. Fact explains nothing," as if spiritual truth can only be implied sideways, or in reverse, or slant, as Emily Dickinson says.

MR: It has to do with thinking about the mind in the way that I was talking about before—that when people choose against something, that doesn't mean they cease to feel it as a choice they have. I think a real problem for writers is the flatness of most characterization, that it comes nowhere near capturing the actual complexity of experience. When you are with somebody you love, that seems as it ought to be. But when they're absent from you, you are more aware of them because of their absence. Loss can create a more profound presence than presence itself.

IV. THE DEATH OF ADAM

CN: This wide-ranging collection of essays is primarily a critique of contemporary American thought. In "Darwinism," you dissect Darwinian theory, pointing out its reliance on discredited paradigms of its day and its unproven elements. And while you scornfully dismiss simpleminded creationist views based on the Biblical account, your introduction argues for the superiority of John Calvin's ideas over those of our contemporary scientists. Have you received response to these arguments from any direction—creationist, Calvinist, Darwinian?

MR: It's a delicate thing; as soon as you talk about Darwinism, you've stirred a hornet's nest. The thing about it is that Darwinism and evolution have been treated as if they meant the same thing, whereas evolutionary theories predate Darwin. There's a collection of essays called *The Fundamentals*—fifteen volumes of it—written by people who were trying to shore up American Protestant theology against the invasion of Darwinism and Agassiz's system, and they say, of course there was evolution.

The question is, what does it mean, how do we interpret it, does it imply the things that were claimed by people of that time that it did imply, for example, eugenics, racial inequality. You can read things about how these theories implied to people in the early twentieth century that they should prevent child-bearing among isolated populations in the, you know, in the Berkshires [*laughing*], whom they just took to be darn inferior!

CN: I thought you were going to say the Amazon basin or someplace, not the Berkshires…

MR: [*Laughing*] The Berkshires! In places outside Pittsfield and so on. I mean, talk about a sword that turns every way. But in any case, the issue was never religion on one side and science on the other. It was the question of this science, in this cultural frame. It was doing the same thing all over the world, of course. It rationalized the extermination of the Tasmanians. It was again a basis for racial policy in fascist Europe. So it was a very serious issue, and it's been very much simplified. At first it was religion in a state of confusion against bad science. Now it's bad religion against bad science. So we're just in a complete swamp at this point.

But Calvinists think I'm a pretty good Calvinist, and that pleases me. People don't read him so they don't know what I mean, except the other Calvinists. One of the things that does please me is that I was cited in the Cambridge book of essays on Calvin, in the essay on metaphysics. So that was devoutly to be hoped. [*Laughs*] And I had a conversation with a scientist that was set up by *Harper's,* in the Rothko Chapel in Houston. He was a Nobelist, a physicist, who writes for the *New York Review of Books,* and he just joked about this kind of crazy contemporary evolution. He said, "You know what they call it, they call it Just-So Stories," which is what it is, if you read it. Nevertheless it has the imprimatur of science, which just knocks people over. If they read any scientific history, they would realize that it has bumbled along in exactly the same way that any other human enterprise has done, and perhaps taken as many victims.

CN: Freud, for instance, is considered to be scientific. You only have to read about what he was actually doing, which was getting his friend Fliess to operate on people's noses to cure their sexual hang-ups.

MR: [*Laughing*] Exactly! Exactly!

CN: What you're saying about how all human enterprise is bumbling reminds me of "Facing Reality," also in *The Death of Adam.* There you suggest that we need to forgive ourselves and each other for being fallible and mortal, as are all of our enterprises. I especially love the last paragraph, which I typed and taped to my office door for a year after a close friend of mine was killed in a plane crash along with both of her parents. There you say, "If the universe is only all we have seen so far, we are its great marvel. I consider it an honor to follow Saint Francis or William Tyndale or Angelina Grimké or Lydia Maria Child anywhere, even to mere extinction. I am honored in the cunning of my hand." What moved you to write "Facing Reality"?

MR: It was one of those interesting invitations that came in the mail. These are all occasional essays, except for "Darwinism." A great problem that we have is a kind of false consciousness that I talk about in "Facing Reality," that we've been sold a bill of goods, a thousand bills of goods. I think that to be a good writer, you have to put yourself on the line, you have to think deeply about what is meaningful to you and you have to make a good-faith effort to speak from the integrity of your own deep experience. There is a tendency to disallow deep experience, as if it were something that we twentieth-century Americans don't have. Nobody doesn't think of something in crisis or in deep difficulty. God help us, maybe there are some poor souls for whom this is not true. But virtually everybody has been acculturated to have some notion of the terms of ultimate human experience. It tends to be religious because that's the way that people generally do deal with these things.

I'm sure there are people who have been brought up to think in terms of returning into the great organism of being, or something like that. But for most people we have what our grandma told us. And people are not encouraged to consult those things, or to acknowledge the fact that they live in the same mythic landscape that the formulators of these difficult narratives lived in also—that the things that have been passed down as ways of understanding it have not ceased to be relevant. And there's a sort of a falseness in the consistent inability. People don't think about accessing what is the deepest narrative for them. I think that that's about 99 percent of the subject of literature. A lot of high-quality intelligence and sensitivity is misspent or underutilized because we have been acculturated to believe, by this great voice around us, that we are trivial people who will not say anything that really matters.

CN: I tell students to figure out what they believe in the way James Baldwin believes in racial equality. To find what matters deeply to them and write about that.

MR: Right. And also write *from* it. I mean, racial equality is not a pressing issue except to people who love justice, who understand the offense that inequality is, just on the face of the earth.

V. MOTHER COUNTRY

CN: What I was hoping when I found this book was that it would be a new novel by you, and I was surprised that it was an environmentalist statement about a nuclear power in the British Isles called Sellafield. The image I still have in my mind from it is of sheep grazing on a green hillside and this nuclear power plant right next to them.

MR: They have done that. They've grazed sheep by it, they've grazed cattle by it, they've put golf courses by it. They sometimes even use the phrase "Sheep may safely graze" [*both laugh*] out of Handel, when it's a real dodgy question whether they may or not. It's a very filthy plant that systematically releases radioactive materials and nitric acid in liquid tons every day into the Irish Sea and has done so for decades. It's in the Lake District, not far from Wordsworth's house. [*Laughs*] They consider it isolated. They've been doing it for so long now that there's really no turning back. They have another one, equally vile, in Scotland, called Dounreay, which was supposed to be a breeder reactor, but it had accidents, as they all do.

Europe has dabbled with that stuff and so has Japan, using British technology. They have built these reactors that are graphite-moderated like the reactors at Hanford that make bomb-grade material, and they consider them "dual use." They produce electricity and then they also produce plutonium and uranium, which

Britain sells, ships into Germany and into Japan by sea. And now the Irish Sea is the most radioactive body of water in the world. All this talk about nuclear proliferation, and people talking about Russia, but Britain is a much older and more important source of nuclear proliferation difficulties.

CN: Why did you chose Sellafield and not someplace here like Three Mile Island?

MR: Nothing to compare in scale.

CN: And you were living in England at the time.

MR: I was. And one of the articles that caught my eye was one that said they had discovered that it was more harmful for children to ingest plutonium than had previously been thought.

CN: So that's part of the bill of goods we've all been sold.

MR: Yes. That's a major bill of goods. And for me, many things go back to racism.

CN: Because the Lake Country is considered full of lesser people?

MR: No, actually, it's quite the other way round. Many Americans who consider themselves extremely liberal have this sort of displaced patriotism, where they will not hear and cannot believe anything negative about Britain. And we liberals, we right-thinking people, can't believe that white people who speak English can do anything dumb. You can't believe how pervasive this kind of thinking is.

I learned a great deal from doing that book. And it was quite respectfully reviewed in general. But it didn't matter. People can't take it in. You say, you know, there's a television program where a British journalist is holding up a Geiger counter into the air, and the wind is coming in off the sea, and the Geiger counter is shrieking. It's nuts. "Well," they say, "but it's still a great place to vacation." I was in Britain and I was becoming aware of all of this because it was in the newspapers, it was on television. I know lots of Americans there. I would say to them, "What do you think about all this plutonium?" And they'd say, "What plutonium?" Our prejudice in favor of Europe is so profound, and it's going to have huge consequences. I think one consequence is that we can look forward to the construction of British and European reactors in this country. We don't know anything about the standards they apply, although the information is perfectly available.

CN: So the audience you're addressing is in this country.

MR: Yes, although it was printed in England. It was published by Faber and Faber. But it had to go out of print because I was sued by Greenpeace under British law.

CN: Wait—Greenpeace sued you? I would have thought they'd be on your side.

MR: One of the things that was very disturbing was that while Greenpeace was active about all this in Britain, there was no information about it in the United States. Or to the extent that there was any, it tended, as it does tend to be, very misleading. For example, they had a brochure that said that Greenpeace claimed that they had helped to create a ban on ocean dumping of radioactive material. But there still is ocean dumping of radioactive material all the time, a great deal of it done by Britain. They not only put this stuff down a pipeline into the ocean, but they dump radioactive waste off the coast of Spain. So, this rouses one's curiosity about what Greenpeace understands its role to be. They collect an enormous percentage of the money that's donated for environmental causes in the world.

There was one particularly ridiculous episode in which Greenpeace figured, and I couldn't get any satisfaction about what they were doing. So in the book itself I raise questions about why did this happen and what were they doing. I made it joking around a little bit, but basically they have this pipeline that since 1957 has been pumping radioactive waste into the sea, right? And according to Greenpeace, they had taken divers out and lowered them to block the thing. In the first place, it's been putting out corrosive material since 1957. How are you going to make a cover that fits the thing? Isn't that a little bit hard to imagine? Then they had lowered these divers to the mouth of what is the source of the most intense radioactive contamination in the world, pulled them back up again. There happened to be a Geiger counter in the boat, which pinned. [*Makes gesture of a dial going over to the max*]

Now, what's wrong with this story? You're going out to block something because it disgorges radioactive waste, and you don't take a Geiger counter? You only accidentally have one there? It only accidentally goes off when the divers come up? Who are these divers that you're going to put them into this intensely radioactive environment? It's all craziness. I simply ask in the book, what can this mean? So I got sued. And among the things that Greenpeace sued me for were hurt feelings.

CN: Did they win?

MR: They won. Well, you know, under British libel law, you can be found guilty of libel if you say something that injures someone's reputation.

CN: So that's why they sued you there instead of here.

MR: In England, yes. They couldn't possibly have sued me here. But the consequence of it was, when a book is sub judice, as they say, it can't be mentioned in print.

CN: So if it can't be mentioned in print, it couldn't be reviewed.

MR: Couldn't be reviewed. Just—poof, disappeared in England.

CN: But here it got attention.

MR: Yes. But here nobody wants to believe what you say about England.

CN: That explains the title! You're speaking about our mother country—

MR: Yeah, the colonized attitude that we basically have. It's like primitive patriotism. We cannot see the "green and pleasant land" people. People act as if I am hostile to England, when in fact I'm trying to say something that might perhaps alleviate a dreadful situation that is very much an English problem. I mean, it's everybody else's because they export the stuff and it flows around in the sea. But they are the primary victims.

VI. THE WRITER IN THE WORLD

CN: The role of the writer in this culture is no longer what it once was, when writers were routinely asked to make statements about public controversies. What do you think about the position of intellectuals in our culture now? How would you change it if you could?

MR: This is such a good question. This country is so various. I'm surprised to find, when I travel around, the cultural life of Minnesota, the cultural life of North Dakota, it's like going from one country to another. And you find people that are intense about where they are, and what is at issue in the place where they are.

One of the things that afflicts this country is that it is so large and so active that it cannot successfully generalize about itself. So it generalizes unsuccessfully. And the unsuccessful generalizations are usually very much to its detriment. One is programmed to think in certain ways, about how much cultural vitality there is, and it's a great privilege to be in a position where one can see it. We have a way of talking as if the intellectual life is something conducted in a drawing room, in New York, probably, when it is vastly larger than that. I think that the people who are noticed as intellectuals, which is an artificially small group, tend to be in a certain sense influenced by the majority about the cultural deadness in this country. [*Laughs*] We continuously get misinformation about ourselves.

One of the ways in which perhaps one is acknowledged as intellectual is by being a spokesman for this misconception, that there is no intellectual life in this country. It is the classic posture of intellectualism, and it goes back to people like H. L. Mencken, "the boobocracy" and so on. And I think it has made an enormous problem, because there is at this point a fair consensus that the culture has failed, and that the public schools have failed, and the public universities need to be revamped because they have failed. We can't acknowledge our own life. I don't think that people who speak about these things publicly are particularly encouraged to do that. And they should be, simply because it is better to say something that is true rather than something that is not true. [*Both laugh*]

CN: If you could say something to world leaders today, what would it be? Or to your fellow Americans?

MR: To my fellow Americans, I would say that I have the deepest admiration for their better potential and I would be so happy and relieved to see it expressed in public. There's nothing in the world that I love and admire more than the best impulses of this country. Nothing that breaks my heart more than seeing it betrayed. World leaders, in general I think I would tell them: Go home. Take a warm bath. [*Both laugh*] Pick a name out of the phone book, appoint him/her as your successor, and we couldn't be worse off.

CN: Including in this country?

MR: I'm not terribly impressed with the current leadership.

CN: That is part of what you were saying about the betrayal of our best potential? You mean who we elect to represent us and speak for us in the world?

MR: Nobody speaks for us. Every day in the newspaper, a new surprise, and I'm never happy with it.

CN: Yes. The image of America one gets from the mainstream

media and the activities of our elected representatives—that's one vision of America. But I can't fit into it, say, this conversation we've had today. You are simply not represented there.

MR: I certainly don't feel represented. You know, I miss many things. I miss generosity. I miss magnanimity. I miss a loyalty to the future that makes people reasonable about how they conduct their lives in the present. The idea of a possibility, for ourselves and others—who is it who said that civilization is planting a tree that you will never sit under? That's what we need to do. We have all these great libraries and all these wonderful resources, museums and so on, because other people planted trees that they were not going to sit under. And now we feel no obligation to leave behind similar legacies, at least in the highest scales of public debate. ✯

JOSHUAH BEARMAN

TALKS WITH

MARJANE SATRAPI

"THE WORLD IS NOT ABOUT BATMAN AND ROBIN FIGHTING THE JOKER; THINGS ARE MORE COMPLICATED THAN THAT."

Found universally:
Crazy people
Good people
Punk rock

Toward the end of Persepolis II, *the second installment of Marjane Satrapi's ongoing project of autobiographical graphic novels, the author/narrator spends seven months designing a huge theme park based on Persian mythology. She takes her Tehran-based Disneyland to the deputy mayor's office, where it is rejected—luckily for us, because shortly after that disappointment, Satrapi left Iran for Paris, a final emigration that led her to discover Art Spiegelman, the power of comics, and the development of her own method of storytelling.*

Satrapi's graphic novels are the opposite of mythology; personal and honest, they humanize the Middle East through memoir. Hemmed in by the tyranny of the mullahs, Satrapi's life is nevertheless cosmopolitan, politically engaged, culturally sophisticated, and, like those of all adolescents, deeply conflicted. Today Satrapi lives in Paris, where she remains deeply conflicted, caught between home and exile, East and West, now all the more complicated by the geopolitics of the post–September 11 world.

The following interview took place at a brasserie around the corner from Satrapi's studio in Paris, where she is working on an animated feature-film adaptation of Persepolis. *She smoked a lot, talked fast, and tied together a multitude of tangents.* *—Joshuah Bearman (Summer 2006)*

I. SUPERHERO STORIES

JOSHUAH BEARMAN: Your books recently came out in Israel and were well received.

MARJANE SATRAPI: In a place like Israel, they're very concerned with Iran, so there's a lot of interest. Especially with what's going on there now, the new government and all. So they want to see what this Iranian from France has to say in her comics. I guess that's good. Now the books are coming out in other countries. And each time, they discover something different to be interested in.

JB: I think the broad appeal probably has to do with how your stories humanize a mostly unknown place. The popular notion about Iran is as a terrifying theocracy, brimming with lunatics who want to kill the West. As if every single Iranian has a bunch of flags in their closet, all lined up for the next Death to America/Israel protest. And then your books come along and tell a different story, about people with the same problems, sorrows, and joys that we have. And fears—here are Iranians who are just as afraid of the Iranian regime as we are.

MS: Absolutely. Here's the problem: Today, the description of the world is always reduced to yes or no, black or white. Superficial stories. Superhero stories. One side is the good one. The other one is evil. But I'm not a moral lesson giver. It's not for me to say what is right or wrong. I describe situations as honestly as possible. The way I saw it. That's why I use my own life as material. I have seen these things myself, and now I'm telling it to you. Because the world is not about Batman and Robin fighting the Joker; things are more complicated than that. And nothing is scarier than the people who try to find easy answers to complicated questions.

JB: Superhero stories are the original territory for comic books, with good versus evil. So by deepening the story, are you also commenting on the format?

MS: I just think that comics have always been more than that. They really haven't always been superheroes. And today, of course, people like Art Spiegelman have shown how truly powerful comics can be. Joe Sacco uses comics as political reporting. So comics are just another medium to express yourself. It's not cinema; it's not literature; it's just something else. It has a specific requirement, which is that images are used to tell the story. There are lots of crappy movies, with guns and action and Arnold Schwarzenegger or whatever. This is not the movies' fault. It's the fault of the directors who made those movies. Any medium can only live up to the strengths of the people working in it. If it's been used to tell bad or boring stories, it's not a problem with comics; it's a problem with the writers of those comics.

JB: Do you think you reach a broader audience because of your use of comics?

MS: Maybe. Because of the images. You see a picture and you understand perfectly, immediately, the basic thing that's happening. It's probably more accessible because we are in a culture of images now. People are used to seeing stories that way. They understand looking at pictures.

II. STUCK IN THE MIDDLE

JB: Was there at a point at which you knew you wanted to draw a memoir?

MS: I always thought about it. And then there was a point that I could imagine what it was going to look like, although I didn't know when I sat down what exactly would appear on the page. Sometimes you're surprised by your own stories. There were things I didn't plan, or didn't really remember at first, that just came out.

JB: Your books are a kind of cultural bridge. If there were only text, maybe they'd be less able to serve that purpose.

MS: Probably so. It would also be harder for me. If I were to write a memoir with words, I'd have to figure out a way to express verbally an image I have in my mind. In my case, it's easier to draw it. And words also are filters. They have to be translated. Even in the original language, there is interpretation and some ambiguity. If there's a cultural difference between the writer and the reader, that might come out in words. But with pictures, there's more efficiency.

JB: You visited West Point and made a cartoon about it for the *New York Times* Op-Ed page. You expected one thing—angry drill sergeants, a summary execution for your antiwar views—but found something else. It seems like that's a synopsis for a lot of your work.

MS: Yes, I learned a lot. In France, all you hear about is how, after September 11, all Americans supposedly eat Freedom Fries. And they don't drink French wine or whatever. The news here makes it look like all Americans are fat patriots with boots who want to start war all over the Middle East. Of course, some people did start talking about Freedom Fries. But in France, you didn't also see the Americans who opposed Bush. So when people here talk about the stupid Americans, I find myself defending America. I say, no, they're not all like that. America's ideals are still strong, and so on.

JB: When you're in America, you probably wind up defending France.

MS: It's funny that way. And everywhere I have to defend Iran. Because Iran is not understood at all, especially in the U.S.—I mean, come on! Bush with his Axis of Evil, and they want to kick our ass and all that. Just like in the U.S., where the people are not all represented by Bush, in Iran the people are not represented by the Ayatollahs. So I'm stuck in the middle.

JB: Like a U.N. goodwill ambassador.

MS: Now my job is to defend everybody. But I don't mind. Because I travel, and I like to talk to people and really listen to them. And I have no prejudices. I figured out a long time ago that, whatever I think I know, I don't know anything. Once I realized that, I really started learning. That's a great strength: I know that I don't know. There are some people in Iran who are fundamentalist and others who are not. I have very good Israeli friends. And I have very good American friends. We come from different cultures but share points of view. It's humanism, which we're steadily losing. That's what the comics are about in a way, trying to stop that loss.

JB: That's something that your books address indirectly. Was that intended?

MS: Absolutely. Of course. The cultural similarities. The human similarities. Maybe the biggest problem is that there's no empathy. Nobody puts themselves in the place of others. Everyone thinks they are the only one to suffer. Or that they're the only ones who like ice cream or take their kids on vacation. People are always so shocked to find out that in Iran we knew about punk rock. Sometimes we learned about it before Americans. I have friends from the Midwest who found out about the punk movement after I did. It also shows the power of anecdotes, a small story, to explain the bigger picture. So I worked in anecdotes of my own to comment on the world. Because the world is not decided by George Bush and Saddam Hussein. They make things happen in the news, but that's not real life. Real life is you and me.

IV. HUNGER EATS CIVILIZATION.

JB: You use comics, a fairly simple format, to tell a nuanced, complex story. And yet somehow, the entire narrative machinery of giant news-gathering organizations and most movies and magazines seems to miss that nuance and complexity. It's a weird reversal: the front-page and cable news, where we're supposed to learn about the intricacies of world affairs and politics, have turned into a comic book, while you've turned a comic book into a window on the world's intricacies.

MS: It's because my kind of story doesn't sell news. I have stopped looking at the TV. Facts and consequences are all they say. Which is never the whole story. The whys are what's important. But violence is news, to a certain extent, and people don't want complicated news. Because as soon as you realize things are complicated, your life becomes more complicated.

JB: It must have been strange for you to watch the recent French riots, since the crisis surrounds identity and East and West, and you straddle both sides. The riots got folded into the grand plot of the clash of civilizations, the first flash point of which was 1979 in Iran, the centerpiece of your memoir. It's like you can't escape that story.

MS: Unfortunately. And it's mostly a made-up story. It was incredible to see how it was created here. All over the news: Muslim rage or whatever. The rioting was not about being Muslim. These people have not been able to integrate. So if they have a crisis of identity, it's forced upon them. If, after three generations of living in France, Arabs are still called Arabs and not French, then of course they will be angry. People ask why the Arabs don't consider themselves French. Well, it's because the French don't consider them French. Then you had the Ministry of the Interior talking about cleaning the scum off the street. That doesn't justify the violence—they don't have the right to burn cities—but it explains what happened.

JB: What about the *mission civilatrice*?

MS: Yes, that exists in theory. But it's a question of money, my dear. Immigrant economics. I never had any problem with the French, but I come from a wealthy family. I'm educated. I live in a nice neighborhood. So they don't care about me. If I had no money or education and lived in the *cité,* then I'd be a problem. Racism is not nearly as important as poverty. That's the same around the world. What look like ethnic problems are really economic issues. If you look closely at all these conflicts around the world, they come down to poverty and economics and resources. The more poverty, the worse the war. Hunger eats civilization. The West is not hungry; that's why they can say they're so civilized. Civilization is the biggest bluff!

JB: I covered the last American presidential campaign. In the process, I talked to a lot of people. I'd say about a quarter of the people I encountered had a politics motivated entirely by the Book of Revelation.

MS: But that's not just a problem with America. The crazy people are not based in one country. They're everywhere. George Bush talks about the Axis of Evil. What's the difference between that and the mullahs talking about the Great Satan? They say, "Read the Koran." The other one says, "Read the Bible." The mullah says he's the best friend of God, and George Bush does too. The problem is that no one has really seen or talked to God, so who can really vouch for what God says? But the mullah is a religious man. He's supposed to talk like that. Bush is the president of the world's leading secular democracy. This is not normal.

JB: In the Middle East, the apocalyptic Christianity of the Bush administration has political implications. There are people in the United States who want instability in Iraq, Iran, Israel—all over, really, because they see it as a sign of the Tribulations.

MS: I never understood that apocalypse stuff. They want the world to end tomorrow. Why? Life's already short. You're going to die. Why hurry? This religion on the rise everywhere really scares me. Are we going to burn old ladies again? Ten or fifteen years ago if you said you didn't believe in God, no one paid any attention. Now it's a political statement somehow to be atheist or agnostic. When people ask me what is my religion, I say I don't have any. And some people are shocked. They don't understand. I say I don't need it. I respect humanity. That's my religion. I can't stand these religions that are really businesses. So much money everywhere that's going to buy a really nice house in heaven—or what? I don't get it.

V. DINNER WITH ART SPIEGELMAN

JB: What do you think about the new president of Iran?

MS: He follows the whole world's movement toward religious extremism. And when the leader of the world's greatest democracy is Bush, then what can you expect in a theocratic dictatorship like Iran? The whole region is run by soldiers or mullahs. In Iran there are social problems behind extremism. Iran is the third-largest producer of oil, but the country has terrible poverty. And so the mullahs come along and make promises. And they use the U.S. as a scapegoat for their problems. Their two biggest enemies, Saddam and the Taliban, are gone, and only the U.S. is left. So the anti-American rhetoric gets louder.

JB: Were you optimistic about the reform movement in Iran?

MS: Who can be optimistic these days? Everyone is losing their head. No one wants to talk anymore. The whole world is run by a bunch of cowboys. I just can't be optimistic the way things seem to be going. I'm extremely worried. Because you can see from history that things can go wrong very fast. Think about how World War I started.

JB: With poor statesmanship and miscommunication and—

MS: And that was when there were diplomats. Now Bush throws away fifty years of diplomacy just like that. So how can I be optimistic?

JB: But then again, your books are rooted in optimism.

MS: Well, of course I do have a little bit of hope. Otherwise, I would just take a shotgun and end it all now. Since I'm alive, I'll always hope that a miracle could descend on us. My intellect sees no way out, but my instinct for survival is hopeful. It says: let's try. The day that I don't have that anymore, I swear to God, I will commit suicide. That's something I do want to communicate to the readers. Not the suicide, but the hope. What I really believe in is good people. It's that simple. The bad ones are really crazy, totally out of their minds, and the problem is, you don't need very many crazies to really screw things up. That's what gives them their power. But there are more of us, I think.

JB: Well, that does sound hopeful. So you must be happy to see the expansion of your medium. If you go into Skylight Books in Los Angeles and other stores, there are shelves of local independent comics that people just bring in and sell. It's really proliferating.

MS: Yes, exactly. It's very exciting. I don't want to be the only cartoonist. There should be many more. I want to see a whole new generation. There are so many writers and filmmakers and photographers in the world. Why not more high-quality cartoonists?

JB: I heard that you bet Art Spiegelman that John Kerry would win the U.S. election.

MS: Yes. I lost that one. Had to pay for that dinner. The problem is that it wasn't just with him. I made that bet with a thousand other people, so that was a lot of dinners I had to buy.

JB: Then again, it sounds like you are an optimist.

MS: I always want to believe in the best outcome. OK, I guess maybe I am an optimist. ✯

BEN MARCUS

TALKS WITH

GEORGE SAUNDERS

"THAT, TO ME, IS ART'S HIGHEST ASPIRATION: TO SHOW THAT NOTHING IS TRUE AND EVERYTHING IS TRUE."

Things for which there is no time to be:
Bloatedly intellectual
Merely clever
Stupid
Programmatic
Cloying

He was born George Saunders and has kept the same name his entire life. Sometimes he moves through the streets beneath a greatcoat designed to keep himself from being killed. Otherwise he is fearless, naked in the evenings, a family man. There has been a mustache, a beard, a bald face. The area locale where he has chosen to live is brutal and cold and produces a large share of lonely people. He sleeps and eats and functions as any person might. But there the similarities end.

For part of each day, Saunders is a hero. He would never agree to this designation. But his modesty, his generosity, his expansive imagination, and his fully developed tenderness-generating technique are a large part of his heroism. His heroism is fitted with a blind spot that keeps Mr. Saunders from knowing about, or being able to acknowledge, the ways that he has beautifully scoured and remade—through artisan-quality writing—the people in many countries. His writing appears in books and magazines and quickly subsumes them, explaining the appearance of horizon fires in the far Northeast. The books of fiction are called CivilWarLand in Bad Decline *(1996) and* Pastoralia *(2000). The Suits call his writing "stories," but they are really soft bodies to wear for a larger experience of life, hollowcore person-shapes that one can slip on in order to attain amazement. Saunders writes bodies, and his readers wear them. Some of these readers are probably in your house. If they are glowing or trembling, now you know why.*

The following conversation took place on an old Toshiba calculator.

—Ben Marcus (Winter 2003)

I. "PAY ATTENTION TO EVERYTHING AS IF THIS WAS YOUR LAST MOMENT ON EARTH."

BEN MARCUS: When I visited your city of Syracuse, New York, I was kept awake all night by crows, who raised such a terrible noise in my motel room that I thought I might get killed. I later heard from other overnight visitors that this had happened to them also. Explain.

GEORGE SAUNDERS: It's true, we have a lot of crows up here. It's part of a Municipal Program to become the West Nile Virus Capital of the Northeast. We actually "recruit" crows from all over the United States—bring them here on special Crow Interview Trips, construct special "GlamorNests" for them all over town, screen weekend-long *Heckle & Jeckle* fests at our local movie houses. And they are loud. We had one in particular around our house who used to sound exactly like he was calling my wife's name ("PauLA! PauLA!") until finally—in connection with the Crow Recruitment Program—we had a translator over, who informed us that what the crow was actually saying was "I could sure use some freaking grapes! I could sure use some freaking grapes! If I don't get some freaking grapes, I'm going back to Cleveland."

BM: Where does the name George Saunders come from?

GS: It actually comes from the fact that my great-grandfather, who emigrated from Greece, was catching a lot of crap for his last name, Vlahakis, and his accent. I think he was working as a fruit seller at the time. So he went for something very British. The accent he couldn't do anything about. He was kind of a wild card—left my great-grandmother and their sons for two years to go back to Greece and fight the Turks. And then as soon as he came home, he ran off with a waitress, to Napa Valley.

BM: Rather than ask who your ideal reader is, since I have met your ideal reader and he hurt me physically, I wanted to ask you how aware you are of entertainment, as a specific gift to a reader, and whether or not there's ever a tension for you between what you feel you ought to do as a writer, and what you actually do. This is not a question about capitulation to a generic sense of what a reader might want, but rather a question of a potential discrepancy between what might please you and what you feel will please others.

GS: This question rattles me, because it makes me realize that I make no distinction between what pleases me and what might please a reader. That is, if I feel the reader will be pleased by a thing, I simply want to do that thing. Period. My feeling is something like this: The basis for literature is the fact that all of our brains are essentially, structurally, identical. First love in 1830, in Russia, beneath swaying pines, is neurologically identical to first love in 1975, back of a Camaro, Foghat blaring. That's why that wonderful cross-firing occurs when we read.

It is not the case, as we sometimes feel, that the writer is making us feel what she felt. It is, rather, that the writer is poking that part of our brain that already felt (or knew, or sensed) what the writer felt (or knew, or sensed). Without getting too Star-Trekky, there really is, I believe, one universal mind, but the basis for the existence of that universal mind is the structural similarity of all those individual minds. Because the brain is a machine, and all those individual minds are just slightly different versions of that machine, only so many mind-states exist, and therefore you can know what I think, because it is what you thought, roughly.

So when I'm writing, I am trying to move myself, or impress myself, or prevent myself from getting bored and walking away—in the faith that, if I succeed in this, the writing will have some equivalent effect on the reader. On every reader? No. On every reader, to some extent? I think so. I hope so. Anyway, that's what I assume. That, to me, is the really magical thing about writing: if I write toward my own best nature, I am also writing toward the best nature of others. It sort of doesn't make sense, and even feels a little fascist, but I think it's true.

Here I have to confess that I also believe that certain effects have more power in prose than others, and that this tendency is, at least in part, universal. I believe in efficiency, action, clarity, velocity. I think these qualities are responsible for the feeling of being "drawn into" a piece of prose. Also, maybe paradoxically, I think that constructing this hierarchy of preferred effects is what style is all about. If one writer prefers some other suite of effects, and energetically tries to construct a prose-world based on the pre-eminence of those effects, style will result.

I will also confess that, for complex reasons of background, etc., I really don't care much about anything but being entertaining—with entertainment, I hope, being defined as "ultimately interesting." Ideally, I aspire to write stuff that takes into account the fact that we are all dying. So there's no time to be bloatedly intellectual, no time to be merely clever, no time to be stupid, or programmatic, or cloying. That's the hope, anyway.

And as for that ideal reader of mine, sorry about that. "Max" is basically a good guy, but he doesn't get out much, and, for him, his fists are his most expressive part. That is, what you construe as "punching" is, for Max, sort of like kissing might be for most people.

BM: Your theory of a universal mind suggests that Buddhism plays a role in how you think about fiction.

GS: You bet. I find Buddhism inspiring in that it says: Everything matters. Suffering is real. Death is imminent. Pay attention to everything as if this was your last moment on earth. And then I see writing as part of an ongoing attempt to really, viscerally, believe that everything matters, suffering is real, and death is imminent. Chekhov said that art prepares us for tenderness, and I think this is also what spiritual practice can do. On a practical level there are also parallels. Buddhism emphasizes honesty and openness, nonattachment. So if you thought your story was going to be a biting satire of a nail-biting patriarchal brutalizer, but then, on page three, a street vendor comes in and makes a really interesting speech about his lifelong love of broccoli, and that speech has more energy in it than anything that came before—openness means admitting to yourself that your story needs to follow that vendor out into the street. That sort of thing.

BM: A cross old man once announced to me that it was impossible to teach writing. I replied, just as crossly, that he meant *he* couldn't teach writing. Nevertheless, nonteachers of writing seem to love to declare its impossibility, to call writing programs scams and money-wasters, and just to generally deride the whole enterprise. Book reviews frequently resort to a shorthand critique, citing "workshop" stories, and a *Village Voice* article claimed that Jonathan Safran Foer's originality stemmed, at least in part, from his outsider status, since he did not attend an M.F.A. program. I was thinking of you and a few other writers—namely Charles Baxter and Aimee Bender—who have a reputation for being extraordinary teachers of writing, not to mention obviously original and productive writers. I'd be curious to hear your take on teaching, what its value might be, and why writing-instruction, unlike other artistic studies—painting or theater or music—seems so susceptible to criticism.

GS: I suspect that what your Cross Old Man was trying to say was: only one young writer in a thousand ever gets a book out, and of those books, only one in a thousand lasts in even the slightest way, so why are you writing-program teachers holding out hope to so many young people, when you know and I know that only one out of a thousand out of an original thousand have any hope of writing an enduring work of literature? And basically, I would agree with that. The chances of a person breaking through their own habits and sloth and limited mind to actually write something that gets out there and matters to people are slim.

But I also suspect that your Cross Old Man is too narrowly careerist. Because he seems to be neglecting the fact that, even for those thousands of young people who don't get something out there, the process is still a noble one—the process of trying to say something, of working through the craft issues, and the world-view issues, and the ego issues—all of this is character-building, and god forbid everything we do should have to have Concrete Career Results.

I've seen, time and time again, the way that the process of trying to say something that matters dignifies and improves a person. I've seen it in my own failures, in writing and otherwise. I think it comes down to the motivation of the individual student. If the student writer wants to get over, become famous, dominate others with his talent—then no matter what, he's going to lose. On the other hand, if he wants to go deeply into himself, subjugate his own pettiness, discover some big truths about life—there's no way he can lose. And the thing is, we all have both of those motivations within us, every second that we're writing. So it's an ongoing, lifelong battle to write for the right reasons. There's a sort of instant karma always working, if you see what I mean.

Having said that, I do think it's possible to "teach writing," in the sense that an older, like-minded person can certainly speed some younger person's progress along that younger person's personal arc. I imagine it this way: The younger writer is racing through some snowy woods, wearing ice skates. The M.F.A. experience, ideally, is a frozen lake that suddenly appears. The writer just gets sped up. The way is easier. The trajectory is roughly the same, but the velocity is higher. The danger of a workshop environment is a kind of groupthink that can creep into even the most enlightened gathering. Since ultimately what we are trying to do as writers (let's admit it) is be iconic and undeniable and breathtaking, setting up a group whose function is to Thoughtfully Regard, then Rationally Critique, may be problematic. But then, I also think it's possible to take that into account—to undercut that tendency, to keep knocking the legs out from under it, so to speak.

Finally: I think the success of the M.F.A. experience is proportional to how closely such a program resembles a salon or a group of friends. So I think small numbers are important, a longer residence time, financial support. I find that the best teaching moments happen when I know my students well enough, personally and artistically, to make certain intuitive leaps with them, leaps that aren't strictly dictated by the work sitting in front of me.

By the way, it may interest you to know that the Cross Old Man lives next door to Max, my ideal reader. Because of the Cross Old Man's impertinence to you, I have just sent Max over to "kiss" the Cross Old Man. I'll let you know how it turns out!

Can I do a follow-up, to you? Because what I am wondering about, in reference to the workshop questions, is what your experience was as a student in a workshop. Did you workshop anything that later became *The Age of Wire and String,* and, if so, how was it received? If you had put some of those stories up, and they'd gotten resistance—would it have mattered? I guess I'm asking because of the extreme originality of that book, and the fact that one of its many charms is that it keeps insisting on abiding by its own new paradigm.

BM: The closest I got to workshopping pieces from that book was in a class that Robert Coover taught called Ancient Fictions. He assigned us to write new mythologies, or creation myths, and a few of the earliest pieces in *The Age of Wire and String* were written in response. It was more of a literature class, with some fiction-writing options instead of critical papers. But it was by far the best course I ever took having anything to do with fiction-writing. The pieces we wrote weren't really discussed. I think we read them aloud and all nodded thoughtfully.

The workshop situation I was in with other teachers tended to err on the side of permissiveness, and actual teaching was more or less absent. It seems strange to say this, but in my own teaching I've tried to reverse almost everything I experienced as a student. Students now also seem to expect far more than I or my classmates ever did: extensive line-editing and lengthy written critiques, follow-up conferences, and then extra critiques of whatever revisions they've done. We were lucky if our teacher showed up or said much at all. At the time, the teacher's silence or reticence seemed like blinding intelligence, but I'm not so sure now.

II. "IT'S NOT A DRAMATIC ARC SO MUCH AS A DRAMATIC VECTOR: STRAIGHT DOWN INTO THE MUD."

BM: Even in your wilder stories, a current of deep ethics seems to run through your characters, an immense desire to do good, and it is this desire, the conflicts it creates, that seems to generate story for you. Big moments of grief seem to result, and these serve as epiphanies, revelations, or just incredible finales. Is this connected to a belief you have about character, or does it derive more from your sense of what might propel a story? Or neither?

GS: I like the kind of story where the reader comes away loving the character, feeling strongly identified with the character. And I think the way to make that happen is to make a character who is as good as the reader. That is, the reader feels the character is doing everything just as he or she would, if put in the same situation. So for the writer this means no slumming, no puppeteering—by which I mean, no manipulating your character to prove a point or illustrate something you believe or service some prejudice you have or fulfill some secret hope for the story. Don't make the character stupider or blinder or meaner than yourself. That is, credit the character with the same basic nature as you, albeit tempered or complicated by whatever is happening to him, or has happened in the past, that makes the character "you," but in a parallel universe. Even if your main character is Hitler, believe that there is some part of yourself that could swell into Hitleresque proportions. Another way of saying this is: believe that there, but for the grace of God, go you. So, in part, this ethical tendency you note is just a strategy to get more warmth into the story.

But to be another degree more honest, I think that's just the way I see the world—in fairly simple ethical terms. I always have. As a kid I was interested in philosophy and religion, and came to reading and thinking via Catholicism, had amazing early experiences in the Church, glimpses into what ideas such as compassion and self-sacrifice might mean at a visceral level, got the sense that life was big and painful and that the purpose of an individual life was to aid other beings in trouble, which runs counter to our instinct, which is to protect our own ass. And then that beautiful heroic narrative of Christ sacrificing himself to save everybody, even when he didn't want to. I found that very moving. That naïve big-question sensibility ("What are we doing here? How should we behave?") stayed at the heart of my ludicrous, spotty reading life through college.

Years later, when I was first working on *CivilWarLand,* I felt like I turned an important corner in my artistic life by letting that sensibility back in, that feeling that things matter, and that literature exists to help us examine the big questions. That there are such things as power, as abuse, as bad luck, and it definitely matters which side of the fence you're on. It matters whether we're hungry, whether your love is returned or rejected, whether we walk into the room with a fireplace and the cheering crowd or are locked out of the room and have to stand out in the cold with wet sneakers, etc. I guess what I'm saying is when it comes to writing stories, I don't know any other way to proceed. As soon as I start writing, things start to unfold around some central moral vector, and that's that. So, sometimes to my frustration, my stories tend to be "problem" stories: will he or won't he do the right thing? And they also tend to be fables, although I didn't realize that until recently. So the tendency you mention is both a blessing and a curse: I have something to write about, but there is a sort of an implicit ceiling, a kind of limit of subtlety I can't get past. The dangers of this approach are oversimplicity, preachiness, and, eventually, fascism.

Can I ask about your relation to this ethical stuff? I feel your work is extremely "ethical," in the sense that I always feel opened up when I'm reading it. I am, in the Chekhovian sense mentioned above, prepared for tenderness. Is this part of your intent?

BM: I'm not sure that in attempting sympathy in fiction I can claim a connection to ethics. It's hard for me to link writing with good deeds, since most of what I wrote for so long was character-free, and then when characters did show up they were interested in killing or at least harming the other characters. Not very ethical. A kind of coldness used to appeal to me. Behavior, if present at all, was mechanized and described the way a tree might be: sort of the stubborn opposite of giving human properties to inanimate things. But if I ever do get lucky and spill out some peoplelike pieces of writing, they are inevitably cruel or pitiful, take your pick. Unfortunately it yields only minimal drama. The cruel people act cruel to the pitiful people, who become more pitiful. It's not a dramatic arc so much as a dramatic vector: straight down into the mud. I'm sure most people get over this narrative paradigm in third grade, but it's about all I can manage so far.

I'm interested in the trace fantastical elements that appear in your stories, as well as the occasional ghost. So much of your stories seem wedded to an emotional realism, yet your settings—the landscapes—are often, if not fantastical, then exceedingly odd or improbable, leading to real emotions in an unreal world. And then your stories, sometimes very slightly, leave the realm of physical possibility entirely (the dead awaken, for instance). Are these three distinct writing-spaces to you? Do you see a difference between "realism" and fantastical writing?

GS: I guess it's strategic on one level: if you're going to have some really crazy things happening, you have a better chance of being believed if you jump off from some believable ground. It maybe comes from a sales instinct: If I'm trying to hustle ten bucks from you, and I've invented a wild story to support my hustle, it's probably best not to sing that story in an operatic voice. Better if I tell it in my normal voice, eyes downcast, acknowledging all your doubts about the veracity of my story. That's how I see the realist touches. I think the fantastical elements are there as my lame-brained attempt to mimic the real strangeness and mystery of even the most ordinary day.

Realism is nonsense, when you think of it. I mean, there is no such thing. Nobody writes realism, if realism is defined as "fiction that is objective and real and not distorted, but is just, you know, normal." But I think that's what "realistic" has come to mean. The nature of all fiction is distortion, exaggeration, and compression. So what we call realism is just distorting, exaggerating, and compressing with the intention of alluding to, or hand-waving at—taking advantage of our fondness for—what I've heard called "consensus reality"—the sort of lazy, agreed-upon "way things are." Which, of course, is not at all how they actually are. How they actually are is: We are walking corpses. Ideas people die for fade within ten years. Murderers walk. The dead don't really die because they can sometimes continue to affect the actions of the living just as much as if they were still around. Et cetera. So realism, as beautifully practiced by Zola, Chekhov, Carver, et al, is a strategy—a strategy to elicit our emotional loyalty by doing some sleight of hand to make the distorted, exaggerated, compressed thing they've made remind us of consensus reality. Why? Power of effect. They want to make a powerful effect.

What I find exciting is the idea that no work of fiction will ever, ever come close to "documenting" life. So then, the purpose of it must be otherwise. It's supposed to do something to us to make it easier (or more fun, or less painful) for us to live. Then all questions of form and so on become subjugated to this higher thing. We're not slaves any more to ideas of "the real" or, for that matter, to ideas of "the experimental"—we're just trying to make something happen to the reader in his or her deepest places. And that thing that happens will always be due to some juxtaposition of the life the reader is living and the words on the page, no matter how unconventional or conventional the representation of those events is—the heart will either rise, or it won't.

I think it's interesting, though, that some writers of our approximate generation have a sort of queasiness around this issue of realism. I know I do. There's something about the normal approach ("Bob, age forty-three, pale blond hair—a senior-level accountant—felt good about his marriage. He got into his tan Lexus, thinking of Maribeth.") that makes me scared and sick. I am always trying to avoid it.

You've written two radically unconventional books. Do you ever feel that pull toward what we're calling realism? If so, what's stopping you? What do you think that pull is about? That is, what do you fear you're missing by not doing "realism"? What concessions/changes would you have to make to be "more realistic"?

BM: I do feel a pull toward realism, but there's always a hand waiting to smack me down off it. From afar, where I definitely am, realism looks like a place of readability, which I very much desire, by which I mean that inscrutability is not something I value. But I can almost watch my fiction turn generic as I attempt realism, and then the trade-off leads to work that is punishingly dull. So what stops me is a total lack of ability. For probably good although unfathomable reasons, a narrative framework, a skin of storytelling—which I equate with a writerly promise that time will pass and that people will move around in a made-up space—seems to justify many kinds of conceptual or innovative approaches to fiction, but I find that, in itself, a kind of fantastical notion. I've seen a few writers I hugely admire, such as Joe Wenderoth or David Markson, become marginalized or called "experimental" because they have forgone the typical narrative skins and pursued more conceptual or subversively informational fiction. Yet their realism is, for me, extremely high.

There are these soporific, safe phrases like "once upon a time" that make nonrealist writing much more OK, and so I'm at the point where I'm wondering if that's a good thing worth pursuing or if it's a capitulation.

III. "HAVE WE SUFFICIENTLY DESCRIBED THE WONDERS OF LIVING IN OUR TIME?"

BM: Several less-narrative pieces of yours ("Four Institutional Monologues," which was in *McSweeney's,* and "I Can Speak!" which was in the *New Yorker*) did not make it into *Pastoralia*. What was the process of selecting work for that book? The above pieces were far less story-driven. Did that play a role in your decision?

GS: If I remember right, "I Can Speak!" was written after the manuscript was finished. So I had all these story-driven pieces and the one monologue, and it didn't seem to fit. But both stories you mention, plus another monologue ("A Survey of the Literature"), will be in the next collection. The monologue-like pieces feel different for me—easier, in some way. They don't depend on surprising myself as much as the more story-driven pieces. But I like them, and my thought for this next book is that they might add a little something—maybe offer a political or institutional angle on stuff that is covered more emotionally by the stories. I can picture a sort of a "spine" of these types of nonnarrative pieces running through the book. I like the way books like *In Our Time* or *The Coast of Chicago* use little spacer pieces that are different in tone and intent than the longer, more narrative pieces.

My usual approach so far has just been to put everything together that feels like it came out of the same aesthetic suite of ideas, which usually corresponds to a certain three-to-four-year time period—and then weed out the weaker links, or the anomalous ones. I usually have two or three pieces I start and don't finish, and another two or three that I finish but am not happy with, and then another couple that I'm happy enough with but don't seem to fit with the rest. They make a sort of goiter on an otherwise smooth shape. And then I figure that, if each of the pieces represents an intense move in some direction, a move that I played out aesthetically, then if I put them all together, with attention to the order—the book should be more than the sum of its parts. That's the theory, anyway.

For this next book, there is a pretty strong nonnarrative presence and also, I think, a stronger political (or overtly political) feeling. This wasn't planned but was maybe a product of the time during which the book was written.

BM: There is a word sometimes used in connection to fiction—*moral*—that can scare the bread out of me because I use it too, and then must secretly admit that I don't really understand it, or what it means, yet it seems to me to be a word that is reached for when something called "serious fiction" is discussed, a word we'd like to assign to the fiction we care about. Does "moral" fiction mean something to you that you can articulate?

GS: The short answer is: all good fiction is moral, in that it is imbued with the world, and powered by our real concerns: love, death, how-should-I-live. This is true, I think, of all great writers, regardless of their approach: Sterne, Chekhov, Barthelme, Morrison, Gogol, Bellow—whomever. But I think that word has taken on additional overtones since the Gardner-Gass debates of the 1980s, where the binary was: (1) Fictional effects are effects of language v. (2) Fictional effects are effects of represented experience. My guess is, most of us who have ever tried to write a sentence in a story know that both (1) and (2) are simultaneously true. If I write, "The cow, ducklike, made a ducklike cow sound, then disappeared down the Shaughnessy Chute," we recognize that there is a pure-sound quality to that, but also that cows and ducks and chutes are somehow "appearing" in our reading-mind. So it's the confluence of these two effects that makes the heart-rise I mentioned above (or doesn't, in this case).

But somehow, at that time, there was this sense that the purpose of fiction was "moral" in the sense of "instructive." That I reject. I mean, it is instructive, it feels that way, but instructive in a deep way, and in a way that does not flow from a writer's desire to instruct, if you see what I mean. Rather, it flows from the writer's confusion in the process of writing, or at least the writer's sense of exploration. Writing can be a formal way of enacting Oliver Cromwell's plea: "I beseech you, in the bowels of Christ, think it possible you may be mistaken." When a writer does that, then I think the result is moral, in the sense of "accounting for all complexities." I think you leave the work of art not instructed, but baffled, baffled in a way that humbles you and makes you move more carefully (but fully) through your life, at least until the effect wears off.

For writers of our generation (and of course, using that expression means I am really talking about me), that phrase "moral fiction" seems to signify something else, though, some deeper fear, a fear that the assumptions "we" have made about writing are self-limiting, especially around the issues of being ironic/edgy/experimental—a feeling that maybe our approach is preventing us from reaching into the more profound aspects of our experience, especially as we get older and less jaded and the checks start rolling in and the grandkids have grandkids and we see that life is not so angsty after all, at least not all the time. That is, the fear that our approach may be omitting significant aspects of our actual experience. I sense a real feeling of discontent hovering over American fiction right now and maybe all American art forms, post-9/11, that have at their core questions like (and please excuse the *U.S.A. Today* "we" in what follows): Does what we are doing matter? Are we writing as big as we need to write? Are we just spoiled-brat sneering aesthetes who are masturbating while looking away from the big questions of our age? Have we sufficiently described the wonders of living in our time? Are we properly accounting for the good and the beautiful and the enjoyable? But also: Are we properly accounting for the fact that evil exists, and exploring the difference between this and not-evil? How much of the irony and cleverness of our experimental writing—and, for that matter, how much of the earnest and uplifting "We"-reinforcement of our realist writing—is just knee-jerk and ultimately reactionary?

In other words, life came brutally knocking at our door, and now we are reconsidering the venture. And I'm not saying everyone should get busy on their Kosovo novel—I think there is a way in which even the most domestic story (or wild, experimental story) can take into account the larger world. But one could argue that American fiction has ghettoized itself by insisting on a self-reifying view (humanist/materialist?) in which all answers are known, the political binary is carved in stone, we all have swallowed whole certain orthodoxies, and the purpose of the fiction is just to reinforce these. At the heart of this lies a selfish agenda, that has (one could argue) really ceased seeing the world as a unity, and has begun aggressively internalizing certain capitalist dogmas that say: of course you are the most important thing, of course you exist separate from the rest of the world.

I'm not sure I actually believe all of the above—but I do find myself thinking about these kinds of things a lot lately. Does this make any sense? Do you feel any of this? It may just be that I am saying: I really really hope to, in the future, write better. By the way, I just came back from the Cross Old Man's house, and am happy to report that, after many many "kisses" from Max, the Cross Old Man has at last admitted that writing can be taught.

BM: I worry that if you smother an old man with kisses, crank up his sexual heat or whatever, he'll admit to anything. These lonely people are just waiting to tell us what we want to hear.

IV. "THAT VOICE OF HEMINGWAY'S CAN'T FUNCTION IN A WAL-MART, ON CHRISTMAS EVE, WHEN YOU HAVE AN STD..."

BM: You have a film project under way. Can you tell me about it?

GS: Back in 1997, Ben Stiller optioned *CivilWarLand* and so for the last year or so I've been working with him on a script. It's been interesting in that film-writing is so much about structure and so little about language. You can just say, "Tens of thousands of chimps emerge from mobile phone booths, speaking French," and that's it. There are the chimps. In other words, you don't have to do what we usually do, which is convince with language. You can just make these little structural units, which will be de facto "convincing" because the viewer will be seeing them. So it changes the nature of the challenge, writing-wise. It forced me to use a different part of my brain; the part that says, if I put A, then B, then C—trusting that each of these will be done well—then I've made resulting Meaning D. Which is not how I think when I'm writing fiction—then, I tend to concentrate on the individual line, trusting that some worthwhile effect will come out in the end, but I don't necessarily know what it is.

It's also been interesting anthropologically—getting some idea of how movies get made, how the larger mass culture might get accessed, how finances play into the whole thing, etc. So much of our storytelling now takes place within this quasicorporate framework, and so it's interesting to see if there is a sort of de facto editing effect working, and if so, what the flavor of it is. Also it's been interesting for me to think about broad appeal—is it possible/desirable for somebody like me? What is the difference between "literary" and "popular"? I've been especially interested to see, in myself, a sort of knee-jerk tendency toward the dark, the negative, the nihilistic—somehow, film-writing made this tendency more noticeable. When I do this knee-jerk thing, it's more apparent, feels more like flinching. In film, it seems like because there are actual people up there, somehow my urge to credit the noble, the good, the simply decent is more easily managed than in stories.

I'm not sure what to think of all that, but I've noticed it, and am sort of mulling it over. It goes back to something we talked about earlier: how much of the brooding, cynical nature of our art-fiction is meaningful (i.e., is telling a deep truth) and how much of it is just limited technical ability and/or sloth? I think there are deep truths about our time that are dark and scary—but I also think that not every dark/scary move that is accomplishable via fiction necessarily has a real-life corollary. Sometimes they're just easier—as Montherlant said: "Happiness writes white."

BM: You've had two amazing and critically lauded collections of short stories. Do you feel pressure to write a novel?

GS: I sometimes do. I just finished reading *Appointment in Samarra* and *Revolutionary Road* and those really made me want to write a novel—they're such beautiful, complicated books, and they show America in so much wonderful detail. My main problem is a very small intersection-set between (1) the abilities it takes to write a novel and (2) the abilities I actually have. Working on a story, I have very strong and intuitive opinions. With novels, I have mostly Ideas, which, in my case, are deadly. I seem decent at compressing, but not so good at elaborating. So for now, I'm just allowing myself to do what I love, which is write stories. The one thing I would love to do in a novel is show the world as a big, stunning contradiction: to show Truth A in all its glory, then show Truth B (which contradicts Truth A) in all its glory.

There's a beautiful story, which sounds like a joke, because it starts: "Once Tolstoy and Gorky were walking down the street." As Gorky described it (in a memoir piece he wrote about Tolstoy), this mob of hussars comes walking up the street, and Tolstoy launches into this brilliant bit of polemic about how that sort of young man—brutal, cocksure, militaristic—represents everything that is wrong with Russia. And Gorky was convinced. Then, as the hussars passed in a cloud of tobacco smoke and cologne and leather, etc., Tolstoy spun on his heel and delivered an equal-but-opposite dissertation on why that sort of young man—fully alive, masculine, passionate, spontaneous—was the hope of Russia's future. And again, Gorky was convinced. That, to me, is art's highest aspiration: to show that nothing is true and everything is true. To work as a kind of ritual humility, and ritual celebration, of all that is.

BM: Like Raymond Carver and Denis Johnson before you, your stories have served as an ideal model—an inspiration—for legions of newcomers. This may be an awkward question, but does being so widely emulated by younger writers change the way you approach what you're doing?

GS: I don't really see that. Every so often, someone will send me a story full of funny franchise names, or composed completely of acronyms. But to the extent that it's true, I'm honored. And it's funny how, as you get older, and look back at your own work—it seems young. In a good way, but... young. And you remember whom you were channeling or admiring at the time. So I say, anything that gets us going. I remember basically rewriting *Red Cavalry* by setting it in an oil camp in Indonesia, where I'd once worked. And also rewriting *In Our Time,* but set in Amarillo, Texas, and Nick had not just come home from war, but was on spring break. And what I felt most acutely, doing those little knockoffs, was how inappropriate and uncomfortable someone else's stylistic tics were, superimposed on my life.

In other words, those imitations helped me realize that there is no Real Life—there is no objective reality. There is just your version of it, and that version has to be in your language. I thought: That voice of Hemingway's can't function in a Wal-Mart, on Christmas Eve, when you have an STD and your uncle is drunk and trying to buy an O'Jays record to give to his new girlfriend, a speed-freak waitress. Hence the constant necessity for new voices. ✯

ADAM THIRLWELL

TALKS WITH

TOM STOPPARD

"I SUSPECT THAT THE WHOLE TRICK IS TO UNDERMINE THE AUDIENCE'S SECURITY ABOUT WHAT IT THINKS IT KNOWS AT ANY MOMENT. I THINK THAT ONE HAS TO TRY TO DO IT ON THE SMALLEST SCALE AS WELL AS THE LARGEST."

This interview takes place:
Driving on the motorway from London
In deck chairs, watching cricket
After cricket, at tea
Driving on the motorway to London

T*om Stoppard was born in Zlin, Czechoslovakia, in 1937, and came to England in 1946. His major plays include* Rosencrantz and Guildenstern Are Dead *(1965),* Jumpers *(1972), and* Travesties *(1975).* Every Good Boy Deserves Favour *and* Professional Foul *were performed in 1977.* Night and Day *came out in 1978,* The Real Thing *in 1982,* Arcadia *in 1993, and* The Invention of Love *in 1997. His trilogy,* The Coast of Utopia*—comprising the plays* Voyage, Shipwreck, *and* Salvage*—opened in 2003. In 1998, he won an Oscar for Best Screenplay for* Shakespeare in Love. *He lives in London, and quite likes cricket.*

—Adam Thirlwell (Summer 2004)

I. TO CRICKET

TOM STOPPARD: You know, I'd like to present myself as somebody who's really on the case when he's writing a play, and I rather admire—hang on a minute, where do we go? We have to go to the M25, and turn off—rather admire the theoretical writer who has an objective in mind and shapes his material in order to convey it and resolve it.

Ages ago I started to do something different from my earlier practice. My earlier practice was to try to work out as much as possible, and not to feel that I didn't know what I was doing while I was doing the writing. But I realized that I wasn't doing that very successfully, and without really understanding what was happening I was actually inventing things as I was coming to them. So I quite quickly became that kind of self-conscious writer—someone who has decided just to start and keep his fingers crossed. And I still think that I ought to do that. *The Invention of Love,* for instance, was really quite a frightening saga. I didn't know where I was going, and if I hadn't got to the point where I realized that I could have a really good solid scene where the old man is literally talking to his young self, which is quite a theatrical, attractive situation for the audience—they have fun with it—if I hadn't somehow blundered my way into that, I don't know what I would have done, frankly. When I look back on my plays I'm absolutely mystified by the fact that I ever began writing them, because I know that in the beginning I didn't know what I was doing, and I think that—OK hang on, yes quite right, M25…

ADAM THIRLWELL: There's a lane on the left.

TS: I do know the way, it's just that I forget to look for the road signs.

With *Arcadia,* I remember writing this academic arriving at this country house and I had to decide whether the manuscript letters from 180 years before were in his briefcase or in the house. I hadn't worked out how it was going to go—which was quite scary and probably beneficial in some way. I'm rambling. Go on. Oh yes, what I was actually trying to say about fifteen minutes ago was that I don't have a play to write at the moment but I have at least two subjects for a play so in a way I do have a play to write, it's just I have no idea what the story will be. And I just don't believe in the kind of theater which I want to write—which isn't a storytelling theater.

There are three or four things I thought, you know, might justify writing a play. I mean, they're all quite interesting, and still are, but I have no idea of any kind of narrative or characters. Usually the problems just disappear, at least somehow—I'd be off. I took it all to France recently and read it all again: I had a suitcase full of offprints and press cuttings, and subjects and God knows what I had. I had more sort of assembled them out of pure *instinct* and I just kept shoving these elements around, and came home not having actually achieved anything at all. So then I got neurotic.

And then I had the realization that there was no necessity for me to write a play, nobody was asking me to. So I then cheered up and stopped trying to, and had a very good period where I was equally nonproductive, writing no play instead of not writing one, if you see what I mean…

AT: Yes.

TS: That sort of exhilaration has now died away and I'm actually going to try again.

My main thing was actually to do with what's called "the problem of consciousness"—the very words sound like a death knell of drama, don't they? There's been a mild academic fight going on, for the last fifteen years, between people like John Searle and Daniel Dennett, who have different notions of what consciousness is and where it comes from. They all agree on one thing—it's just the brain, physics. And I was just an unreconstructed dualist, actually. So, I thought, that would be interesting to write about. That was one thing. And then there was Sappho. I had a period of getting excited about exploiting fragments as an art form. I mean, faute de mieux, one has these pages of Sappho, and most pages don't make any sense.

God knows whether it's anything to do with a *play* or not, but it's interesting in itself.

They used a lot of papyrus for bandages—so if you imagine one of your pages, or Shakespeare's sonnets, being torn longitudinally into three strips, and just the middle one remains… It looks very interesting on the page, and all kinds of people have tried to write the whole poem on the basis of the fragments left.

AT: There's an Ezra Pound one, isn't there?

TS: Yes. There is. So that was another thing, and there were a couple of other things… And, quite perversely, I mean, without any real rationale, I decided to somehow jam them all into the same narrative, like cats in a bag fighting. And I think probably I was overambitious, which is why I didn't even get anywhere.

I'd write a page and a half, six or seven times, the same page and a half, and then I began not avoiding cliché, and I began to think about Martin Amis's "war against cliché." I got sidetracked. I began to think that he was completely wrong about that because one of the things one uses is familiarity, it's actually a useful thing to have in one's locker. The phrase goes home better because you don't have to think, Oh that's nice and new. So I began to look for clichés in things I liked, and I began to realize very quickly that there are a lot of things I like, where the only right word was the obvious word. That Betjeman poem about the girl in the inglenook, and he's such a thumping crook—if you had something besides "thumping" it just would not be as good.

AT: There are writers like Betjeman who use cliché—Joyce, Ionesco, Beckett, who also do this: they don't use the cliché without consideration; they arrange clichés musically, with care. I think

Betjeman's often the same, although he's not seen as an experimental writer like them. He's doing something quite clever…

TS: I don't know how clever it is, in the sense of being conscious cleverness, but I think his instinct is right. That the poem is not a clichéd poem, simply because it's using some cliché. But that was something else.

But the *fragment* thing—I began to visualize the madness. I think in the end I thought, No, you can't, this would have to be a film. Then you could just cut into the middle of a conversation, and out of it—and then do it again, and then do the other bit of it, and so forth. I don't think you can do that on the stage: I think it would be terribly irritating, and pretentious.

Yes, well, my Sappho play: nothing exists. I'm going to try again. I'm so depressed. I'm just sort of full of self-disgust actually. This morning I weighed more than I've ever weighed in my entire life. Literally. And that's really a low point isn't it—just thinking, I've never ever, in all these years, weighed as much as this.

AT: Gaining in gravitas?

TS: Eating sandwiches and ruing the day.

The fact that *The Coast of Utopia* turned out to be three plays was something I didn't plan until I was on the point of starting to write—it's just that I got addicted to the background reading. And ended up finding this enormous nine-hour saga. And I was really very fascinated by the people but I was also aware that I had to massage the historical narrative into something which had some sense of being a play, having the architecture of a play.

AT: In my arrogant, novelistic way I had this theory that you were borrowing from the novel—in the matter of length. A play has two hours, whereas a novelist has 450 pages in which to explore minute aspects of character. Obviously, in *The Coast of Utopia,* one of the things you're interested in is irony, ironic undercutting—the way that a character's ideas can be undermined by their behavior, and it's intriguing that this kind of thing is more interesting and easier to do, onstage, if you've got more time to do it.

TS: I think that's right.

[*Pause*]

AT: I can give you an example.

TS: All right.

AT: One of the things I was thinking was the infidelity between Alexander Herzen and his wife, Natalie, in *The Coast of Utopia*—the way the entire theme runs throughout the play is very delicate. It's first mentioned actually in relation to Herzen, with Natalie saying to Herzen's best friend, Nick Ogarev, "I suppose you're going to say it was only a servant-girl." But evidently she's not devastated by it. She's sad from it and hurt by it but it's not ruined their marriage. And then later Herzen announces: "Fidelity is admirable, but proprietorship disgusting." It's the naïveté of Oscar Wilde in his essay "The Soul of Man under Socialism": "Jealousy, which is an extraordinary source of crime in modern life, is an emotion closely bound up with our conceptions of property, and under Socialism and Individualism will die out." But Herzen is devastated and proprietorial when he finds out that Natalie has been unfaithful.

TS: That was completely conscious on my part.

AT: Then I think what's lovely is that it's complicated further so that Natalie is flighty, romantic: she's not perfect. So that when Herzen sentimentalizes the affair after her death and says, "Her devotion to me, her remorse, her courage when she faced the madness that man infected her mind with..." that's a falsification after the fact. And the further irony is that when Natalie Ogarev is unfaithful with Herzen, Ogarev does not mind—and yet Natalie wants to believe that he does—"He's in pain. We've broken his heart. His worst enemy couldn't have hurt him more."

That's an example of a theme that runs the length of two plays, and the complications and mirrorings of that would just not have been possible in a play that only lasted two hours.

TS: I think it would be possible in a play that was about nothing else. I think you could write a two-hour play that was only about that. There is something very attractive in having this vast canvas, in which you can really balance things against each other when they're separated by all kinds of other but no less equally interesting events.

The thing you've just been describing became for me what I *had,* all I had by way of a story. That was really it. Because Herzen's intellectual and ideological development didn't really go very far after 1848. By 1851–'52, he's pretty much worked out what he'd been disenchanted by and where the future for Russia ought to lie—that people were just too corrupted and the answer had to be to go back home and do it with the unpolluted peasantry. So by the time we get to the beginning of the final play, *Salvage,* he doesn't have anywhere to go as regards changing his mind about things, which is why I felt myself in trouble.

AT: Writers who are stylists are often writers who dislike ideas. And one of the things that I was thinking, in *The Coast of Utopia,* is that essentially you're sending ideas up. Ideas are things which people take very seriously, and yet there is this area of ordinary domestic experience which somehow manages to upend them—which washes over and ironizes the theoreticians in *The Coast of Utopia.* So you get Bakunin, say, the prophet of libertarianism, who's simply a domestic despot.

In *The Coast of Utopia,* the same idea is uttered by more than one character, but in different contexts. I imagine that this is to show that ideas are like suitcases, as it were: an idea is a suitcase into which you pack your own clothes.

TS: Yes. It's interesting, actually. We have to look for a gate on our right. It's to do with the bad fit between private and public demeanors. It doesn't spring from a sense of confrontation. I mean what I write about—it doesn't spring from an urge to refute or to detach oneself. It's much more to do with recognizing, or feeling that I recognize, a displacement between public and private utterance, and public and private posture; that people find it quite difficult to match up the private arena and the public arena so their emotional and domestic lives sometimes seem quite irrelevant to their intellectual lives. Hang on. Hello. My name is Tom Stoppard, is this the cricket?

II. AT CRICKET

AT: Where were we?

TS: Yes, where were we?

AT: Turgenev. Herzen and Turgenev.

TS: I think Turgenev had a good sense of what he himself was capable of doing. He had a good sense of what he was put on earth to do. And he also had a good sense of his ultimate usefulness rather than uselessness. His fictions lived longer than Herzen's essays; they didn't have an obvious and direct utilitarian function, but they did have a function—Bazarov and so on became part of the language of a crucial movement. Because he's clear-eyed and honest, and an artist, people return again and again to the stories he wrote: the mortar between the bricks seeped into people's thinking. So Turgenev played a larger role than Herzen, the way things went in Russia.

They were both people who enjoyed and liked having the finer things in life, and they were aware of the anomaly. Herzen was aware of it. Herzen was actually the rich guy among this crowd: he inherited his father's estate, he never had any money problems, and he was aware of some kind of contradiction and referred to it occasionally. But his humanitarian and egalitarian instinct was extremely strong: a sense of justice and fairness. He was willing to have it all taken away from him, because he could see that it was unfair, and that's rather wonderful, because he was working against his own class, ultimately. At that stage, he had a sort of faith in other people's humanitarian impulses. Turgenev looks a bit cynical compared to Herzen.

AT: I think it's Turgenev's brand of skepticism that I find interesting. A militant aestheticism, as it were, has to be completely skeptical at all points of political action or political ideology. It's constantly aware of all the contextual motives. It isn't idealistic. And certainly someone who believes in the value of politics is going to find Turgenev rebarbative. There's a toughness to Turgenev: a rigor in his relativism.

TS: Turgenev had an absolute horror and terror of violence. Turgenev was a monarchist if the alternative was violence. And when Turgenev was under some kind of suspicion by association, he absolutely panicked, and wrote to Moscow saying: "Look, you know, everyone knows I'm utterly against anything like that," and so on.

Herzen's possibly trying to dissociate himself from apparent shared values with the system of Turgenev—although he did share a certain level of living, he enjoyed the same things and valued the same things, and liked them to survive.

Oh, it's very difficult to get at this one.

Turgenev is a bit like that story about John Braine in the southern states of America, at a cocktail party, with an Episcopal bishop, having a glass of sherry. And Braine said: "This is the most wonderful country in the world—America." And the other man said: "Well, not if you're black." And Braine looked slightly bewildered and said: "But I'm not black."

I think Turgenev was saying: "Yes, but I *am* a Western liberal, who was brought up to enjoy opera. That's what I *am*. How else can I see anything? I'm not a Sandwich Islander. I can only function from this point of view." Whereas Herzen was not doing that, not saying that: he had a much wider view and a deeper view of the context. But in the end—it'd be cruel to say he was ineffective, as people continue to get inspiration from him, so it wasn't as if he were dead—but he got overtaken by the traffic, just sort of run down, it came up behind him and squashed him. Turgenev made sure he wasn't in the road.

AT: This relationship, or nonrelationship, between the political and the literary, is there in your work, too. It intrigues me, say, reading Kenneth Tynan's *New Yorker* profile of you where, although it's full of love and admiration, there is this tiny undertow of Tynan thinking: "Why isn't this guy writing Brechtian plays?"

TS: I know. The thing is that he had the bad luck to write his profile just before *Professional Foul*. And then a month later *Every Good Boy Deserves Favour* was published.

AT: Did you ever discuss those plays with him?

TS: No, I didn't really. The truth of the matter is that he was broke and was terribly glad to have a long profile paid for with a lot of money. He asked Harold Pinter to cooperate for a profile. Pinter said he wouldn't. So then he asked me. I found out later. His main motive was to write a profile of *somebody*. Having written it, I don't think he was that interested in the fact that I followed with two plays about politics.

AT: The argument in the profile seems to center on Wilde.

TS: I used to have these conversations with Tynan about Wilde's essays, particularly "The Soul of Man under Socialism." I was slightly dishonest with him because I pontificated about Wilde on the basis of the plays I knew, and nothing else. Tynan would then say, "This is all nonsense, this wonderful essay 'The Soul of Man under Socialism,' blah blah blah." So I would think, Oh, Christ, I better read that. And then I'd read it, as it were, with demolition in view—to undercut any effect. I'd dismiss it as being simply another form of his pirouetting.

I think that 9/11 and the Iraq war are events which... You can't behave as though they changed nothing, you know? Everything has to be changed in some way: your thinking is changed, your thinking about what you should be writing about, certainly. Well, I'm thinking about it. Well, put it this way: while the emotion is at its height, while the consciousness is at its most acute about what's happening, while you're living in that kind of atmosphere, your view or your assessment of the purity and validity of that sonnet somehow... It doesn't mean you think, Oh I have to stop, there's no point in writing sonnets anymore, that's all over. It's not that. But the decades which led up to the end of what Fukuyama would call "the previous history" went on for so long. Occasionally there'd be a bit of a frisson called Cuba, but generally speaking it just went on for so long that it became the climate. You felt that Max Beerbohm would have written what he'd written, in the same climate.

I kept very quiet after 9/11. Everybody sort of bounced into print in a self-questioning way—and I can understand why, I felt much the same—but I thought, Don't say anything because the times are distorting: they're distorting your ability to think clearly at the moment.

AT: I think I feel that the two are perhaps incommensurate.

TS: Go on with that one.

AT: Well, there are things that I care about concerning art, and that is evidently, on one level, a very important concern, and on another level an absolutely minuscule and irrelevant concern. Evidently art is a luxury. And so were I to be reduced to living in fur, in Siberia, tomorrow, I would not be caring particularly about Oscar Wilde and style.

It seems to me that sometimes there is a melodrama of self-questioning about art: if you believed before 9/11 that it was important to care about not using cliché, say, then there's no reason why 9/11 might change that. It might make you think that sometimes you should be thinking about other things as well, but then it surprises me that it would take something like 9/11 to make you realize that: the actual concern seems to me to remain...

TS: It alters the emphasis you put on it, doesn't it? For a while.

AT: I just think that there can be a tough kind of aestheticism, a pragmatic type, which thinks that obviously these concerns are limited within their own sphere, but that doesn't mean that the entire sphere has to disappear just because there are other things of importance. It's evidently true that the other things of importance will always rise and fall—so that at some point suddenly it will seem imperative to be thinking about terrorism, or thirty years ago to be thinking about communism—but it seems to me also that in the end the really good writers do have a slight autism to them, an earned independence.

I think sometimes you can see this kind of problem where writers try to make a link between being a good writer and being a good person, or a good reader and a good person. But there's no reason why there should be a correlation between your ethical ability and your aesthetic ability—and that kind of statement is made by someone haunted by the unnecessary worry that art needs to be justified on a further, moral level.

TS: No, I agree with that. Things get more interesting when the artist uses the event as his subject matter. I mean, in the trenches of the First World War, there were tens of thousands of copies of Housman. There's an edition published in a size you could fit into a battle-dress pocket. That's a different thing from, say, David Jones's *In Parenthesis,* which was an attempt to bring his aesthetic values to the subject matter. And there of course nobody has a problem—

basically they say, "Well that's what artists should do, that's what they're for, they must remember, and relive, and see more clearly." And what *you're* saying is "What about the guy who wasn't there, and who wants to continue perfecting his sonnets?" And what *I'm* saying is that whatever the values one invests in the work he's doing, the fact that he's doing it is a moral statement. It's not like saying, "I'm not actually committing myself here": in a way you *are* making a statement by detachment, by detaching yourself.

AT: The guy who makes bicycles—you would think it was rather odd if he were to say to you: "I've had to rethink everything I've been doing since 9/11."

TS: Yeah, that would be odd, wouldn't it?

AT: And I'm not sure how different that is from the idea that the guy who writes plays, say…

TS: But you see, this is exactly where one sees that artists are not bicycles. I mean, PEN doesn't have a committee for pastry-cooks in prison, or bicycle-makers in prison. So you think, Well, what the hell is this? What's going on here? When did society constitute itself in such a way that this figure of the artist had some kind of special status? How far back does that actually go? And the answer seems to be, it actually goes back to the beginning.

AT: I wonder how far this problem of art is really a category mistake, of people wanting a word to mean more than one thing.

TS: A lot of questions which present themselves as problems turn out to be a failure of vocabulary.

Decent shot, wasn't it?

AT: There was one thing you said earlier. I said that style was the most important thing for me. And you said that the idea never grew on you. Do you mean that actually now you don't believe that style is all important, that you grew out of it—or that you instinctively knew that it was something you never had to ponder?

TS: The question is, what do I mean now, or what did I mean then?

AT: Well, it could be either. Either is fine.

TS: What I would say is that it's different for a novelist.

I thought when I was young, and I think now, that a style-signature is why you read somebody. And, when I was young, finding and keeping and impressing that style-signature led me into a liking for certain kinds of writing in an attempt to emulate or simulate certain kinds of style-writing—which maybe put a strain on what I was writing. I mean, when I was starting off I remember a short story I wrote that had a one-legged person in it, and I remember some translation showing up and I was thinking, Well, this actually says in English "intrepid uniped"—what is the *point* in Lithuanian, there's simply no point in *saying* it, if you can't have fun with the language. And I think that there are writers for whom that's not an important issue. Writers who are possibly very great writers, writers I revere—Hemingway for example. I imagine Hemingway in German would be absolutely fine. But there are writers for whom that can't possibly be true.

And I still feel that a writer's style, if that's the word—tone, signature, whatever—is the reason for reading him. But, where it stops is you begin to realize that the way a play can work upon you—event, physical event—is very effective indeed. When you refer back to the source of all this—the page—it doesn't seem to be there. Furthermore, there's no authorial voice in a play, every single voice is a person—and how can it be, why should it be, that each of these people should have a style? People are not, on the whole, stylish speakers. So one has to be careful of the word. Although as you perceive a thought, there always seems to be one more corner to go around. You might then say, "Well, look at Mamet, for example." Yes, well, look at Mamet! I mean, the artifice in that! The care that goes into every utterance! I think that when I started off, I probably didn't have enough confidence in myself to suppose that I could capture and hold the attention unless there was something startling going on all the time—and the notion that the attention would be held by something deeper than that *struck* me, but I didn't know how to do it, or felt I didn't know how to do it. So I always turned, somehow without even willing it, into comedy. But I may have got the chicken mixed up with the egg, actually.

Oh that's a just *beautiful* shot. [*Claps*] I'm always mystified by drives, the cover drive, which hits the bat higher up than I feel I could cope with. A cover drive which comes off the bottom three inches of the bat I understand. One which comes off the middle of the bat I find very hard to work out.

AT: A comment I love about dialogue in the *novel* is a moment where Lampedusa is talking about Stendhal. He says that in Stendhal "the fault of so many novels has disappeared, this fault which consists in revealing the soul of the characters through their dialogue..." Whereas in Stendhal, *"there is no famous dialogue."* It's just, "How are you?—I'd like some scrambled eggs please." And I was thinking this is impossible for a dramatist—if you didn't reveal the soul of the characters through their dialogue in some way, the play's going to be impossible.

TS: Yes, yes. But the power that a play has over its audience, I think, in the end is not in the dialogue. It's the situation. I've always envied playwrights who are knockout situationists—Ayckbourn is, for example. Who probably would be delighted to be bracketed suddenly with Stendhal, but I say this equally as the same compliment: he doesn't write memorable lines, but you're absolutely gripped by the situation onstage. I recognized this very early on, and I've become aware that plays of mine which worked better are the ones where the style element just becomes a bonus. But it's good if you find that your wisecracking people are actually in a situation which has the audience agog, and not really feeding off the style of utterance at all.

AT: I think somewhere else you said that the problem with your plays was that for a long time everyone spoke the same.

TS: Well, I did used to say that: I used to think it.

AT: But I think it's arguable about even your early plays, and it's certainly not true of plays from even *The Real Thing* onward…

TS: I think it was true early on in some ways. I have an African dictator, in one play—and I remember thinking to myself, quite cold-bloodedly, I'm going to have to find a background for this guy, which will enable me to write his dialogue, because I sure as hell can't write African-dictator dialogue. I can only write the dialogue for somebody who was at the LSE and then went back to Africa. Which is more or less what I did.

I think that it's a slightly out-of-date quote. I think I learned to do things as time went on, or perhaps I just discovered they weren't as difficult as I assumed that they would be.

AT: I think that realizing how little you need to create a character's voice is an interesting thing: I think I always believed that it requires an incredible ingenuity of invention, that you had to be able to think up seventeen things that this character—

TS: It requires an *ear*—it's not actually inventing, if you're remembering it. And some people are better than others. I'm very bad at it. I know that from the way that I can put on a record, an album, which I've heard fifty times—it's a long way into the track before I work out which one it is. Or something comes on the radio, and I think, It's one of my favorite records, which one is it, *which* of my favorite records is this? And I'm sure for writers there's a strength there or a weakness, and I simply don't think of it as being a strength of mine at all.

There's another way of putting this.

How do you avoid being boring when you're writing a boring character? Well, the answer is really that we don't have a boring person in a play unless the point is that he's boring, and then you've got a situation which is interesting or funny or whatever because the boring element is there for a particular reason. There's a Peter Nichols play I remember where people show up at somebody's house and there seems to be—in my memory—reams and reams of dialogue on how they got there, which road they took—"Oh, no, you should have taken the A35." This is a conversation without any redeeming interest, either in subject or phrasing. But of course it was hilarious because—it's to do with recognition, isn't it?

Let's go and have a cup of tea.

III. TEA

TS: I've got a nice after-lunch feeling now.

AT: What is it you think is charming about cricket? I think I like its unpredictability—that this is a game which is played as a game of skill, but is essentially a game of chance.

TS: I never think of cricket as being anything to do with chance. It seems to me entirely about skill. Yes, the weather might intervene. But that's not really about cricket, that only possibly impinges on the result of a particular match, but the actual cricket is something separate.

But *my* involvement with cricket came through playing, not through watching it. I'm not sure I ever found it terribly interesting to watch. But being inculcated from the age of eight or nine, cricket—no more than any other sport I played—became interesting from the point of view of doing it. I was never that good at it, but I did aspire to being a wicket-keeper.

There's something about the position of wicket-keeper which appealed to me very deeply—I was very bad-tempered if I had to play in a match where while fielding I wasn't allowed to keep wicket. Cricket seemed more or less pointless to me if you weren't actually a wicket-keeper. And I could see that it might be a viable game if you opened the bowling and continued to bowl for the entire course of the innings. That also could be interesting, I suppose. I loved being involved in every ball bowled—which is your situation when you're keeping wicket. It isn't *even* true, really, of somebody who's bowling, who gets a rest every six balls. And consequently I hero-worshipped, in succession, Godfrey Evans, Alan Knott—I suppose I was too old to hero-worship people by the time we got to Jack Russell. But I find when I'm watching cricket on television even now—I rarely go to cricket—I still find myself mostly fascinated by what the wicket-keeper's doing.

It's partly to do with the fact that every ball is frightening, if you're keeping wicket, because there's a very good chance that you'll have to *deal* with it if the batsman doesn't. And, as you know, when it comes to catches being offered, probably three out of five go to the wicket-keeper, generally. So you feel that there's a lot of responsibility on you, and one is constantly frightened of publicly shaming oneself—by dropping an easy catch or missing an easy stumping—which of course happened to me all the time, but nevertheless that's what I liked doing.

AT: Whereas for me the thing I hated about fielding was the knowledge that at any point this thing could come toward you.

TS: But, when fielding, somehow you feel that there are so many other directions that the ball may go in. Whereas with wicket-keeping, if the batsman doesn't hit it, it's yours. And I loved, I suppose, the gloves and the pads and all that, and the sound the ball made going into a glove. It's quite a complex little thing, keeping wicket. And this tremendous sort of pride in standing up to a bowler who wasn't particularly slow, if you got to know him very well.

AT: It reminds me—talking of weather and cricket and chance. In *The Coast of Utopia,* in the second play, *Shipwreck,* Herwegh says: "*Stoical* freedom is nothing but not wasting your time berating the weather when it's bucketing down on your picnic." And in *Salvage,* Herzen mentions "picnics ruined by rain" in his list of things he's moved beyond. And the final scene is of an outdoor party where it's starting to rain. Is this a deliberate pattern?

TS: No, it's not. It was unknowing, I think. I mean, even if it wasn't unknowing, it wasn't supposed to mean anything. But it's nice that there is a pattern. The thing is, Adam, that things that are sort of *spottable* in that way are, as it were, rare—and sometimes are conscious. But they're there like jokes for the attentive reader, they're not there to provide vital clues to the thrust of the play, or a vital piece of symbolism—not to me, I don't think.

AT: It's true that it's not the key to the play, but it does link up to a larger theme: things happen beyond our control, as it were the future is not reliable. Herzen says that people mistakenly want to believe that they can own the future. That was the pattern that I thought it linked up to, you plan a picnic, but you have no idea if it's going to be pissing down.

TS: No, I completely see that, and I absolutely feel the same way about it as you do, but also from the same perspective as you do. These things emerge, and you think, Oh, that's good because it's *x, y, z*. What it is *not* is somebody sitting down with a piece of graph paper at ten in the morning and thinking, Now how can I plant something which will convey, perhaps, no no no... So it's all true but it's not that significant, that's all. I think it's very flattering, I think it's a great compliment when you come across somebody in conversation or print who actually has remembered a detail in a play. It's hardly what one expects but it's very nice.

AT: You said you aren't the kind of writer who has an objective in mind and shapes the material in order to convey that. And I don't like that kind of writer, either, who simply has a thesis and wants to expound it. But there's still scope for artistry, for organization, for theme, for formal play—and it's as if you are also trying to shut that off as well.

TS: Well, I think I know where the truth lies. What I mean is that

I can sort of see why I'm contradicting myself. When you're writing the speech about picnics ruined by rain, you're not thinking, Ah, I'll have a picnic later where it starts to rain. What is going on is that you find yourself at a picnic and you remember it would be a good fit if it rained. So, you know—it's true from one angle and untrue from another angle.

I actually rather relish—in other people if I can spot it, and certainly enjoy it in my own things—echoes which bounce back at you, or echo down the play. I like that happening, and in fact occasionally I stumble into something which becomes actually structural, like the penknife in *Voyage*.

The great thing about the penknife in *Voyage* for me is that I didn't know that I'd be able to do this, until things emerged, and then it becomes the nicest thing in *Voyage* for me. It's not premeditated, but it's very knowing when you do it.

AT: I absolutely know what you *mean,* that no good writer is going to be thinking in terms of a play's architecture as a whole, at every moment. And yet although some of the formal tricks that I love about your work are things that might be lovely flukes, some things are too intricate.

It's interesting, say, following the penknife. If you think about the structure of *Voyage,* progressing forward in time, twice, filling in the gaps from the first half in the second half—I love that the first time you hear about the penknife is actually when you don't know you're hearing it—when Tatiana says, "Did you catch anything?" You assume she means a fish.

TS: Yes, it's backward.

AT: The penknife is a lovely miniature of the play's structure.

TS: One has seen quite a few good documentary drama plays where you're just shown what happened and what people said as near as one can endeavor that way. And what I remember thinking and feeling and I still feel the same way now, is that there's something disappointing, something missing, if that's all you manage to do. So, I'm intensely encouraged and cheered up by finding things which are not happening on the level of history, but which are happening on an entirely different level, like the penknife, because they seem to me to save the play. To put it another way, they *make* it a play. That odd bit of artifice, odd bit of shimmer in the silk, I think saves the situation for the writer.

AT: They also link to one of the main themes in *The Coast of Utopia:* the misinterpretation of the present.

TS: There's something about shuttling back and forth, through time in the case of *Arcadia,* which I adore. I just love things which aren't exactly written at all—that in *Arcadia* a twentieth-century apple is cut by a nineteenth-century knife and fed to a tortoise. I find that more theatrical than three-quarters of a page which took a week to write.

And although I always claim that I like to come out of a different box each time, actually I think that the things they have in common are greater than I've allowed for. Although there are no time threads in *The Real Thing,* the same thing's happening as is happening in *Arcadia:* there's a man in a chair, and he gets a present from a woman and he opens it up and picks up the box and that's the end of the scene—and it's different and the same each time. It's that layer which I think separates a play from its fellows. Because one thing for sure is you don't change very much as a *writer:* the actual jokes you make, the kind of metaphors you like, the way people talk, that doesn't change very much, frankly.

I sound as though this is a very interesting subject. I can see it's objectively quite interesting, but it's not something which I think about much. Is that true? I think that's the problem at the moment, probably. I mean, it's not true. I think the reason that I'm a mess at the moment is that I'm too conscious of the things I've just been talking about.

What I think I mean is that there is a distinction between talking about work, and presuming to explicate it in some way. The most famous question in modern drama is "Who is Godot?" What a total and utter calamity it would have been if Beckett had said, "Oh, it's the collective unconscious," or "It's the inspector of highways," or "Jehovah." What an appalling thing to happen to that play, because it just shuts off what that play actually does—which is that it's about what happens to you while you're watching it, isn't it?

But the *actual* reason why I came back from France without having started—is that I didn't know what the plot was, or who the people were.

AT: I think sometimes that plot is a slight embarrassment to a writer who cares about form. Without a genuinely interesting story, any amount of formal experiment is irrelevant.

TS: I could write a play tomorrow, no problem, if my take on it was that the audience would be so fascinated to know what I was going to do next that they would be very happy just to see what these people were talking about for a couple of hours. I'm up to here in cognitive science, no problem. But it's not possible. The gulf which is supposed to separate the next Hollywood film from the next fringe drama is actually quite narrow. Both of them need a good plot. Because unless you want to turn the page, you're not really winning, are you? This thing of the page turner—it's true of *Hamlet*. So, however clued up I am, and however brilliant I am, having speeches about neurons, unless someone's saying, "Yes, but what happens next?" you're dead.

I don't think I used to realize that. I don't think I wanted to.

AT: But form can make something interesting too: a lot of interest is the plot's form, not its content—the organization of the material.

TS: I suspect that the whole trick is to undermine the audience's security about what it thinks it knows at any moment. I think that one has to try to do it on the smallest scale as well as the largest. When I got going on *The Coast of Utopia,* I was very aware of this. I think I lost sight of it somewhat. The first scene ends with somebody saying: "One thing for sure, we're not going to let this marriage take place." And then, the first line of the next scene is: "The newlyweds are here." And then you think: Oh well, he was wrong about that. And then think: Oh no he wasn't, it was somebody else. This thing of undermining the audience's sense of what's going on—I think it is drama, a lot of drama is that.

AT: I think it's in one of your conversations with Mel Gussow where he says to you, "I'm not suggesting that you should write like Hemingway. I'm just trying to understand the admiration."

But I have a theory why you like Hemingway. Which is in this kind of occlusion. There is the famous thing Hemingway says: "It was a very simple story called 'Out of Season' and I had omitted the real end of it which was that the old man hanged himself. This was omitted on my new theory that you could omit anything as long as you knew that you omitted and the omitted part would strengthen the story and make people feel something more than they understood."

His writing is based on occlusion. Is that something similar? You like presenting characters, and the audience, with a situation they don't quite comprehend? You like pushing things to the side, so the reader or audience has to infer the rational situation that is going on.

TS: It's true. But you must know the people you like really have very little to do with what you like to write yourself. And anyone who loves Hemingway the way I love him would be well advised to just get past it, you know: do your Hemingway pastiche and move on. I did mine, actually—short stories and things, really embarrassing. I was at a Hemingway conference once, where they have a Hemingway library, and I read my Hemingway short story without telling them who'd written it. A self-humiliation.

AT: Do you believe there could be a good play with bad technique?

TS: I worked out once that technique was actually about controlling the flow or the trajectory of information—from the play to the audience—just controlling it, so it gets there in a certain order, in certain stages: a lot of it boils down to that.

IV. FROM CRICKET

TS: Do you think that most people are integrated and coherent about what they are as writers? The way it works with me is that I stumble across some kind of formulation which has a certain persuasive quality, and because I get used to how to say it, I get very good at delivering that line. And then after a while, time goes by, and I no longer think it—if I ever did think it. I was just delivering the line because I knew how.

Did you ever read the *New York Review* talk I gave in the *New York Review of Books*? I just couldn't *do* it. I stood up there and did my usual thing, and they all said it was fine but I knew it wasn't. They sent me the proofs, and I sat down and wrote new stuff and gave it back to them. They printed that as what I'd said. So anybody who'd been present would have thought, Oh, what a terrible memory I have, I don't remember him saying any of *this*—and I hadn't said any of it.

But, in writing it, I discovered things I thought, completely new thoughts, which I've hung on to ever since, and think, Oh, yes, that's what I think. Some of them were quite central. One of them was getting sick of the whole denouement idea. I fell into this thing, and by the time I'd come out of it, I emerged with this completely coherent intact philosophy of the anti-denouement writer, and it hasn't actually collapsed yet.

I still think that's what I think.

AT: One of the things I love in your work is a running joke—it's there in *Travesties* and it's there also in *The Coast of Utopia*—where you use Wilde for revolutionaries. So that in *Travesties* Lenin says:

This seems to me the core of the play: how far a genuine love, the sentiment, can somehow in retrospect get shaded into nostalgia, into sentimentality.

TS: It's not a bad interpretation.

If you think of love letters, other people's or your own, there's tremendous—there's a sort of, there's a, there's a, there's a tremendous, Jesus God—there's a tendency for them to veer off into the most embarrassing pathos and sentimentality which is all too evident in retrospect but which at the time of writing seems to be an accurate expression of feeling. So it makes one wonder whether there's something which is relative to the observer which is not the same thing which is relative to the writer. And I think when I said they always seem to be a hair's breadth apart, it's that difference between how it is being felt by the writer and how it is being received by the audience.

AT: The thing is—this examination of sentiment, of feeling, is there in all your plays. Often you're described as a playwright of ideas: but most of the people called playwrights of ideas are people with very definite ideas: their plays prove ideas. Whereas in your plays, although there are a lot of people coming up with ideas, the interest is never for the ideas—it's to do with the process by which they come up with them, the emotions which are creating the cerebral theories.

TS: It's also to do with how one might rebut those very same ideas. But you can see that there *is*—God help me, I'm not wrong about this, am I?—that there is the ghost of a promise of a play if I… There's this poem written in roughly 600 B.C. about a woman looking at the woman she loves talking to a man, and she just actually describes the symptoms and they're very precise: there's this wonderful phrase about how thin fire races under the skin. There are all these physiological things which happen to the narrator of the poem. So you can see that to explore or undermine that by

"Really, if the lower orders don't set a good example what on earth is the use of them?! They seem to have absolutely no sense of moral responsibility! To lose one revolution is unfortunate. To lose two would look like carelessness!" And then Bakunin says in *Salvage*—"Our first task will be to destroy authority. There is no second task." Which seems to me to point to a continuity. You're replacing political belief with paradox and contradiction: aestheticism replaces sincerity.

TS: Do you think writing something because you feel it invests writing with a quality that distinguishes it from the unfelt?

I'll try and pose this in a get-at-able form. To somebody who is unaware of either, is there actually a real difference between Henry James and Max Beerbohm's parody of Henry James? What actually distinguishes them? We know that in the case of James there is sincerity and in the case of Beerbohm there is no sincerity, but can you find that difference when you look at the two?

AT: I think the interest of a parody is that, like all works of art, it is and is not like the thing it's representing. A parody exists in the same relation to a work of art as a work of art exists in relation to reality. It's a joke on the same theme. When you read Beerbohm's James parody, would you really believe it was by James? I'm not sure you would. Because James's style has a subject but Beerbohm's subject is only a style.

TS: I think you're absolutely right—you know James wouldn't have bothered to expend his style on this.

AT: I suppose the reason why the parody works is that sometimes James is examining velleities of feeling that basically don't exist, or only exist to Henry James, and therefore Beerbohm has this space to work on: sometimes you feel that James is giving too much emphasis to things which no one thinks about really.

But on the other hand, he's also brilliant at showing people that actually they think far more closely about very minor things than they thought they did. You have to revise what you mean by important or unimportant when you read James.

TS: For me, the reason it's become more political, now… A desire for the play to be moving was not part of my thinking in any way. I was interested in abstract ideas and I liked making jokes. From the very beginning, even Rosencrantz talking about being dead [in *Rosencrantz and Guildenstern Are Dead*] wasn't an *emotional* moment. It was, as it were, just logic-fun or word-fun or think-fun. But for the last fifteen years, I found myself writing things which moved me at a certain point, and move other people, and *now* I don't want to write a play which doesn't.

So I sit in France and I've got all these bits, and I can manipulate them quite cleverly, for a couple of hours, and that's what I would have been doing I suppose—but *now* I can't start because unless there's some kind of human pain here, or redemption, I don't want to do it, or don't want to bother.

In *Indian Ink* there is a moment about a woman brushing petals off her sister's gravestone, so she could read the name on the stone, and then she says good-bye to her dead sister, and I remember having a bit of a gulp when it was being acted, even though I'd written it.

And this is quite a good way to close one of these circles, because the actual phrase was, you know, par excellence, without style, without finesse. It consisted of three words, "Bye bye darling": that was it. But because of the situation—this is what we were talking about—because of the situation it sort of made one gulp a little bit, and, if I've made any kind of journey at all, it's the journey from discounting that—discountenancing, I suppose I'm trying to say, that—to a place where it's central to the point of writing a play, the desire to write a play.

I think that's the one thing which has emerged from the chaos of conversation, from all our very enjoyable chat, as something which I do recognize has happened. I understand why I can't be

bothered to write the play yet, because there isn't this em
available in it.

AT: There's a lovely thing Nabokov says, defending Dicken
House against the charge of sentimentality: "I want to sub
people who denounce the sentimental are generally una
what sentiment is." The problem is that sentiment is so
sentimentality.

TS: It's very close, it's a hair's breadth, isn't it? I'm always d
myself when I think I've brought off a moment of sentimen
I think, Oh, God, this is actually TV.

AT: If you take *The Invention of Love,* say, the title's ambiguit
to both sentiment and sentimentality. It's about the fact th
ally you invent the love object, so that Jackson and Bosie a
inadequate to the emotion expended on them, and yet the
them is entirely real, entirely irrational, and entirely rig
completely true.

And this is very similar to Housman as a scholar. W
you're in love with Moses Jackson, or doing an edition of
ius, both involve "useless knowledge"—but that doesn'
them wrong or invalid.

But the second sense of the title is brought out in the w
use Wilde at the end. Like Housman, Wilde is in love with
who is not worthy of him. But Wilde is also shown to be
mental—when he says, "Once, I bought a huge armful of l
Convent Garden to Miss Langtry, and as I waited to put t
a cab, a small boy said to me, 'Oh, how rich you are!'… 'O
rich you are! [*He weeps.*] Oh—forgive me. I'm somewh
worse for cake.'" It's slightly theatrical—the sentiment has b
sentimentality. And it links to the earlier moment where
describes "False nostalgia"—which he glosses later: "all the r
archaism, anachronism, the wayward incontinence that only
sight can acquit of non sequitur…"

describing it in terms of what's happening in her brain at that moment, in purely physical terms…

I'm sure there's something quite strong in *feeling* being the refutation of thinking: that the feeling that she expresses—in some way—cannot be accounted for by the neurologist, cannot actually be fully described and accounted for by the scientist.

And this… So there's a play there. There… There must be. ✯

GARY ZEBRUN

TALKS WITH

EDMUND WHITE

"I'VE CONDUCTED MY SOCIAL AND INTELLECTUAL LIFE ALMOST BY ACCIDENT AND IN THE MARGINS OF MY SEXUAL AMBITIONS."

Intellectual mentors:
Paul Goodman (though not for his writing)
Susan Sontag (though later they became enemies, alas)
Michel Foucault (though they seldom talked about ideas)

The first time I met Edmund White, I was twenty-six years old and he was the fifteen-year-old nameless narrator of A Boy's Own Story *(1982). Until then, my only glimpses of forbidden homosexual encounters in literature were the plague-filled streets of* Death in Venice *or the room at Peter Coffin's Spouter-Inn where Queequeg and Ishmael shared a bed at the start of* Moby-Dick. *In 1982, White's novel was a rare example of a story about a gay character whose struggle with his sexuality was at the heart of a piece of fiction.*

For all his notoriety among gay literary circles in this country, White truly crosses over on the other side of the Atlantic. In France, for more than a decade, he's been a Chevalier de l'Ordre des Arts et des Lettres. He's as well known there and in England and Italy as his American contemporaries are recognized here: Philip Roth, Norman Mailer, John Updike, and Princeton colleague Joyce Carol Oates.

He has a trail of astonishing books (nearly two dozen) which include the great trilogy A Boy's Own Story, The Beautiful Room Is Empty *(1988), and* The Farewell Symphony *(1997); the giant* Genet: A Biography *(1993), which won a National Book Critics Circle Award; the little gem of a biography* Marcel Proust *(1999); the anguished AIDS love story* The Married Man *(2000); and even* The Joy of Gay Sex *(1977). His book of collected essays—*Arts and Letters*—was published by Cleis Press in the fall of 2004. His memoir,* My Lives, *was published in January 2006.*

Edmund Valentine White III was born in Cincinnati in 1940 and moved to Evanston, Illinois, with his mother and sister after his parents divorced, when he was seven years old. He graduated from the University of Michigan in Ann Arbor in 1962 and moved to New York City. For decades, when he wasn't living in Paris or Rome, he was a writer for Time-Life Books, a senior editor at the Saturday Review, *and a teacher at Johns Hopkins, Columbia, Yale, Brown, George Mason, Temple, and New York universities.*

These days, at sixty-five, he lives in Manhattan's Chelsea district and teaches creative writing at Princeton University. He travels widely and voraciously explores a landscape of cultures that, at a time when America seems so obsessed with itself, makes him a marvel in the quest for passion and engaging art. —*Gary Zebrun (Spring 2005)*

GARY ZEBRUN: In 1983, shortly after *A Boy's Own Story* was released, in an interview with Don Swaim, a New York radio talk-show host, you said that you sensed a thousand gay men struggling with their sexuality were watching over your shoulders while you were writing the novel. There was a touch of embarrassment in your voice. Now, more than twenty years later, how do you feel knowing that you are a literary icon?

EDMUND WHITE: You and I both know that literary celebrity, even when it's of a brighter magnitude than mine, pales beside that of movie stars, politicians, and television and sports personalities. If I'm an icon it's a very small, dark one in the corner of the chapel without even a single candle guttering before it. That said, I must confess that I have always felt it was the greatest good luck to be published at all much less read by my small band of patient, faithful, knowing readers. As for my status in the gay community, I am well known enough to be asked what I think of gay marriage, for instance, though I seldom have an opinion about politics that is more interesting than anyone else's.

What I do like is the feeling that gay people are still figuring out who they are and that fiction is the best—virtually the only!—public place for exploring questions of ethics and identity and destiny. My chance has been to be a part of that dialogue for three decades.

GZ: Well, shaping a dialogue, whether it's cultural or social, is pretty political, I think. Your nephew Keith Fleming recently wrote *Original Youth: The Real Story of Edmund White's Boyhood*. In the introduction, David Leavitt is struck by the young White to whom it was "self-evident that the world was very phony (as well as heartless, deluded, and selfish)," and how "this deep-seated distrust of humanity throws interesting light on his subsequent aloofness from political concerns." Funny, even though you say you seldom have an opinion about politics that's different from anyone else's, I don't see the detachment from politics in your fiction, even in the fiercely "autobiographical" work. And in *Fanny* one of its astonishing strengths is its political satire. So are you a "closet" political or social activist, even though you don't march in the streets?

EW: I guess I think of myself as political, though I've never voted once in my life. In *The Farewell Symphony* the narrator isn't interested in Watergate, since he thinks of the American government as "their" government, certainly not his as a gay man. I suppose it's difficult for young gays to understand, but in the '50s and early '60s, when I was coming out, there was very little sense of a coherent gay community. We used to say that if we were leaving a gay cruising place and it caught on fire we'd just keep on walking and not look back. That double alienation—from a cold, self-hating world of gay men and from a violently disapproving dominant culture—certainly scotched any nascent sense of political involvement and responsibility.

To be sure, at the University of Michigan I hung out with Tom Hayden and the authors of the *Port Huron Statement* and I thought of myself as a radical, at the very least a socialist. But by 1971 I had the brilliant Simon Karlinsky, a Russian expatriate, nipping at my heels and attempting to force me to face up to the horrors of the Soviet regime. He gave me Nadezhda Mandelstam's *Hope Against Hope* to read, although it took me another ten years to wake up to historical reality. Now we know that many more people were tortured and killed in the name of socialism than by the fascists, but that recognition was a long time coming. I was as guilty of blindness of that sort as other so-called leftists of my generation in America.

So much for politics in the old sense. In the newer acceptation of the personal-is-political I've certainly always felt that my books had a political dimension. I felt that I was showing in my trilogy, for instance, the deforming power of the Eisenhower years, the heady sexual liberation of the 1960s, the New York artistic effervescence of the 1970s, and the debacle of AIDS in the '80s—and in my case a flight to Europe. Since I am at least as interested in sociology and class analysis as I am in psychology, a "political" approach to styles of life comes to me naturally.

GZ: These days, I often feel like flying off to Europe and staying there, though I'm not sure, as an American, I'd be very welcomed. You're one of the few American writers of your generation who has spent enormous chunks of time abroad, and your affection for places such as France and Italy is a wonderful force in your fiction. In *The Farewell Symphony* the narrator on the eve of returning home from Rome says, "An English guy had tears in his eyes... He told me he was sad to be going home. As an American I was used to the idea that 'home' was superior to everywhere else (richer, more powerful, trend-setting)... Suddenly I saw that for an American travel abroad is always a form of slumming." Tell me a bit about your passion for places outside the United States and the necessity for you to return home.

EW: It's true that I've known Scots in Crete and Dutch in Spain and they would never dream of returning to their cold, rainy countries full of spotty countenances and tepid beer and limp french fries. To be sure, I've also known Americans in Paris who refused to speak English and who had thoroughly replaced their American with Gallic souls. But that sort of "traitor" is rare among Americans. We love our country or at least feel that it is setting world standards. These days, of course, the standards can be downward trends—toward isolationism, military intervention, a two-tiered society of very rich and poor getting poorer, of inadequate medical care, polluted environment, declining academic levels, even inadequate nutrition.

Even so, America for a working writer remains a great artistic environment. We may not worship art as Europeans do, but at least we make a lot of it; America has bad readers but great writers, just as France right now has great readers but few good writers. America is so complex, violent, inassimilable, raw, and religious that it never bores an observer nor comes entirely clean in any social analysis.

A punk kid once interviewed me on British television and said, "Mr. White, you are known as an American, a writer, and a homosexual. When did you first discover you were an American?" My answer: "When I moved to Paris." Like many cultured Americans of my generation I wanted to impress Europeans with how civilized I could be, speaking foreign languages, knowing how to kiss a hand, daringly sexual in conversation but otherwise markedly discreet, etc. We wanted to jump through all those golden European hoops. We wanted to be "polished." Now I feel most at home with other Europeanized Americans. We can laugh at French humorlessness and trumpeting American voices, remark on the lack of a French word for "name dropping" or an American word for *frileux* (sensitive to the cold), etc. Certainly living in two languages (French and English) made me much more self-conscious about language than ever before. The French insist on clarity, have an allergy to figurative language, appreciate a simple style devoid of slang, and some of those predilections have worked their way into my prose.

GZ: In many of your novels, as Robert Lowell or William Carlos Williams did in their poetry, you draw your characters and narratives from an autobiographical well. If anyone asked me, I'd say you're really a devilish manipulator. I'm always surprised when critics or book reviewers confuse your sources of material with plain confessional writing. In the essay "Nabokov's Passion" you write about his "particular delight to invent sinister or insane or talentless versions of himself, characters who are at least in part mocking anticipations of naïve readers' suspicions about the real Nabokov." I wonder, does this also describe the way you treat your own life in those novels, such as the trilogy, that appear so autobiographical?

EW: I'm a good deal less playful than Nabokov. A lot more prim and serious. More devoted to the truth as I conceive of it than to beauty. At the same time I am always conscious of the reader's response to my work, which means that in my autobiographical fiction I have made my first-person teenage stand-in a bit less precocious sexually and intellectually than I really was; I wanted people to identify with the young hero of *A Boy's Own Story*. At the same time I dared to end the book with the boy's betraying the only adult man who has accommodated his sexuality, and that stroke certainly turned off many readers, not to mention potential filmmakers. I suppose at every moment of writing for me there is a trade-off between my desire to woo the reader and my debt to the truth (in real life I did betray a prep-school teacher, and I wanted to acknowledge that dark stain on my youth). As the trilogy moves through time I suppose I was willing to take on board more of my real experience and complex personality. For one thing a gay man who is thirty in 1970 will be entirely different from a gay man who is thirty in 2000. If childhood—at least middle-class suburban childhood—sometimes feels timeless and "universal," adulthood is far more inflected by the contemporary setting and moment.

GZ: Yes, I love the way you almost effortlessly portray the actual moment of your life in much of your work. In the Nabokov essay you discuss the philosopher Theodor Adorno's defense of the artist's attention to experience, to the concrete. You point out that Adorno said, "The universality of beauty can communicate itself to the subject in no other way than in an obsession with the particular." In *The Farewell Symphony,* the nameless narrator puts it this way: "The writer's vanity holds that everything that happens to him is material. He views everything from a distance and even when the cops arrest him for sucking a cock through a glory hole, he smiles faintly and thinks, 'Idea for Story.'" So talk about stealing parts of your narratives straight from life.

EW: Right now I'm living through the most painful moment in my romantic life that I've known since I was in my twenties. Even though I cry all the time, can't sleep, and talk to myself, forget things and respond emotionally to the most inappropriate cues, nevertheless I'm taking notes of my moods and quirks, since in the past I failed to map out the shape of a broken heart—its strategies and lies and illusory victories. Probably when I'm lowered into the grave I'll still be writing "Idea for Story."

I've been influenced by the theater and actors all my life, and the prevailing doctrine of my day (and still today) was Stanislavski's. He puts a great emphasis on the impossibility for an actor to body forth any emotion at all unless he can find a concrete example of it in his own memories. Maybe an actor has never lost someone close but he can still remember a devastating parting or the death of a pet or something. He must re-create that memory within himself not by going directly for the emotion but by feeling his way into the sensory recollections of the setting—the unclean feeling of the velvet upholstery, the depressing smell of carbolic acid, the look of a fluorescent light behind shutters.

In *Fanny* I wanted to write about Mrs. Trollope's affair with an escaped slave. Fortunately I've had the experience of submitting my aging white body to the frequent attentions of a black athlete I've known for the last three years—with a few substitutions, voilà! There are things I wouldn't dare to describe (childbirth, for instance) unless I accompanied a woman friend through the whole process, *et encore*...

GZ: I'm shifting gears here, but I know you love the work of Marcel Proust and Jean Genet, one bourgeois and the other iconoclastic. Is this a tension that fuels your imagination?

EW: If Proust is bourgeois he's also gay and half-Jewish (Jews would say all-Jewish since his mother was a Jew). He publicly denied both affiliations; he fought a duel to clear his name of the slur that he was gay and when a newspaper listed him among promising young Jewish writers he stiffly reminded the editors that he was a baptized Catholic. In *Remembrance of Things Past* the narrator is very Old France and Catholic and one of the few men left standing at the conclusion as an uncompromised hetero. I contend that Proust's constant lying to his friends and readers—his unending transpositions of men into women, Sodom into Gomorrah, illicit gay sex into illicit affairs with "butcher girls"—that all these lies trained his memory and imagination and made him a great writer. It's precisely in the ten thousand passages where he lies that he is most creative.

If Genet is iconoclastic (and he was), he inverts Catholicism to create his own devil-worship, he crowns his drag queens with a tiara of ripped-out dentures in a ceremony worthy of the Cathedral of Reims, he describes a thug's penis with words worthy of Racine. (Once, to a cute boy he was trying to pick up, he improvised a pun on Phaedra's line "O Prince, I languish, I die for Theseus.")

GZ: Maybe that's why gays love to tell stories; like Proust, we've all lied about our sexuality at one time or another. God, I lied about it until I was forty. I'm curious: I've heard you say you were interested in reinventing, much in the way you reimagined Fanny Trollope, a gay companion piece that Stephen Crane had written to *Maggie: Girl of the Streets* but was forced to destroy by his editor. I've read that some literary scholars believe Crane spent his life suppressing his homosexuality. You've been so utterly open about yours for so long. Why are you interested in Crane?

EW: Was Crane gay? I've never heard that before. It wasn't his editor but his friends who insisted he destroy the manuscript to *Flowers of Asphalt*. No, I'm more impressed by Crane's kind of naturalism that led him to want to document homosexual prostitution despite the social onus against it. In the end he chickened out, but even his initial attempt was very daring. I subscribe to the constructivist notion that homosexuality is invented anew by each epoch, and I'm eager to imagine what it could have been like in the suddenly burgeoning big-city excitement of New York in the 1880s, a moment when the old don't-ask-don't-tell silence about sodomy was giving way to a new sociological descriptiveness about "vice."

GZ: Well, you never chicken out about painting the vibrant underground of gay life. You celebrate it, even when it's touched by so much loss. The nameless narrator in *The Beautiful Room Is Empty* says, "The appeal of gay life for me was that it provided so many glancing contacts with other men." Some people, especially straight people, think the gay experience is filled with passionless promiscuity. That's garbage, isn't it? Can't a multitude of glancing contacts be a kind of love? Evanescent maybe, but still love?

EW: A key experience for me was when I was in my twenties and I'd go to the "meat rack" on Fire Island between the Pines and the Grove. It would be two or three in the morning, the surf was pounding on the beach just beyond the dunes, the stars would be swirling because I'd drunk too many gin tonics, a fog would be floating over the scrub brush and wind-trained trees, my calf muscles would be tired from walking so far off the path and into the sand—and up ahead someone would be sending signals with the pulsing end of his cigarette. Then suddenly there he would be, wrapped around me, my hands full of hard dick and soft skin, his finger pushing up inside me, our mouths exchanging smoke and saliva… Soon we'd be three or four but as the daylight began to crack the code of the night's secrets I'd be lying in the sand next to that first all-blond whose weary, happy face was now developing like a photo in the pan to reveal the little aerodynamic lines around his eyes, the sheen on his well-kissed lips, the scribble of blond hair around his absurdly small dark nipples…

Oh, those were the days, and if all that was anonymous sex (technically it was) then I can only say it was more powerful and poetic than what goes on in any marriage bed.

GZ: Yes, powerful and poetic and one of the loveliest pieces of erotic remembrance that I've heard. Proust would approve. I'm a bit jealous you celebrated your sexuality so young and made so many gay friends. Your fiction possesses a dizzying patchwork of friendships. In your latest novel Fanny Trollope obsessively wants to befriend others, particularly Fanny Wright, but she ends up disappointed and alone again. Can you discuss the importance of friends in your life and how they intersect in sustaining or melancholy ways in your work? And I suppose we're coming to a close, so let me ask one of those final, stupid interview questions, which you can ignore: if you could have dinner with three or four other writers long gone from this earth, who would be at the table?

EW: I've never been very interested in celebrities, not even in meeting celebrated writers. When I was in my twenties, however, there were two New York writers I longed to meet—Paul Goodman (*Growing Up Absurd*), who's now long dead and largely forgotten, and Susan Sontag, who much later became a friend for a couple of years before we became enemies, alas. In both cases I was hoping they'd help me to get published. In my daydreams they'd read me, see the merit, and miraculously open doors for me. In fact, when I did know Sontag fifteen years later she did help me to get a Guggenheim and an award from the American Academy of Arts and Letters, and she wrote a blurb for *A Boy's Own Story* (which eventually she demanded I remove from the cover of subsequent editions).

I wasn't particularly interested in Goodman's writing, though his diary *Five Years* was an early gay confession about the exciting artistic and sexual milieu that was developing in New York in the late '60s and throughout the '70s. Sontag's writing, on the other hand, always fascinated me, and thanks to her I became interested in Roland Barthes and [Antonin] Artaud. Her terse, impacted style—so different from the flowing, easygoing belletristic essays that preceded hers in America—demanded concentration and invited genuine intellectual participation from the reader.

Now I am well past the stage of having literary crushes of that sort. I don't expect anyone to take me up and make me better known. Foucault in the early '80s was perhaps the last vital intellectual idol of my life, though we seldom talked about ideas and I never wanted him to "help" me. Other French friends have meant a great deal to me: Marie-Claude de Brunhoff, one of my two or three best friends, who introduced me into all the closely packed circuitry of Paris social and cultural life. Albert Dichy, who helped me with the research for the Genet biography and who is one of the few people I've ever known who is always rethinking virtually every question. To listen to him is to hear a first-class mind at work. Nor does all this work exclude a wild and boyish sense of humor. He is the ideal companion. Then there is Chantal Thomas, a new friend whom I've met since leaving Paris though she is a Parisian. Chantal, who has written a remarkable novel about Marie-Antoinette (*Farewell, My Queen*), is someone who is a pure pleasure to be with. She is responsive as much as she is stimulating. She knows everything but is never guilty of pedantry—and she, too, like Albert Dichy, never repeats herself.

I have spent so much of my life pursuing handsome men, like a bloodhound led on by the odor of sperm, that I've conducted my social and intellectual life almost by accident and in the margins of my sexual ambitions. Nevertheless friendship has brought me as much pleasure as sex or love, though friendship is a mild pleasure, neither addictive nor a good subject for obsessiveness. Many of my friends, of course, are ex-lovers. I've seldom broken with anyone who was ever important to me sexually. Since my main erotic emotion is gratitude, even the dim remains of this feeling are a good basis for friendship, which combines complicity with admiration.

I feel I've learned nothing about "life," that is, how to have a good one. As a novelist I distrust general ideas and moral conclusions. The realm of fiction is all about morality—the testing of conflicting values, the staging of competing claims—but I would never want to reduce those conflicts to a message, an endorsement.

As for that dinner party—I guess I'd be most excited if I knew I'd be spending it with three or four (or just one!) young men who'd like me. Moody, difficult, affectionate guys. ✯

MILES MARSHALL LEWIS

TALKS WITH

AUGUST WILSON

"BLUES IS THE BEDROCK OF EVERYTHING I DO. ALL THE CHARACTERS IN MY PLAYS, THEIR IDEAS AND THEIR ATTITUDES, THE STANCE THAT THEY ADOPT IN THE WORLD, ARE ALL IDEAS AND ATTITUDES THAT ARE EXPRESSED IN THE BLUES."

Favorite play topics:
Love
Honor
Duty
Betrayal
Ex-enslaved people who sell dog shit

On May 10, 1988, I met my Bronx high school's black alliance club at the Forty-Sixth Street Theatre, a shrink-wrapped copy of Lovesexy *(released that day) tucked under my arm. Amazingly, Prince was the last thing on my mind after more than two hours of* Fences *(1986), a riveting treatise on a father-and-son conflict over their visions of black identity.* Fences *was my first taste of Wilson's ongoing drama cycle, which encompasses the black experience in each decade of the twentieth century. Enthralled by Wilson's blues-tinged voice, I followed his subsequent successes:* Joe Turner's Come and Gone *(1988),* The Piano Lesson *(1990),* Two Trains Running *(1992),* Seven

Guitars *(1996),* King Hedley II *(2005), and revivals of* Jitney *(2001) and* Ma Rainey's Black Bottom *(1985).*

Born Frederick August Kittel in Pittsburgh, Pennsylvania, in an impoverished neighborhood known as the Hill, the playwright was one of six siblings. Dropping out of high school after a teacher's racist accusation that he had plagiarized a paper, Wilson soon became a poet under the inspirational aegis of Dylan Thomas and Amiri Baraka. He began writing plays in the 1970s after a brief stint with the Black Horizon Theater. Ma Rainey's Black Bottom *caught the attention of Dean Lloyd Richards at the Yale School of Drama in 1982, which led Wilson to the Great White Way. He swiftly kicked its ass: the playwright has been awarded a Pulitzer Prize and a Tony Award for* Fences *and another Pulitzer and Tony nomination for* The Piano Lesson.

Outdoors at an Au Bon Pain in Boston, the fifty-nine-year-old Wilson took a break from rehearsing a pre-Broadway production of his latest play, Gem of the Ocean. *Lighting Marlboro Lights proved difficult under the chilly, gusty wind as we bound from the blues to hiphop, Bearden to Basquiat, and beyond.* —*Miles Marshall Lewis (Summer 2004)*

I. "I THINK THAT'S THE CORE OF BLACK AESTHETICS: THE ABILITY TO IMPROVISE."

MILES MARSHALL LEWIS: Despite the similarities between *Fences* and *Death of a Salesman,* and the art of playwriting as a predominantly white discipline, you've cited your greatest literary influence as poet/playwright Amiri Baraka. How would you say he influenced you?

AUGUST WILSON: I'm not sure what they say about *Fences* as it relates to *Death of a Salesman*. At the time I wrote *Fences,* I had not read *Death of a Salesman,* had not seen *Death of a Salesman,* did not know anything about *Death of a Salesman.*

My greatest influence has been the blues. And that's a literary influence, because I think the blues is the best literature that we as black Americans have. My interest in Baraka comes from the '60s and the Black Power movement. So it's more for Baraka's political ideas, which I loved and still am an exponent of. Through all those years I was a follower, if you will, of Baraka. He had an influence on my thinking.

MML: Were you exposed first to his poetry or his plays?

AW: The poetry in particular. The book called *Black Magic,* which is sort of a collection of several books. That's sixty-nine—I wore that book out, the cover got taped up with Scotch tape, the pages falling out. That was my bible, I carried it wherever I went. So that in particular. I wasn't writing plays back then, so I wasn't influenced by his playwriting—although, to me, his best plays are collected in a book called *Four Black Revolutionary Plays,* with *Madheart, Great Goodness of Life, A Black Mass,* and *Experimental Death Unit 1.* They contributed a lot to my thinking just in terms of getting stuff on the page.

MML: How specifically was the blues an influence on your work?

AW: Blues is the bedrock of everything I do. All the characters in my plays, their ideas and their attitudes, the stance that they adopt in the world, are all ideas and attitudes that are expressed in the blues. If all this were to disappear off the face of the earth and some people 2 million unique years from now would dig out this civilization and come across some blues records, working as anthropologists, they would be able to piece together who these people were, what they thought about, what their ideas and attitudes toward pleasure and pain were, all of that. All the components of culture. Just like they do with the Egyptians, they piece together all that stuff. And all you need is the blues. So to me the blues is the book, it's the bible, it's everything.

MML: Baraka himself said that if you want to know where black people are at any point in our sojourn in this wilderness of America, listen to the music of that period.

AW: Yeah!

MML: Your characters also often riff off of each other like jazz musicians, particularly in *Seven Guitars.* Your work in general is like improvising on a theme: the life of Southern blacks who migrated to the North in the twentieth century. How has jazz impacted your creative process?

AW: I think that's the core of black aesthetics: the ability to improvise. That is what has enabled our survival. I came to jazz late, man. I wasn't interested in jazz. I remember guys walking around with John Coltrane, Archie Shepp albums under their arm and I go, "Aw, man, it ain't got no words!" If it didn't have any words, I wasn't that interested.

All that changed on an October night in 1966 when I came up on Kirkpatrick and Wylie Avenue in Pittsburgh and saw about two hundred people standing out on the corner, which was unusual. The first thing I thought was that somebody got killed. [*Laughter*] So I run down there and I say, "Hey, man, what's happening?" and they go, "Shhh!" And they were listening to John Coltrane out of the Crawford Grill, you see. And the people inside the Crawford Grill—cause the drinks cost ninety cents, in sixty-six that's a lot of money—the people inside, they don't even know how to spell John Coltrane's name. They inside talking about what they gonna do Friday night and so-and-so's cousin got a new Lincoln Continental, you see. John Coltrane ain't playing to them, man, he playing to the brothers out on the street, cause the music's coming straight out over their heads and out on the street. And the brothers outside, they prayin. This is their music. This is what has enabled them to survive these outrageous insults that American society has forced on them.

So when I saw two hundred niggas stunned into silence by the power of art in the music of John Coltrane and his exploration of man's relation to the divinity, that's when I got interested in jazz. And also, as a young man wanting to be a writer, I said, This is what I want my art to do. I want to accomplish that. I can't say I went out and found me some John Coltrane, cause I didn't have no record player. [*Laughter*] But I did perk up and I started paying attention at the jazz club. We had a guy named Kenny Fisher in Pittsburgh, he played saxophone. I just got more interested.

Other than just improvisation and being a master of the power of black aesthetic, I can't really say I've been influenced by jazz, although I've come to it late. I've been trying to catch up, man. Charlie Mingus?

MML: Mingus is a master.

AW: Yeah, baby.

MML: I got to see Miles Davis twice as a teenager, at the JVC Jazz Festival at Avery Fisher Hall. Seeing my namesake before he passed away was a very big deal. I know *The Piano Lesson* was directly influenced by the Romare Bearden painting of the same name, and that also his *Miss Bertha and Mr. Seth* and *Millhand's Lunch Basket* were on your mind in creating *Joe Turner's Come and Gone.* How did Bearden come to you?

AW: With Bearden, there was a book called *The Prevalence of Ritual.* Bearden painted a lot of collages. He was painting a collage of rituals attendant to everyday life: burials, funerals, and things of that sort. Bearden, I know he spent some time in Pittsburgh, his maternal grandmother lived in Pittsburgh then. I look at them collages, I know everybody in there! [*Laughter*] Ah, there's my uncle, yeah, that's Charlie, there's Dick over there. They even look like em. It was the first time that I'd encountered art that was black America in all its fullness, its richness. And it wasn't sentimental. It wasn't that "Aww, we sufferin." It was like, "We're the people, we're here, we're vibin and this here."

I said, I want to make my plays the equal of one of them canvases. Put Bearden here and put Wilson up there. I'm not a painter but I want to be able to hang in the same gallery with him, man.

And then someone asked Bearden about his art. He said, "I try to explore in terms of the life I know best those things which are common to all culture." So I go, the commonalities of all culture within the life I know best—which is black life, that's who I am—I'm gonna express that. That's what I want my art to be about. This is the way *we* do things. We all bury our dead, we all have parties, we all decorate our houses, but we do it different. And it ain't nothin wrong with it.

I watched, in a bus station in downtown St. Paul, these four Japanese guys have breakfast. They sat there and chatted politely among themselves. One of em got up and took pictures. Now I found out from their conversation that they were taking Greyhound across the country to California to go to college. They can all afford to fly first class but they takin a bus, they havin adventure, to have some fun. So when the bill came, they all reached for their American Express cards to pay the bill. They paid the bill and they left.

So I asked myself, If it had been four black guys in here having breakfast, what would be the difference? The first thing I noticed is that there's a jukebox there. It never occurred to any of these four Japanese guys to play the jukebox. But four black guys walk in, the first thing they do, *some*body going to go over to the jukebox and put a quarter in, right? The other guy gonna come and say, "Hey man, play so-and-so!" "I ain't playin with you, man. Put your own money in!" So he ain't gonna play his music, right? The second thing I noticed, nobody said nothing to the waitress. The four black guys, I don't care what she look like, somebody gonna say something to her. "Hey baby, how you doin?" "Look here, mama, what's your phone number?" They gonna do that, right? "Nah, nah, don't talk to him, he can't read, blah blah." And then the guy gonna get up to play another song, somebody gonna steal a piece of bacon off his plate, and he's gonna come back and say, "Hey man, I ain't playin with y'all, man, quit messin with my food." Other than that, when the time comes for the bill, it's that, "Leroy, lend me two dollars, man." Right? It's just the way we do it.

Now, somebody sitting over here would say, "They don't like each other. The guy didn't let him play the record, he stole some food off his plate, they harassed the waitress." So to them, the way you do things is all wrong. If you bring four white guys in, they'll do it differently than the Japanese and the black guys. What white America does, it accepts the way the Japanese does it. It accepts the way the Czechs from the Czech Republic might do things different. But blacks are supposed to act like them; they say, "Y'all still ain't learned how to do things."

MML: As a hypothetical, how do you think the artwork of Jean-Michel Basquiat might affect your plays?

AW: I suspect it would be closer to what we moving toward, which is [a] hiphop play. If he had been around in the '60s when I was twenty-three, twenty-four—a young man searching for the world—I'm sure I would've embraced that much more than when I was forty-five and coming to know his work. It's a different person coming to know his work, and I'm already trying to absorb these other influences. But I could see somebody being influenced by him, and the best way to say what it would be like is: it would look like them paintings. And I'm trying to make my stuff look like Bearden's paintings, the literary equivalent of that. I hear more and more hiphop plays being written. And they're written in poetry, they're written in verse, they're written in rhyme the same way you do a lyric. Only now, it's a larger canvas and we gonna tell the story; instead of using the three-minute thing here, we're gonna use a larger canvas. And I encourage that. There gotta be a future, and it can't be what it is now cause you gotta build on a present and keep moving and going down. It's supposed to be something that you can't think of now. That's part of life, man.

II. "TO ME, HIPHOP IS WHAT I CALL THE SPIRITUAL FIST OF THE CULTURE. THAT'S PROOF THAT THE [BLACK] CULTURE'S STRONG, ROBUST, INVENTIVE."

MML: What do you imagine the influence of hiphop might be on your work?

AW: I don't think it's any different than a blues influence or a jazz influence, because it's just an extension of music. It's just another way of doing it. You couldn't have hiphop unless you had Charlie Patton and Skip James and Sun House and all the rest of them. Although it is different; I recognize that, man. I recall when Baraka and the Black Power poets of the '60s tried to wed jazz in poetry. And, see, that didn't work, because it didn't have the beat. You have to have the beat. The blues and poetry are closer than the jazz and poetry. To me, hiphop is what I call the spiritual fist of the culture. That's proof that the [black] culture's strong, robust, inventive. That's not saying we ain't got some problems. I mean, it's the way we used to do with some of them lyrics and whatnot... [*Laughter*] But I look past that and I go, yeah, now we're here, we're strong, we're alive, we're robust, we're inventive, and we still doin it. That's proof of that. So I embrace it.

MML: Whose decision was it to put some Public Enemy into your last play, *King Hedley II,* which took place in the '80s?

AW: That's the director, Marion McClinton, that was his choice. I think it was not so much they were big in the '80s but what that particular song ["Fight the Power"] said as a relationship to the character, King.

MML: I've got a quote from you here that says, "If I were going to write a play set in 1980, I would go and listen to the music, particularly music that blacks are making, and find out what their ideas and attitudes are about the situation, and about the time in which they live." What music did you eventually listen to while writing *King Hedley II*?

AW: Blues. [*Laughter*] I said that, but I did not do that. All the ideas and attitudes that hiphop-generation people in the '80s had, that's where they got it from. They got it from they daddies, it was rooted here. So I really didn't have to do that. I listened to Tupac. Relative to my blues collection, I got a small hiphop collection, or what I call "rap collection." It's not my favorite music; blues is favorite. I pay attention, keep my ear to the ground. I do recognize what's going on. I'm trying to think: I know I listened to Tupac back then, but still, basically, I thought the core impulse of people is still coming out of the blues. So I tried to make the other elements of my play reflect the '80s more.

People say, "Well, you writin a play in 1911 and you weren't alive in 1911. Did you do any research?" I say, I don't do research. They say, "Well, how do you know?" Because the plays ultimately are about love, honor, duty, betrayal—what I call the Big Themes. So you could set it in the '80s and make use of various things, but you're telling a story that is using the Big Themes. It's a love story, *King Hedley II*. It's a lot of things. It's really jam-packed, with King as a Christ figure, there's a lot of little ideas that I was working on in there, or echoes and suggestions of.

MML: What else is in your rap collection?

AW: Wu-Tang Clan. I got Snoop, his first album. People give me some over the years. I got some Biggie.

MML: There was a controversy in 1990 over an article you wrote about turning down director Barry Levinson to direct a film of *Fences*. You wanted a black director, which raised the question: can whites master a black style? That said, what's your opinion, if any, of Eminem? Do you think he's capable of mastering the black aesthetic of hiphop?

AW: Yeah. He's imitatin, he ain't creatin. There's a very big distinction. He's not an innovator. He can't create in that style, so everything he do is just imitatin. Anybody can imitate anybody.

MML: I've read someone say, "Sure, whites can box like Muhammad Ali, once they see him do it."

AW: The same thing with jazz. Benny Goodman could play jazz, but they ain't creatin no music, they not innovators. So the music, it's gotta be there for you to step into it. I wanna see you create it; it would be something different. Different aesthetics at work. But you can be influenced by, you can imitate anything. Got some Japanese guys that play some great jazz. Man, they really good, too! It's already been done, man.

MML: Many of your plays deal with the disconnect between the vantage point of different generations, in their respective ways of reading society. Do you find a correlation between that and this year's controversial comments from Bill Cosby that were critical of black youth?

AW: Let me say, first of all, I did not hear the comments, I hear people talking about them. My understanding of it is that he went on a tirade against poor black people. I say, if you want to go on a tirade, there's a whole lot of things to go on a tirade about other than poor black people, starting with the systemic conditions that create these poor black people. I have an uncle who lived in America and died in America, seventy-three years, was born a poor man and died a poor man. How is this possible when they comin over with two cents and become multimillionaires?

There's a reason why. Of course, the reason is he's black, and the opportunities, truncated possibility, et cetera. Let's go on a tirade about the United States Department of Agriculture, which admittedly discriminated against black farmers by denying them loans over the course of sixty years. So it's not one individual secretary of agriculture. It happened to be the same sixty years while this other hand [of government] over here is signing laws against discrimination, this other hand over here is fighting war against poverty, while they over there systematically denying these black farmers loans until the farms come down from $1,200,000 to $3,000. They go, "Oh, we've been discriminating against you, here's what we'll do: we'll offer you a settlement," which the *Washington Post* called a mere pittance, of $50,000. The average value of the farm is $500,000. And then, you look up two years later, they gotta fight like hell to get their $50,000. They've denied over 50 percent of the claims, they spent over $12,000,000 fighting the claims. Let's go on a tirade against *that*. Let's see what happens. Because you take the white farmer who was given the loan and track him down: his farm is now worth $5,000,000, he's now a productive member of society all them years. The black guy has to go drive a truck, drive a cab, do something to stay alive, and all because of discrimination.

Now, was the secretary of the Department of Agriculture fired from his job? No. Was there an outrage about this? No. When they said they were gonna change the anchor on NPR, seventeen thousand people called up and they were mad about it because they're getting a different anchor on the goddamn radio. It's America—why didn't seventeen thousand Americans step forward and say, "No, we don't want that in America, we don't want discrimination"? Let's go on a tirade about that. And after we finish going on all these tirades, eventually we goin to get to wanna tirade about the way niggas act and the way they don't speak correct English and et cetera. My point is, there are systemic causes for that, so let's look at the causes. I have a special problem with a billionaire beating up on people because they poor.

III. "I CAN'T APPROACH [MY FEMALE CHARACTERS] ANY DIFFERENT THAN I HAVE, MAN, CAUSE ALL MY WOMEN ARE INDEPENDENT."

MML: What is *Gem of the Ocean* about?

AW: Love, honor, duty, betrayal. [*Laughter*]

MML: Well, how about a "plot synopsis"?

AW: There was a man who arrives at Aunt Esther's house seeking. He's in spiritual conflict. Then you find out that there's a man accused of stealing a bucket of nails from the local tin mill; he runs and jumps in the river and stays there till he drown. The people in the mill is upset about it, right? The whole plot point is about this bucket of nails and why the man drowned in the river rather than to come out the river and take his thirty days and admit to something he didn't do. He'd rather die in truth than live a lie.

Then we come to find out that the guy who arrives at the house of Aunt Esther, Aunt Esther takes him on a journey on a magic boat to a place called the City of Bones in the middle of the Atlantic Ocean, which is a half mile by half mile. It's a beautiful city unlike anything you've ever seen. The city is built of the bones of the Africans who were lost in the Middle Passage. So he traces his journey back on a boat, essentially on a slave ship, to the City of Bones, where he discovers a way for him to redeem himself. He takes that road to redemption. I don't want to say any more cause I don't wanna give the plot away [*laughter*], but that's what it's about.

MML: You set *Joe Turner's Come and Gone* in 1911 to take advantage of the African retentions of the characters. How do those retentions play out in *Gem of the Ocean*?

AW: When I set *Joe Turner* in 1911... In school, I was taught to start counting [decades] at one. So I put 1911, I'm working on my 1920s play, and my wife said, "What about the aught years?" And I go, "What?" And she say, "The aught years, the zero years." Then I realized I had another decade to do [*laughter*] and it was even prior to 1911. That would be the one that was closest to Africa, so I had to find a way to do that, and that's where Aunt Esther—who is 285 years old at that point—and the City of Bones come from. Because anyone who was like forty-seven years old in 1904 was born in slavery.

For instance, one of the cats is a runaway slave and he made it up to Canada. Instead of staying up there, he joins the Underground Railroad. He took sixty-two people there and now he's walking the streets of Pittsburgh trying to find something to do. He actually collects dog shit and he sells it, it's called "pure." The shoemakers use it to patent leather and all that kind of stuff too. He found a way. So this is what's happening in 1904. You got a lot of people wandering around who were ex-slaves, born in slavery—he was twenty years old when he ran away—so it's very close.

MML: Is that true? Did Africans escaping enslavement sell dog shit?

AW: The pure collectors? Well, in Europe they did that. There were pure collectors in Europe. I don't know about the United States, but I figured...

MML: Do you have an opinion about hiphop actors on Broadway? In the past few years we've seen Sean Combs in the revival of *A Raisin in the Sun,* Mos Def in *Topdog/Underdog,* and Mary J. Blige off-Broadway in *The Exonerated.*

AW: They were actors, right? They were actors who were hired to do the role and they did that, right? I don't have any problem with that. As a matter of fact, they did the *Def Poetry Jam on Broadway.* So when you look up there's gonna be like forty, fifty of em. Somebody should put them in the same play.

MML: Somebody should. [*Laughs*]

AW: I am aware that some of the actors have a problem: "They're in our thing and they just come in and do this..." That's who they hired to do it, man. Let him stand or fall based on his talent, not on who he is.

MML: What's your opinion of playwright Suzan-Lori Parks?

AW: I like Suzan-Lori Parks, I like her work, man. I saw *Topdog/Underdog.* I was on a panel once that selected an award for her, wrote her a citation and everything. It was the Laura Pels Award that's given by PEN.

MML: Essayist Sandra Shannon has criticized the women in your plays, saying, "His feminine portrayals tend to slip into comfort zones of what seem to be male-fantasized roles." Feminist critic bell hooks said of *Fences* that "patriarchy is not critiqued" and "sexist values are reinscribed." I was wondering if you've given thought to this in relation to approaching the final play in your cycle, which takes place in the 1990s, a time when women are arguably their most liberated and independent.

AW: I can't approach them any different than I have, man, cause all my women are independent. People can say anything they want, that's valid, they're liable to say anything they want. I don't agree with that. You gotta write women like… they can't express ideas and attitudes that women of the feminist movement in the '60s made. Even though I'm aware of all that, you gotta be very careful if you're trying to create a character like that, that they don't come up with any greater understanding of themselves and their relationship to the world than women had at that time.

As a matter of fact, all my characters are at the edge of that, they pushing them boundaries, they have more understanding. I had to cut back and say, "These are feminist ideas." My mother was a feminist, though she wouldn't express it that way. She don't know nothing about no feminist women and whatnot but she didn't accept her place. She raised three daughters, and my sisters are the same way. So that's where I get my women from. I grew up in a household with four women.

MML: My grandfather was a numbers runner in Harlem; Amsterdam Earl they called him. You wrote a numbers runner into *Jitney*—I wondered if you had any numbers-runner stories from Pittsburgh.

AW: At a bar, a guy put a gun to his head and was gonna shoot him unless he paid him fifteen dollars. And the guy didn't have no fifteen dollars, so Harvey stepped forward—he's a number runner—and said, "Man, here's your fifteen dollars." "No, Harvey, I don't want it from you. I want it from him." And Harvey said, "C'mon, what kind of sense that make? He don't have anything." Finally he say, "OK, Harvey, I'm doin this for *you*." So he took the fifteen dollars and he kicked the guy, he didn't shoot him. The police are standing across the street watching the whole thing.

I wrote a poem about a friend of mine, Ahmir Rashid. Ahmir is like everyman. I'ma try to say my poem. "Ahmir has big days / Standing on the corner of 125th and Lenox / Thin lips curled around a reefer / He is waiting for the number man / So he can go to Hackensack to see the woman in the red dress / The edge of impatience rides his upper lip / The loaded .45 tucked in his pants." Aw, shit, something about the loaded .45. [*Laughter*] "Makes a soft bulge under his coat / The number man is late / Ahmir knows he will either be in Hackensack tonight / Or booked for murder in the 4th Precinct / The number man knows this also / Which is why he is, right now, on a train to Atlanta." I hope it wasn't Amsterdam Earl. [*Laughter*] That was "Ahmir Rashid #1." I just got an idea. I might write about twenty more Ahmir Rashid poems and put me out a book, man.

IV. "YOU CAN WORK SO HARD AND REWRITE SO MUCH THAT YOU GET CONFUSED OR CAN'T REMEMBER WHAT'S IN HERE, AIN'T IN THERE, OR WHY THIS PARTICULAR THING IS IN THERE. THEN YOU'RE LOST."

MML: What ever happened with the film of *Fences*?

AW: In 1987, when I wanted to make the movie, I told them I wanted a black director. In 1990 they agreed to hire a black director and then for a long time we battled over who that black director should be. Once it was a black man, "It can't just be anyone. Now let's find the *right* one." So we stood there awhile. Eddie

Murphy was a producer and then they got another someone to take over from Eddie Murphy. I just finished a rewrite, a draft of the script. We ready to do it whenever we ready to do it but I don't sit by the telephone, man. [*Laughter*] I just keep moving, doing my things. If it happens, it happens. It's gotta happen the way I want it to happen because I gotta look in the mirror, face myself.

At the time, they told me there were no black directors, and about a month after that the *New York Times* put about thirteen new black directors in a photo. I sent it to them after I told them it was criminal that the guy didn't know no black directors. At the time, there was Gordon Parks, Bill Duke, Spike Lee. There were a bunch of black directors; he didn't know any. Marion McClinton, who is the director of this play, Paramount Pictures actually hired him and I've been working with Marion on the script. When we get the green light, we'll go ahead and do it.

MML: Baraka told me that Bill Duke directed *Hoodlum*—about Harlem numbers runner Bumpy Johnson—from a screenplay he'd written, but he went uncredited. Will you eventually write some screenplays for Hollywood?

AW: Yeah, I got ideas for about four of em. When I finish writing my plays, then I can do that. I'm not gonna do that and interfere with what I'm doing. If I did that, I would only have three plays written, man. When that's done, I'll write my book of poetry, do my paintings, I might even start singing, I don't know. [*Laughter*]

MML: Black playwright Woodie King Jr. told me that poets make better potential playwrights than prose writers because of their mastery of the economy of language. He was criticizing Toni Morrison's play *Dreaming Emmett,* saying that fiction writers' plays tend to be too verbose. As a poet, do you agree?

AW: I would agree with him, but I wouldn't say that's the reason why. I think poets deal with ideas of metaphor, they deal with the idea of story. Every poem is a story but it's condensed in a small space. What's lacking mostly in American playwriting is the idea of metaphor, storytelling, et cetera. It's the way poets think that would lend themselves to dramatic structure. They're used to condensing ideas into small spaces, that's true.

I read somewhere that poetry is the enlargement of the sayable. In other words, the impulse to write the poem, that impulse is a great dramatic impulse. But, hell, anybody could write a play. [*Laughter*] I do know this: All writers are not dramatists. You may be a great writer, but that doesn't necessarily mean you're a dramatist. Very few people have done both. I'm writing a novel when I finish my plays and then we'll find out. I know I'm a dramatist; we'll find out if I'm a novelist.

I always say that any painter that stands before a canvas is Picasso until proven otherwise. He stands before a blank canvas and he takes his tools. Paint, form, line, mass, color, relationship—those are the tools, and his mastery of those tools is what will enable him to put that painting on canvas. Everybody does the same thing. His turn out like that because he's mastered the tools. What happens with writers is that they don't want to learn the craft. That is your tools. So if you wanna write plays, you can't write plays without knowing the craft of playwriting. Once you have your tools, then you still gotta create out of that thing, that impulse. Out of necessity, as Bearden says: "Art is born out of necessity." Most writers ignore the very thing that would get them results, and that's craft. And how do you learn craft? In the trenches. You've got to do it. You got to get in there, you got to write. I say write and then write and write and write some more and go write some more.

Charles Johnson is a friend of mine in Seattle. Charles threw away 2,500 pages! It blows me away to this day. I said, How many? That's like ten books, just to get to that one. And that's work, but he wasn't afraid to do the work. And that's how you learn it, in the trenches. Do it, do it, and do it.

MML: I know you do a lot of rewriting—your plays may change substantially between their first production and the Broadway run. How much rewriting is excessive/obsessive? How do you know when it's done?

AW: First of all, let me say, I'm blessed to have the opportunity to go back into rehearsals with a play and get it right. Sometimes you sit there opening night and go, "Oh, man." You don't see it until you see it. You can't make yourself see it, but when you see it… Sometimes opening night, I see something I could've done that could've improved the play. I don't write with a hammer and chisel. It's not set in stone.

How much is too much? At a certain point, you can overwork something. I've seen painters overwork a painting. I've done some drawings and my wife, I'll go show her the drawings, she'll go, "It's overworked." I'll go, "Yeah, I worked real hard on that." And working hard, I missed my original idea that I started with. That can happen in the plays, too. You can work so hard and rewrite so much that you get confused or can't remember what's in here, ain't in there, or why this particular thing is in there. Then you're lost. That's too much. But as long as you can have control of your material and you're working to make the story clearer, working to improve it… As long as you don't get lost up in the rewrites, you're OK. Once you get lost and you don't know why you're doing what you're doing, you're in trouble.

MML: The *New Yorker* once reported that you'd only seen two movies between 1980 and 1991: *Raging Bull* and *Cape Fear.* From 1991 to now, have you managed to hit the cinema?

AW: I just don't enjoy movies. It's not my thing. Even when I was a kid, I went to movies and stuff but I never became a movie person. That's true, I didn't step into a movie theater in them eleven years, but during them eleven years there was this invention of this thing called the VCR. So that doesn't mean I haven't seen any movies. I saw a few. To this day, I got DVDs now, I still don't see that many movies cause it's not my thing.

One year, I went twenty-three times. Me and my wife said we'd go every Wednesday. [A young black man staying in a homeless shelter approaches with quarters for dollar bills. I give him the dollars, Wilson gives him some more. He walks off and we don't mention it.] *Amores Perros,* I liked that. *Memento,* I saw that too. *Master and Commander*—a piece of junk, man, I didn't like nothin about that. I saw *Sankofa* in a movie house in Baltimore with my daughter. I loved that. I've seen Spike's stuff. I saw *Barbershop,* that was fun. I just would rather read a book or listen to some records.

MML: When I was four years old, my mother took me to *The Wiz* on Broadway, and at thirteen, my grandmother took me to *The Tap Dance Kid*. But seeing *Fences* at seventeen really helped cultivate my love for theater. It seems my peers don't really bother. So thanks a lot, Mr. Wilson.

AW: You're welcome. We're gonna change that with your peers, man. We workin on it. I think Puffy had a lot to do with that. He brought a lot of people in there that otherwise wouldn't have went to see the play. And if they come to see him as opposed to the play, that's OK. They come to see him and *discover* the play. People came to *Fences* to see James Earl Jones and they discovered the play. "This is a good play, too, but I saw James Earl!" All that helps, man. ✯

JULIE ORRINGER

TALKS WITH

TOBIAS WOLFF

"AS A WRITER YOU BEGIN WITH INFINITE FREEDOM, AND THEN YOU MUST IMMEDIATELY START HEMMING YOURSELF IN. PART OF THE BEAUTY OF WRITING ABOUT THE ARMY, OR SUCH WORLDS, IS THAT THEY OFFER YOU AN ENCLOSED THEATER OF HUMAN FOLLY, OF HUMAN ASPIRATION AND FORMATION."

Recommendations from Tobias Wolff:
When guessing a woman's weight, aim low
Never land a helicopter in a confined space
If you want to sweet-talk a girl, say you're into Ayn Rand

Tobias Wolff is a short-story writer, a memoirist, a novelist, a father, a husband, a jazz aficionado, a hiker upon remote mountain trails, a neophyte pianist, and the mentor of many young writers. He was born in 1945 in Birmingham, Alabama; grew up in Florida, Utah, and the Pacific Northwest; attended Concrete High School in Washington State, the Hill School in Pennsylvania, Oxford University, and Stanford University, where he was a Stegner Fellow and a Jones Lecturer, and where he is now the Ward W. and Priscilla B. Woods Professor in the School of Humanities and Sciences. He is the author of short-story collections, memoirs, novellas, and novels, including In the Garden of the North American Martyrs *(1981),* The Barracks Thief *(1984),* Back in the World *(1985),* This Boy's Life *(1989),* In Pharaoh's Army: Memories of the Lost War *(1994),* The Night in Question *(1996), and* Old School *(2003).*

Wolff's writing makes us recognize those aspects of ourselves that are hardest to acknowledge: our selfishness, our pride, our cowardice. But he also brings to light our potential for self-understanding and compassion—the knowledge that comes from years of honest introspection, from the desire to make sense of the decisions that shape our lives. For his rigorous intelligence and his deep, empathic understanding of humanity, he has been compared to Chekhov; his writing is Chekhovian, too, in its gorgeous simplicity and in the way characterization gives rise to the shape of his narratives. He is a tireless reviser, a believer in the process of writing. In answer to an anxious question of mine a couple of years ago, he told me, "The only way to learn how to write a novel is simply to do it."

This interview took place at Wolff's office at Stanford, where he and I had spent many an office hour hashing through drafts of my own stories when I was a Stegner Fellow. *—Julie Orringer (Summer 2004)*

I. WORLD'S FAIR

JULIE ORRINGER: In the time I've known you, I've known you only as a writer and teacher. But I understand you've also been a waiter, a night watchman, a busboy; you've guessed ages and weights for a living, you spent several months as a reporter, and of course you spent four years in the army, which we'll talk about later. So I'm wondering if you can guess my age and weight.

TOBIAS WOLFF: [*Laughs*] What I've learned to do with women is to go low. But I'm not going to do that today.

JO: Go high.

TW: I would say… stand up.

JO: Is it always standing up?

TW: Oh, yeah. This was at a booth at the World's Fair. [*Takes a moment to assess, and then guesses interviewer's weight and age.*]

JO: Close!

TW: I'm out of practice. Was I at least within three pounds?

JO: Nearly. Did you always give yourself a window of three pounds?

TW: Yeah, that was the range. Which actually allows you seven pounds, three on either side and the one in the middle. You really had to win when you were doing this, because otherwise people were just buying the prizes, which were cheap-ass little things. If you lost, they'd start looking at the prizes and thinking, This isn't worth my fifty cents. So you had to win in order to get a crowd—or, in carny speak, a "tip." When you get a tip, people keep gathering to see what's going on. If they sense a real challenge, they'll play and pay. It's like having your own private mint. They can't wait to come up and give you money, but only if you're already winning. I was good at it. And it was clean; there was no way to cheat.

JO: Was there a scale?

TW: Yeah, there was a big scale. What you'd do to get going every night is have a couple of plants in the crowd. And you'd have a line of patter. If there was a pregnant woman, you'd say "Come on in, we'll weigh the both of you for the price of one!" You lay down a steady line to bring the crowd toward you and get a nice tip built up. It was hard to get it going during the day. Sunlight is not conducive to the mob mentality you need to create. But at night, under the carnival lights, with people screaming on the rides—it was a snap to pull in a crowd. I had a blast that summer. I'd lied about my age and was hanging out with all these old carny types.

JO: How old were you?

TW: I was sixteen.

JO: Where was it?

TW: Seattle's World's Fair. The rather squalid carnival section, not the World of Tomorrow, the culturally edifying part of the fair.

JO: Were you home on break from school?

TW: I was between years at boarding school at the time. When I got home I needed to scrape some money together to make up the shortfall of my scholarship and also to come up with my train fare back East. I started off working at a coin toss. Very quickly I figured out that the age-and-weight gig was much better. I had a friend over there and he segued me into the age-and-weight-guessing business. After the fair broke up in the fall, the carnival was headed on a big swing through the country, attaching itself to various state and county fairs. I was sorely tempted to stay with it; I'd met so many characters and was having so much fun. But I had just enough sanity to know that was probably not a good idea.

II. THE THEATER OF HUMAN FOLLY

JO: When I read the initial excerpt of *Old School* that appeared in the *New Yorker,* I thought back to "Smokers," your first published story, which appeared in the *Atlantic Monthly* in 1976. In both stories you perfectly portrayed the ways in which we manipulate the truth to our own advantage. What was it that pulled you toward that material?

TW: When I went off to boarding school, I already knew I wanted to be a writer. This might sound unlikely or at least opportunistic, but when I got there I knew that someday I would write about that place. It was so different from anything I'd experienced before, and it was such an intense wash of experience that at the time I could hardly parse it out. But I knew that someday I would. I remember discovering Salinger in my first year at that school because everyone was passing him around, still. The school he'd based his own recollections on was just down the road from us—we used to play them in sports—Valley Forge Military Academy, which he calls Pencey Prep. The book was forbidden there. The students were not allowed to have it, so of course all of them had read it. It was like a required text. I thought, What idiots! Can you imagine that?

Anyway, it had a local notoriety in addition to being interesting on its own. I laughed my ass off at the book when I read it. I enjoyed it so much. Of course I saw certain facets of life at my own school pictured there, but I was also very aware of some fundamental differences. By and large, the masters and boys at my school were not phonies. There was a sort of strange high-mindedness there, which I now understand to have grown out of a certain Anglophile tradition, and which was easy to satirize. Nevertheless, it was different. Salinger could not have written his novel about my school. But by the very act of reading it and correcting for it even as I read it, the seed of *Old School* was planted.

I have always loved reading school stories. I don't know why, exactly, but I do. I love William Trevor's school stories; he's got one in every collection, sometimes two. And there's the section in *Eminent Victorians* where Strachey talks about Dr. Arnold, Matthew Arnold's father, who was the headmaster of Rugby School. It's fascinating as an essay on education, and also very funny. Orwell's "Such, Such Were the Joys." School is a fantastic theater. A lot of writers certainly have found it so.

JO: It must have something to do with being in transition between childhood and adulthood. That's fertile ground for narrative. But in a way, being at boarding school also seems akin to being in the army. Both situations are bound by strict rules and codes of conduct.

TW: Exactly. They're both closed worlds.

JO: How does that affect the writing?

TW: It's akin to the advantage a poet has in consenting to working within a form. As a writer you begin with infinite freedom, and then you must immediately start hemming yourself in. You have to choose a genre, you have to choose a voice that precludes using other voices. You have to choose a time that precludes other times. Part of the beauty of writing about the army, or such worlds, is that they offer you an enclosed theater of human folly, of human aspiration and formation.

JO: One of the particularly notable aspects of your school's culture was its focus upon the literary world, its love of writers, and its idea of the writing life as something to aspire to. Did you know that about the school before you went there, or was it a fortunate coincidence?

TW: It was a fortunate coincidence. I hadn't been there two months before Robert Frost came. He was revered in the wrong ways by the teachers I'd had up till then, because they saw him as a Hallmark card writer, which, I'm afraid, is what we were taught good writing was—uplifting sentiment.

JO: He is actually quite a dark poet. "From the time when one is sick to death, / One is alone, and he dies more alone."

TW: Oh, God, he sure is. He's a tough poet. And complicated. Not overcomplicated or perversely complicated, but he is complicated. And yet there is that face of his work which is deceptive, and can allow you to read him simplistically, and that is a great mistake. Before a visiting writer came to the school, the masters had us read this person's work, and they introduced me to a different Frost than I had been reading before. So when he arrived, it was an extraordinary experience, really. I had never seen a real writer before—certainly not one of that Olympian stature. He was the great American poet then. And indeed he went on to read at Kennedy's inauguration, as you know; he traveled to Russia on a goodwill mission, met with Khrushchev. It attested to the position a poet could have in society—bringing the vision of the world of poetry into the world of affairs. You just don't see that anymore. Is there anyone like that now? I guess Robert Pinsky would come about as close as you can get. Frost was very interested in politics. If you read his letters, you find he had lot of ideas about education too; he'd been a schoolteacher. Some of his ideas were really cranky and mischievous. He would advise young people to leave school and go off to strange places like Brazil and Kamchatka.

JO: Did he talk about that at the Hill School?

TW: Not to my knowledge. I ran across that in a book, a little monograph called *Robert Frost as a Teacher.* Then there was something in the Lawrence Thompson biography that confirmed it. Frost was very, very mischievous, and manipulative. But I've taken the long way around the barn here: no, I didn't really know about the literary nature of the Hill School.

It's funny—I just met a guy the other day who said, "That school you wrote about—was that the Hill School?" and I said, "Well, I did go there, and it was partly drawn on my experience." And he told me how he went to be interviewed after a hockey game at Hill—he wanted to do a postgraduate year there. Our headmaster was the hockey coach, so he went to talk to the headmaster after the hockey game. He'd had his nose broken by one of our hockey players. They were very rough, even then. And I said, "Well, he would have loved you if you'd gotten your nose broken by one of our players. That's your badge of honor. You're in." But when he went up to the headmaster's study, William Golding was there and the two of them were talking and drinking, just totally shitfaced.

He did indeed get in and chose not to go, after all—he got into some good college and went there instead. But here's William Golding lying back with our headmaster, who's a very literary guy—used to publish essays about education in *Life* magazine and places like that. He taught the senior honors English seminar every year. A very smart guy, widely read, advised the school literary magazine. If a kid was disgruntled about not getting his work published he could submit it to the headmaster, who would look it over and give him some comments, to help him do a little better next time.

JO: Did you do that?

TW: I did. Boy, I didn't like what I got back. He really gave it to me. He was right. I didn't want to know it at the time, but I certainly recognize the truth of his criticisms now.

JO: What were his criticisms?

TW: Lack of specificity. This woolly idea that the less you say about a person or a place or a situation, the more universal it will seem.

JO: We're really drawn to that idea as young writers.

TW: Yeah, because it's so easy. We like the symbolic. It's very seductive when we're young.

III. THE COMPANY OF OTHER WRITERS (OR, "THE COMMENTS THAT DISTURBED ME MOST WERE THE ONES THAT WERE TRUE")

JO: One of the ideas I found particularly compelling in *Old School* was the notion that as young writers, we have some need or desire to be taken up by more established writers, to be introduced into their society—to shake the hands of writers who have touched the hands of other writers. Can you talk a little bit about how you developed that idea in the book, and also about how that was part of your own experience as a young writer?

TW: I was certainly conscious of the lore of writers. Even before I actually read anything about it, I was aware that Hemingway had been brought along by people like Gertrude Stein and Ezra Pound and F. Scott Fitzgerald. I mention Hemingway because he was the focus of my interest at the time. As I read writers' biographies later on, I noted that many of them met other writers and received help from them. Maupassant was a writer I loved; I read a biography that talked about how Turgenev took him up and put him through his paces. It's a natural enough thing.

Part of what my novel concerns is the way this boy is trying to move away from the orbit of his own father. He has decided—rather unfairly—that it isn't satisfactory, and he is looking, as you do when you abandon one father, for another. That blessing touch he's after gets embodied for him in literature. He's looking for that hand to fall on his shoulder, that anointing. Of course we discover as we get older that it doesn't work that way.

JO: In your experience, how does it work?

TW: Seldom the way it seems. For example, it's known that Sherwood Anderson helped Faulkner along. Well, yes, he did—he sent a novel of Faulkner's off to his publisher, but did so only under the condition that he didn't have to read it. He didn't read the book! He didn't *want* to read it. He never read it. A funny story. Anyway, writers when they're young tend to seek the company of other writers—some community of writers with whom they can share their work and get a response to it. I would imagine that the competition between Greek playwrights served as a kind of workshop. They were certainly aware of each other. They lived in the same town, or polis. Literature has always been written under the scrutiny—in the presence, if you will—of other writers. This idea of the writer as the *figure isolé,* it simply doesn't ring true to experience. You will feel the discipline and presence of other writers through the books you read, if nothing else. Influence is inescapable.

JO: In your own development as a writer, you spent some time as a Stegner Fellow and then as a Jones Lecturer at Stanford. How did that affect your work?

TW: I was thirty when I came here, and I'd been writing on my own. I had never given my work to a roomful of other people and had them mark it up and tell me what they thought of it. It was kind of a shock, really. Some of what I got back was silly stuff, I thought. But the comments that disturbed me most were the ones that were true—the ones that pointed out things I was doing that I wasn't aware of, for good or ill.

There were some good critics in that workshop, foremost among them Allan Gurganus, who is also a wonderful writer. Allan was very humane but truth-telling as a critic, and very good at catching tics he could tell you weren't aware of—tics of language, of manner. We had the same standard of writing, which was that every word should count, but I wasn't as far along in living up to that standard as I'd hoped I was. The workshop was very useful in helping me see what I was doing, making me more self-aware, to the point that I kind of had a hard time writing for a time after I got here. I did it, but the self-consciousness has a constipating effect at first. Then you drop those habits and you're off again. I wouldn't undo that experience for anything. It was infinitely useful to me.

JO: I think there's something essential about learning the nitty-gritty, the craft of writing—it helps you make rather large leaps in your work. But it does sometimes have a stymieing effect. I felt that very much at Iowa, when I was in Frank Conroy's workshop. He taught us so much about craft all at once that every time I sat down to put words on the page I felt a barrage of rules descending upon me. But eventually the craft becomes second nature, and the work becomes stronger for your having learned it. People talk about whether or not writing can be taught—that seems like one of the things that *can* be taught.

TW: I came to Stanford with some very ambivalent feelings about joining a workshop. For one thing, before I came here, I often wrote as a kind of subversive activity, something done in spite of the distractions that life presented, other jobs obviously being among them. Then there were personal relationships that seemed to represent a kind of obstacle to writing. At the Hill School and later at Oxford, writing was obviously valued, but they didn't do workshops—you wrote on your own, as an individual expression, something done almost in spite of the school. Because they asked so much of you in other ways, you had to steal the time to do it. I wrote even when I was in the army—not in a disciplined way, of course, considering the life I led.

JO: You were working on a novel.

TW: Yes, I was working on a novel. It wasn't any good, really, and probably couldn't have been, considering the halting way in which I was forced to write it. Nevertheless, I always felt as if I was getting over on them when I was writing, you know what I mean? I wasn't *supposed* to do it, and that made me want to do it. When I went to Oxford, after I got out of the army, the university had no interest in creative writing at all. They would have laughed at the idea of a creative writing workshop as part of the university curriculum. I wrote a novel when I was at Oxford, and I did it in spite of my studies. And I did it again when I was working at other jobs. I always wrote outside of the realm of what anybody expected me to do. It wasn't an approved activity. And I liked that about it. It gave it a flavor—let me put it that way.

In some ways, that flavor was essential to the activity itself. So to suddenly enter a world where it was the expected and approved and institutionally encouraged thing! I was really worried that I wouldn't be able to write at all. In some ways that happened, but more because of the self-consciousness than because of anything else. I was old enough to know that I didn't have time to waste, so when I was given the gift of time I used it. Nobody taught me lessons in craft as such. It was more a question of learning to be a good reader of my own work, and of other people's work as well. Not just the writers in the workshop, but more canonical writers. I think the great use of the workshop is that it teaches you to be a good, close reader. Not to read through the lens of an ideology, or the theory of a self-enclosed world of language, but what's here, what's right in front of you. Attend to it. What does it say? What are these words doing? What is the form of this piece? Why this form rather than another?

And the workshop also teaches you to think about human problems. It's not about craft for me. If it were, it wouldn't be interesting. When I'm talking with my students I'm really interested in the human springs of a story—what is there in the necessities of this particular character that produces this narrative? What has mattered to the writer in the writing of this story? We try to understand those things because craft without them is exercise. As you know from having been in a workshop of mine, I don't assign exercises. I think that each time out should be a swing for the fences. Don't do base-running drills. You can do those on your own time. The experience of reading other people's work with that kind of attention, and then having your own work read with that kind of attention and reported to you in detail, even by voices you don't agree with—even in your resistance to criticism you are educating yourself about writing and about your own writing. And if you don't end up becoming a writer, it's still got to be good for you.

JO: Because it increases your understanding of how the human world works.

TW: Absolutely. And how all our experiences and memories, in order to become intelligible and useful to us, must be shaped in some way. We impose a form on experience; there's no other way to live. We don't have a choice about it. We do it. But why do we do it the way we do it? Why do we choose one form rather than another?

IV. ONE HAS TO FACE THESE THINGS

JO: A number of critics have mentioned that there's a certain moral structure embodied in your work. How would you describe the way you arrived at your own sense of morality in fiction writing, and how did it affect the way you tell your stories?

TW: Well, I'm not sure, but the experience of reading and writing fiction is what gave me a sense of morality, more than anything else, because it helped me think out and objectify the question of character. In our everyday lives, we're mostly lost in the soup of ourselves. Where are we going to stand to see ourselves? We have to achieve some vantage point, and the continual experience of being inside oneself doesn't give you that. The vantage point must be different for different people. For some it's religion. I wouldn't equate religion and literature—I wouldn't want to make a religion of literature, it doesn't function well as a religion, but it does offer a place to step outside yourself, as much as one can, anyway.

So much of what I've come to think of as my character has been the result of my recognizing in other stories aspects of my own experience and my own inclinations, bad and good. That kind of heart-rising-to-heart you feel sometimes when you read, even if you're embarrassed to admit what it is that you're recognizing—you achieve in that way an escape from the imprisonment of the self.

JO: I was thinking about *In Pharaoh's Army.* The narrative tone throughout the book is self-effacing and often very self-critical. The scene I keep coming back to is the one in which you're about to be released from service and your replacement has come in—he's very self-important, a real jerk, and he thinks you've failed in your duties in Vietnam—and he's trying to direct a helicopter to land in a space that's too small, and you decide not to deter him, and the result is that a lot of people's homes are destroyed.

TW: Yeah, these little makeshift shelters they've thrown up.

JO: In that scene, and throughout *In Pharaoh's Army*—really, throughout all of your nonfiction—you avoid one of the dangers inherent in memoir, which is that the memoirist will portray himself as being larger or more humane than we suspect he actually was, or that he'll draw a veil over his failings. It seems to me that in your work, in a sense, you do the opposite of that.

T.W: You know, that's a really astute point—when you say "the opposite of that." I think that, indeed, I may have sometimes exceeded what was required in self-revelation, especially of weakness and vice. I wanted so much not to do the kind of thing Lillian Hellman did in her memoirs, which was to constantly show herself in the most heroic light: always the smartest person in the room, always the one with the integrity. There are any number of memoirs like that. They seem written to show what a wonderful and superior person the writer was. Well, I know I'm not.

On the other hand, sometimes I wonder if in doing this—in making a vow to myself that I would not be any easier on myself than I was on anybody else I wrote about—if I didn't sometimes go too far in the other direction. That is, I think if I were writing such a book now I would be a little more understanding of myself, as I try to be of other people. Not in a sappy way, not in an exculpatory way; one has to face these things. But I think, perhaps particularly in *This Boy's Life,* the hand may have fallen a little too heavily on the narrator. Anyway, in my anxiety not to make a special pleading for myself, there was a danger—I might have been a little harder on myself than I needed to be in the interest of being truthful.

JO: Do you think that the tendency to be hard on yourself in your memoirs translates to the tendency to be hard on the protagonists of your fictional narratives?

TW: I hope not. I do write, as indeed most writers do, about things that have gone wrong. There's not much of a story if things have gone right. Stories are about problems, and not the kinds of problems that result from a safe falling out of a window, but from somebody having a choice and having a problem with that choice, and then the series of consequences that follow from making that choice. To portray that honestly is to show the way people parse out their choices, and self-interest naturally comes into play. It isn't so much a matter of wishing to be hard on people as wishing to be truthful. If there's a moral quality to my work, I suppose it has to do with will and the exercise of choice within one's will. The choices we make tend to narrow down a myriad of opportunities to just a few, and those choices tend to reinforce themselves in whatever direction we've started to go, including the wrong direction. Our present government likes to lecture us on the virtue of staying the course. Well, maybe it's not such a good idea to stay the course if you're headed toward the rocks. There's something to be said for changing course if you're about to drive your ship onto the shoals.

JO: *Old School* seems to a large extent to be about evasions of truth—about the characters' evasions of the truth with regard to religion, social class, and personal connections. I was fascinated by the way that theme developed across the various narrative threads of the novel.

TW: It's not so much about the evasion of truth, which has an active quality. A lot of what happens to this narrator grows from an accumulated sense of fraudulence. For example, you mentioned the question of religion. He doesn't really lie about that at all. What would be his lie, anyway? He feels like he's lying because he's not telling people his father was Jewish—something he's just discovered himself. Yet he has no Jewish relations that he knows, and he hasn't been brought up at all in this faith; he was brought up in another faith altogether. Even under Jewish law he's not Jewish. Mostly he feels himself to be Jewish because he's not saying anything about it. It's what he keeps secret that he feels to be truest about himself. His sense of holding something back gives it an obsessional character and, in that sense, confers an imaginary identity upon him. He does this with other things too. He doesn't really lie—and in fact no one would be that interested anyway. They may not be as fooled as he thinks they are, either. When he finally publishes his story it's no big deal to anybody. It's kind of like, "I thought that all along." It really doesn't seem to come as a great revelation to anybody.

JO: When he publishes his story—

TW: —that isn't his story—

JO: That isn't his story, yes; that's when it comes out that his father was Jewish. And it seems there must be a connection between this suppression of his Judaism and his sense of the unacceptability of his social class, too.

TW: That's right. But again, he's not entirely to be trusted in this matter. He intuits that there is something, some spirit in the school, that does not fully accept Jewish boys or boys of a different social class. But then he admits that never once has he ever heard anyone say anything to that effect or behave in that way. So where is that coming from, really? I mean, it probably is, in fact, partly coming from the school—but I think it's also coming from him. He's conspiring with the school to produce this feeling.

JO: Did you understand that aspect of the character when you began the book, or was it something that came out of the writing?

TW: I understood it when I began the book, though I didn't understand just how pervasive it would be. Certainly this character takes it farther than I ever did, but again it's a question of recognition. In writing a book, you can use things you recognize in yourself as points of inspiration. He's playing out on a large scale aspects of myself that I played out on a smaller scale.

JO: And you chose to write the book as a novel rather than as a memoir.

TW: Oh, God, yes. I always knew it would be a novel. First of all, nothing interesting happened to me at my school. Yeah, we had Frost come, but Ayn Rand never came, and Hemingway certainly didn't—nor did he ever agree to. But these were the writers who were most influential on me. The writing competitions in the novel were largely an invention, too. I wanted to write about vocation, and I wanted to write about influence, and since I'm a writer, the influence I wanted to home in on was literary influence, and how it works—the omnivorous, ruthless way we consume and reject influences when we're young, the trail of dead writers we leave behind us as we progress.

Most of the boys at Hill had read Ayn Rand. At the girls' schools, they were even more into it than we were. At the dances we would have, I remember endless conversations with girls about Ayn Rand—they were really big-time into her. After all, she was writing about women who ran railroads, and nobody else was doing that. I mean, look at the women in other fiction at the time, popular fiction. And at that age, you know—it's a rare reader of fifteen or sixteen who is aware of the cheesiness of Rand's style. You're quite apt to get caught up by its very partisanship and by the heat of her own beliefs, which so animates all her fiction.

JO: Were you in high school when you began to reject those ideas?

TW: More just after. The narrator comes to his senses before I ever did, because you accelerate things in a novel. Again, it's the sense of form that compels it. It can't just be "and then, and then, and then," endlessly. There has to be a decisiveness to achieve literary form. You're giving an impression of life, but you can't actually record it just as it happens or it dissolves into mush.

JO: I'm curious to know more about your experience of writing the novel—how it was different from writing those early longer, novelistic memoirs, and perhaps even from writing *The Barracks Thief,* which is sometimes classed as a novella but which feels to me like a novel.

TW: *The Barracks Thief* is a short novel, but it was originally written at novel length. I'd also published another novel much earlier.

It was never my wish to represent *Old School* as my first novel; I always have to set the record straight on this. Back in 1975 a novel I'd written at Oxford was published in England and was going to be published over here by Macmillan, but for reasons that I still don't know, it fell through at the last minute and was never published in the U.S., thank God, because after it was published in England I withdrew it from circulation. When it came out, I realized it was awful. I had thought it was good, but somehow the light came on when I actually read it again.

JO: What was awful about it?

TW: Oh, it was just terrible, just an embarrassing book. It's like a first draft of a novel. I learned something, no doubt, in writing it—made a lot of mistakes I wouldn't repeat. I do indeed wish it hadn't been published, and I never name it on my list of publications, and that was thirty years ago. My next book didn't come out until six years later, a collection of stories. I've always considered that my writing life really began with that collection of stories, not with the novel. I never mentioned it to my publishers; it was never listed in any of my books. I never thought to mention it to anybody. My own editor didn't know I had done it, so when they made up the publicity for *Old School* they said it was my first novel. In each interview I've had to correct that.

Having said all that, I don't know how to characterize the difference. I could give you a trite answer about how when you're working on short stories you do know they're going to end sometime, and how when you're writing a novel you spend years deepening your experience of the characters and the world you're writing about. But also a kind of anxious wonder sets in as to whether or not you'll really finish it, whether it will be any good, whether all this time will have been wasted—and we all hate to waste our time.

Everything I've written, including this book, has seemed to me, at one point or another, something I probably ought to abandon. Even the best things I've written have seemed to me at some point very unlikely to be worth the effort I had already put into them. But I know I have to push through. Sometimes when I get to the other end it still won't be that great, but at least I will have finished it. For me, it's more important to keep the discipline of finishing things than to be assured at every moment that it's worth doing.

JO: Sometimes it seems so hard to hold off the skepticism.

TW: You just learn to do it.

VI. WRITING ABOUT WAR

JO: You've taken on the subject of war in both your fiction and nonfiction; what were the challenges it posed for you?

TW: The hardest thing about writing about a war you've been in is that you're terrified of getting it wrong, because of the people who have suffered such losses—and I'm not just talking about Americans. I'm talking about the Vietnamese, too. There were around 5 million Vietnamese killed, most of them civilians. You're aware that whenever you write anything about war, even with the intention of showing what it's really like, you're covering it with that inevitable glamour that war has for people except when they're in the middle of it. This last April, when those troops headed across the desert in their tanks, doing those "We're gonna go get these guys" interviews, like kids going to the next town to play a basketball game or something—those were the same kinds of things we were saying when we first went over. And now—talk to them now.

JO: A lot of people have drawn comparisons between what's going on in Iraq right now and what went on in Vietnam.

TW: It's very different, really. I don't think the comparisons work except in the folly of the enterprise and the mendacity of those who led us into it, and the willful blindness to reality, and the failure to appreciate anything about the country that we were going into, and the failure to seek out people who knew what the situation actually was, people who could plan reasonably for it, and maybe even decide not do it on the basis of what they learned. To start off with their minds made up, and to allow only those things into consideration that further strengthened decisions made in utter ignorance—in those ways, yes, it's similar.

But on the ground, in the place itself, they could not be more different. To begin with, there was no civil war going on when we went into Iraq. There was not a legitimate movement, a nationalist liberation movement we were going in to oppose. There was a despot, an evil regime in charge, unambiguously so. That didn't mean that we should've gone in. There are a lot of despots and evil regimes in the world. I don't know why, for example, we didn't take measures against Charles Taylor before we did, while he was slaughtering his fellow countrymen by the hundreds of thousands. If that really is the reason we went into Iraq, we should have been doing it elsewhere, with others.

JO: Of course, that wasn't really the reason.

TW: No, it wasn't, and it's not even the reason we were given. For them to appeal to that as their justification now is very dishonest. They fudged it, and now they're paying for it. At this point, we are actually creating a resistance that was not there before. In that way, I guess it could come to resemble Vietnam, but it will be a Vietnam of our own creation. Won't that be ridiculous?

JO: The ways in which we've managed to make ourselves villains in this war are just astounding. They're happening both on a very high level and on a personal level. We Americans used to be able to defend ourselves in the face of our government's actions overseas by arguing that those acts were coming down from our leaders, rather than from the people themselves. But the atrocities committed at Abu Ghraib made us question that defense.

TW: They did, absolutely. And people kept supporting the war in the face of those revelations. There was a piece in the *Times* by a guy named William Broyles who was the editor of *Newsweek* for a while, editor of the *Texas Monthly* before that, and a marine in Vietnam. He was ruminating about the polls that show that support for the war among Americans is still pretty high. He was saying this is only possible because most of these people don't have anybody at hazard over there, and that if you brought the draft back, those statistics would evaporate overnight. And he's right. We've created this mercenary army, essentially, made up disproportionately of people from minority and economically disadvantaged backgrounds. If our own kids were at hazard our feelings about the war would change very quickly. I hate the idea of the draft; I've got two boys who would be eligible. But the truth is, to make these things real, we need to share the danger.

JO: In a way, it brings to mind one of the things we're always trying to do as writers: to help people understand the humanity of others, the importance of other lives.

TW: Absolutely. That is exactly right. I think that's the greatest thing literature can do, and it is a very great thing indeed.

JO: In light of what's going on in Iraq right now, what kind of responsibility do you feel we have as writers? Do you feel like we have special responsibilities as writers?

TW: We have responsibilities as citizens. I don't think we have special responsibilities as writers. All you can do is try to humanize people's imaginations. I don't know any better way to do it than to just keep on writing as you write. What is a fiction writer to do? I don't know, except to insist on the value of what you do by continuing to do it. Because this world is continually trying to negate the value of what you do. That's your resistance. And then, to act as a citizen in other ways—to vote, to try to get other people to vote, to protest, to boycott, to do whatever a good citizen does in support of one's beliefs—yes, absolutely, all that. But not to turn your work into propaganda, because then you've become what they are. It will suck the humanity right out of your work.

JO: And in what direction do you see American fiction writing going now? What are some of the things you're noticing about the work that's different from what you were seeing ten or twenty years ago?

TW: I guess I'm seeing a little less interest in literature as a game. There's a tremendous faith in narrative, I think—a sense that maybe it isn't just a piece of criminal naïveté to believe that something valuable can come out of the telling of human stories. Postmodernism has forced tremendous self-consciousness upon us, perhaps against our will at times. After such knowledge, what forgiveness? You can't ever escape what you know. We're very self-aware as writers now, but it's interesting to see that narrative has been reinvigorated by that, rather than abandoned. It's given writers a new arsenal of forms, a new sophistication with which to tell their stories. Aside from that, I'm infinitely respectful of, and always in wonder at, the variety of ways that people tell stories and keep making them new. ✯

CONTRIBUTORS

Daphne Beal's first novel, *In the Land of No Right Angles,* will be published by Anchor Books in 2008. She is a regular contributor to *Vogue,* and her nonfiction has appeared in *McSweeney's*, *Artforum,* and the *London Review of Books.*

Joshuah Bearman is a writer and, along with his girlfriend, a jewelry proprietor. He lives in Hollywood, and has contributed to *This American Life*, *Wired*, *L.A. Weekly,* and elsewhere.

Dave Eggers, the editor of *McSweeney's,* has written books and lives in California.

Ben Ehrenreich is the author of the novel, *The Suitors.*

Nell Freudenberger is the author of a novel, *The Dissident,* and *Lucky Girls,* a collection of stories.

Novelist Tayari Jones is the author of *Leaving Atlanta* and *The Untelling.*

Jonathan Lethem is the author of seven novels, including *The Fortress of Solitude* and *You Don't Love Me Yet.* He lives in Brooklyn and Maine.

Sarah Manguso is the author of four books, most recently the memoir *The Two Kinds of Decay* (FSG, 2008) and *Hard to Admit and Harder to Escape* (McSweeney's, 2007), which was included in McSweeney's One Hundred and Forty-Five Stories in a Small Box. At present she is the 2007–2008 Joseph Brodsky Rome Prize Fellow at the American Academy in Rome.

Ben Marcus is the editor of *The Anchor Book of New American Short Stories.* His books include *Notable American Women* and *The Age of Wire and String.*

Miles Marshall Lewis is native to the Bronx and currently lives in Paris with his wife and their baby boys. Lewis is editor of the urban lit journal *Bronx Biannual* and is completing his third book, *The Noir Album: On Mulitcultural Life in Paris,* a memoir.

Alec Michod wrote *The White City,* a novel. His new book involves World War II espionage and the sexual proclivities of the elderly.

Cornelia Nixon's books include two novels-in-stories, *Now You See It* and *Angels Go Naked,* plus a book on D. H. Lawrence. Her awards include two O. Henry Prizes (one of them a first prize), a Nelson Algren Award, two Pushcart Prizes, and fellowships from the N.E.A. and the Bunting Institute. She teaches in the M.F.A. program at Mills College.

Julie Orringer is the author of *How to Breathe Underwater,* a collection of short stories. She is a graduate of Cornell University and the Iowa Writers' Workshop, and she was a Truman Capote Fellow in the Stegner Program at Stanford. Her stories have appeared in the *Paris Review*, *McSweeney's*, *Ploughshares*, *Zoetrope: All-Story*, *The Pushcart Prize Anthology*, *The Best New American Voices*, and *The Best American Non-Required Reading.* She is working on a novel set in Budapest and Paris in the late 1930s.

ZZ Packer is the author of the short story collection *Drinking Coffee Elsewhere,* and was a 2004 PEN/Faulkner Award finalist. Her stories have been published in the *New Yorker*, *Harper's*, and *Zoetrope All-Story,* and have been anthologized in *Best American Short Stories 2000* and *2003*. She lives in the San Francisco Bay area.

Alexandra Rockingham wrote, directed and produced films for fifteen years. Most recently she produced the three-hour-long documentary *Gambling, Gods and LSD.* She is writing her first novel.

Zadie Smith was born in north-west London in 1975, and continues to live in the area. She is the author of *White Teeth*, *The Autograph Man,* and *On Beauty.*

Adam Thirlwell was born in 1978. His first novel, *Politics,* was published in 2003; it has been translated into thirty languages. In 2003, *Granta* magazine placed him on their list of the Best Young British Novelists. He lives in London.

Vendela Vida is the author of two novels, *Let the Northern Lights Erase Your Name* and *And Now You Can Go.* Her first book, *Girls on the Verge,* was a journalistic study of female initiation rituals in America. Vida is a founding co-editor of the *Believer* magazine, and a board member and teacher at 826 Valencia, a non-profit youth writing lab. She lives in Northern California.

Sean Wilsey is the author of a memoir, *Oh the Glory of it All,* and the co-editor, with Matt Weiland, of *The Thinking Fan's Guide to the World Cup,* and the forthcoming *State by State,* an updated version of the great WPA guides to the United States.

Gary Zebrun is an editor at the *Providence Journal.* A graduate of the University of Notre Dame and the Brown University writing program, he is the recipient of Yaddo, MacDowell, and Bread Loaf fellowships. His first novel, *Someone You Know,* was a finalist for a 2005 Lambda Literary Award. He lives in Newport, Rhode Island.

ACKNOWLEDGMENTS

Heidi Julavits, Ed Park, Andrew Leland, Alvaro Villanueva, Sarah Manguso, Marc Holcomb, Barb Bersche, Heidi Meredith, Dave Kneebone, Eli Horowitz, Sam Potts, Dominic Luxford, Jim Fingal, Alex Carp, Jory John, Caitlin Van Dusen, Chris Ying, Soo Oh, Mac Barnett, Jordan Bass, Brian McMullen, Aran Baker, Sydney Goldstein, Carolyn Gan, Elise Winne, Jennifer Carr, Rachel Bolten, Melanie Glass, Juliette Linderman, Sophie Klimt, Jennifer King, Jacquelyn Moorad, Matt Werner, Polly Bresnick, Greg Larson, and Rebecca Goldman: thank you.